D0802964

Illuminated Manuscripts

John Bradley

BRACKEN BOOKS
LONDON

Illuminated Manuscripts

First published in 1905 by Methuen & Co. Ltd, London.
This second edition published in 1920 by
Methuen & Co. Ltd, London.

This edition first published in 1996 by Bracken Books,
an imprint of Random House UK Ltd,
Random House, 20 Vauxhall Bridge Road, London SW1V 2SA

Copyright © this edition Random House UK Ltd 1996

All rights reserved. This publication may not be reproduced, stored in a
retrieval system or transmitted, in any form or by any means, electronic,
mechanical, photocopying or otherwise, without the prior written
permission of the publishers.

ISBN 0 09 185052 5

Printed and bound in Guernsey by The Guernsey Press Co. Ltd

CONTENTS

Book I

CHAPTER I

INTRODUCTORY

CHAPTER II

VELLUM AND OTHER MATERIALS

CHAPTER III

WRITING

CHAPTER IV

GREEK AND ROMAN ILLUMINATION

v

CONTENTS

CONTENTS

CONTENTS

CHAPTER II

RISE OF NATIONAL STYLES

CHAPTER III

FRENCH ILLUMINATION FROM THE THIRTEENTH CENTURY TO THE RENAISSANCE

CHAPTER IV

ENGLISH ILLUMINATION FROM THE TENTH TO THE FIFTEENTH CENTURY

CHAPTER V

THE SOURCES OF ENGLISH FIFTEENTH-CENTURY ILLUMINATION

CONTENTS

CHAPTER VI

ITALIAN ILLUMINATION

CHAPTER VII

GERMAN ILLUMINATION FROM THE THIRTEENTH
TO THE SIXTEENTH CENTURY

CONTENTS

CHAPTER XI

ILLUMINATION SINCE THE INVENTION OF PRINTING

ILLUMINATED MANUSCRIPTS

Book I

CHAPTER I

INTRODUCTORY

What is meant by art?—The art faculty—How artists may be
compared—The aim of illumination—Distinction between
illumination and miniature—Definition of illumination—
The first miniature painter—Origin of the term "miniature"
—Ovid's allusion to his little book.

THE desire for decoration is probably as old
as the human race. Nature, of course, is
the source of beauty, and this natural beauty
affects something within us which has or is the
faculty of reproducing the cause of its emotion
in a material form. Whether the reproduction
be such as to appeal to the eye or the ear depends
on the cast of the faculty. In a mild or elementary form, probably both casts of faculty exist
in every animated creature, and especially in the
human being.

Art being the intelligent representation of that
quality of beauty which appeals to any particular
observer, whoever exercises the faculty of such
representation is an artist.

Greatness or otherwise is simply the measure of the faculty, for in Nature herself there is no restriction.   There is always enough of beauty in Nature to fill the mightiest capacity of human genius.   Artists, therefore, are measured by comparison with each other in reference to the fraction of art which they attempt to reproduce.

The art of illumination does not aim at more than the gratification of those who take pleasure in books.   Its highest ambition is to make books beautiful.

To some persons, perhaps, all ordinary books are ugly and distasteful.   Probably they are so to the average schoolboy.   Hence the laudable endeavour among publishers of school-books to make them attractive.   The desire that books should be made attractive is of great antiquity. How far back in the world's history we should have to go to get in front of it we cannot venture to reckon.   The methods of making books attractive are numerous and varied.   That to which we shall confine our attention is a rather special one.   Both its processes and its results are peculiar.   Mere pictures or pretty ornamental letters in sweet colours and elegant drawing do not constitute illumination, though they do form essential contributions towards it; and, indeed, in the sixteenth century the clever practitioners who wished, in bright colours, to awaken up the old wood-cuts used to call themselves illuminists, and the old German books which taught how the work should be done were called *Illuminir bücher*. Illuminists were not illuminators.

In the twelfth century when, as far as we know, the word illuminator was first applied to one who practised the art of book decoration, it meant one who "lighted up" the page of the book with bright colours and burnished gold.

These processes suggest the definition of the art. *Perfect illumination must contain both colours and metals.* To this extent it is in perfect unison with the other mediæval art of heraldry; it might almost be called a twin-sister.

As an art it is much older than its name. We find something very like it even among the ancient Egyptians, for in the Louvre at Paris is a papyrus containing paintings of funeral ceremonies, executed in bright colours and touched in its high lights with pencilled gold. But after this for many centuries there remains no record of the existence of any such art until just before the Christian era. Then, indeed, we have mention of a lady artist who painted a number of miniature portraits for the great biographical work of the learned Varro. We must carefully observe, however, that there is a distinction between illumination and mere miniature painting. Sometimes it is true that miniatures—as *e.g.* those of the early Byzantine artists, and afterwards those of Western Europe—were finished with touches of gold to represent the lights. This brought them into the category of illuminations, for while miniatures may be executed without the use of gold or silver, illuminations may not. There are thousands of miniatures that are not illuminations.

At the period when illuminating was at its best the miniature, in its modern sense of a little picture, was only just beginning to appear as a noticeable feature, and the gold was as freely applied to it as to the penmanship or the ornament.   But such is not the case with miniature painting generally.

Lala of Cyzicus, the lady artist just referred to, lived in the time of Augustus Cæsar.   She has the honour of being the first miniaturist on record, and is said to have produced excellent portraits "in little," especially those of ladies, on both vellum and ivory.   Her own portrait, representing her engaged in painting a statuette, is still to be seen among the precious frescoes preserved in the museum at Naples.

The term "miniature," now applied to this class of work, has been frequently explained.   It is derived from the Latin word *minium*, or red paint, two pigments being anciently known by this name—one the sulphide of mercury, now known also as "vermilion," the other a lead oxide, now called "red lead."   It is the latter which is generally understood as the *minium* of the illuminators, though both were used in manuscript work.   The red paint was employed to mark the initial letters or sections of the MS.   Its connection with portraiture and other pictorial subjects on a small scale is entirely owing to its accidental confusion by French writers with their own word *mignon*, and so with the Latin *minus*. In classical times, among the Romans, the "miniator" was simply a person who applied the *minium*, and had nothing to do with pictures or portraits at all, but with the writing. That the rubrication of titles, however, was somewhat of a luxury may be gathered from the complaint of Ovid when issuing the humble edition of his verses from his lonely exile of Tomi :—

> "Parve (nec invideo) sine me liber ibis in urbem :
> Hei mihi quo domino non licet ire tuo.
>
> .   .   .   .   .
>
> Nec te purpureo velent vaccinia succo
> Non est conveniens luctibus ille color.
> *Nec titulus minio,* nec cedro carta notetur
> Candida nec nigra cornua fronte geras." [1]

Tristia, Cl. 1, Eleg. 1.

There are many allusions in these pathetic lines which would bear annotation, but space forbids. The one point is the use of minium.

[1] "Go, little book, nor do I forbid,—go without me into that city where, alas ! I may enter never more. . . . Nor shall whortleberries adorn thee with their crimson juice ; that colour is not suitable for lamentations. Nor shall thy title be marked with minium, nor thy leaf scented with cedar-oil. Nor shalt thou bear horns of ivory or ebony upon thy front."

CHAPTER II

VELLUM AND OTHER MATERIALS

Difference between vellum and parchment—Names of different
preparations—The kinds of vellum most prized for illuminated books—The "parcheminerie" of the Abbey of Cluny
—Origin of the term "parchment"—Papyrus.

AS vellum is constantly spoken of in connection
with illumination and illuminated books, it
becomes necessary to explain what it is, and why
it was used instead of paper.

We often find writers, when referring to ancient
documents, making use of the words parchment
and vellum as if the terms were synonymous;
but this is not strictly correct. It is true that
both are prepared from skins, but the skins are
different. They are similar, but not the same,
nor, indeed, are they interchangeable. In point
of fact, the skins of almost all the well-known
domestic animals, and even of fishes, have been
used for the purpose of making a material for
writing upon. Specifically among the skins so
prepared were the following: the ordinary lamb-
skin, called "aignellinus"[1]; that prepared from
stillborn lambs, called "virgin parchment."

From sheepskins was produced ordinary
"parchment," and also a sort of leather called

[1] Strictly *agnellinus*.

"basane" or "cordovan." Vellum was produced from calfskin ; that of the stillborn calf being called "uterine vellum," and considered the finest and thinnest. It is often spoken of in connection with the exquisitely written Bibles of the thirteenth and fourteenth centuries as of the highest value.

Besides these were the prepared skins of oxen, pigs, and asses ; but these were chiefly used for bindings, though occasionally for leaves of account- and other books liable to rough usage.

Before the tenth century the vellum used for MSS. is highly polished, and very white and fine. Afterwards it becomes thick and rough, especially on the hair side. In the examination of certain MSS. the distinction of hair side and smooth side is of importance in counting the gatherings so as to determine the completeness, or otherwise, of a given volume. Towards the period of the Renaissance, however, the vellum gradually regains its better qualities.

Thus it may be seen that the difference between vellum and parchment is not a mere difference of thickness ; for while, in general, vellum is stouter than parchment, there is some vellum which is thinner than some parchment. Not only are they made from different kinds of skin, but the vellum used for illuminated books was, and still is, prepared with greater care than the parchment used for ordinary school or college treatises, or legal documents.

The fabrication of both parchment and vellum in the Middle Ages was quite as important a matter as that of paper at the present time, and

certain monastic establishments had a special
reputation for the excellence of their manufacture.
Thus the "parcheminerie," as it was called, of the
Abbey of Cluny, in France, was quite celebrated
in the twelfth century.   One reason probably
for this celebrity was the fact that Cluny had
more than three hundred churches, colleges, and
monasteries amongst its dependencies, and therefore had ample opportunities for obtaining the best
materials and learning the best methods in use
throughout literary Christendom.   As to the name
"vellum," it is directly referable to the familiar
Latin term for the hide or pelt of the sheep or
other animal, but specially applied, as we have
said, to that of the calf, the writing material thus
prepared being termed *charta vitulina*—in French
vélin, and in monastic Latin and English *vellum*.

The name "parchment" had quite a different
kind of origin.   It is an old story, found in Pliny's
Natural History (bk. xiii. ch. 70), that the ancient
use or revival of the use of parchment was due to
the determination of King Eumenes II. of Mysia
or Pergamos to form a library which should rival
those of Alexandria, but that when he applied to
Egypt for papyrus, the writing materials then in
use, Ptolemy Epiphanes jealously refused to permit
its exportation.   In this difficulty Eumenes, we
are told, had recourse to the preparation of sheepskins, and that from the place of its invention it
was called *charta pergamena*.

Pliny and his authority, however, were both
wrong in point of history.   Eumenes, who
reigned from about 197 to 158 B.C., was not the

inventor, but the restorer of its use (see Herodotus, v. 58). It was called in Greek μεμβράνα (2 Tim. iv. 13).

We may mention, by the way, that neither vellum nor parchment are by any means the oldest materials known. Far older, and more generally used in Italy, Greece, and Egypt, was the material which has given us the name of our commonest writing material of to-day, viz. paper. The name of this older material was *papyrus* (Gr. πάπυρος and χάρτης). As a writing material it was known in Egypt from remote antiquity. It was plentiful in Rome in the time of the Cæsars, and it continued, both in Grecian and Roman Egypt, to be the ordinary material employed down to the middle of the tenth century of our era. In Europe, too, it continued in common use long after vellum had been adopted for books, though more especially for letters and accounts. St. Jerome mentions vellum as an alternative material in case papyrus should fail (Ep. vii.), and St. Augustine (Ep. xv.) apologises for using vellum instead of papyrus.[1] Papyrus was also used in the early Middle Ages. Examples, *made up into book-form—i.e.* in leaves, with sometimes a few vellum leaves among them for stability—are still extant. Among such are some seven or eight books in various European libraries, the best known being the Homilies of St. Avitus at Paris, the Antiquities of Josephus at Milan, and the Isidore at St. Gall.

And in the Papal Chancery papyrus appears to

[1] Thompson, *Greek and Latin Palæography*, p. 33.

have been used down to a late date in preference to vellum.[1]

In France papyrus was in common use in the sixth and seventh centuries. Merovingian documents dating from 625 to 692 are still preserved in Paris.

[1] Thompson, *op. cit.*, p. 34 ; Aug. Molinier, *Les Manuscrits,* Prélim.; Lecoy de la Marche, *Les MSS. et la Miniature,* p. 24.

CHAPTER III

WRITING

SEEING that illumination grew originally out of the decoration of the initial letters, our next point to notice is the penmanship. The alphabet which we now use is that formerly used by the Romans, who borrowed it from the Greeks, who in turn obtained it (or their modification of it) from the Phœnicians, who, lastly it is said, constructed it from that of the Egyptians. Of course, in these repeated transfers the letters themselves, as well as the order of them, underwent considerable alterations. With these we have here no concern. Our alphabet, *i.e.* the Roman and its variations, is quite sufficient for our story. In order to show as clearly as may be the varieties of lettering and the progress of penmanship from classical times to the revival of the old Roman letters in the fifteenth century, we offer the following synopsis, which classifies and indicates the development of the different hands used by writers and illuminators of MSS.

It is constructed on the information given in Wailly's large work on Palæography, and in Dr. de Grey Birch's book on the Utrecht Psalter. The former work affords excellent facsimiles, which, together with those given in the plates published by the Palæographical Society, will give the student the clearest possible ideas respecting these ancient handwritings.

Omitting the cursive or correspondence hand, the letters used by the Romans were of four kinds—capitals (usually made angular to be cut in stone), rustic, uncials, and minuscules.

The rounded capitals were intended to be used in penwork. Uncials differ from capitals only in the letters A, D, E, G, M, Q, T, V, for the sake of ease in writing. It is said that this class of letters was first called uncials from being made an inch (*uncia*) high, but this is mere tradition; the word is first used on Jerome's preface to the Book of Job. No uncials have ever been found measuring more than five-eighths of an inch in height.

For the assistance of such students as may wish for examples we must refer to certain MSS. and reproductions in which the foregoing hands are exemplified.

CIRCA FOURTH CENTURY.

Capitals, yet not pure.

> The Vatican Vergil, No. 3225, throughout (Birch, p. 14; Silvestre's *Paléographie universelle*, pl. 74).

With regard to the relative antiquity of capitals and uncials, M. de Wailly observes: "The titles in pure uncials, but less than the text itself, give an excellent index to the highest antiquity. This is verified in MSS. 152, 2630, 107 of the Bibl. du Roi, etc. MSS. of the seventh or eighth century, whether on uncial or demi-uncial, or any other letter, are never constant in noting the title at the top of the page, or the kind of writing will vary, or if uncials be constantly used, the titles will not be smaller than the text. These variations become still greater in the following centuries. The ornaments which relieve the titles of each page commence about the eighth century" (i. p. 49 C).

Capitals and *Uncials.*

The Homilies of St. Augustine (Silvestre, pl. 74).
Augustine Opera, Paris Lib., 11641 (Palæograph. Soc., pl. 42, 43).

Rustic.

The Second Vatican Vergil, No. 3867 (Wailly, pl. 2), called the "Codex Romanus."

Sixth Century.

Rustic and *Uncial.*

The Montamiata Bible (Birch, 35 ; Wailly, pl. 2, 4).

Rustic and *Minuscule.*

The Cambridge Gospels (Westwood, *Palæograph. Sacræ Pictoria,* pl. 45).

Uncials.

Gospels in Brit. Mus. Add. MS. 5463.
Paris Lib., Gregory of Tours (Silvestre, pl. 86).
Vienna Imp. Lib., Livy (Silvestre, pl. 75).
Brit. Mus., Harl. 1775 (Palæograph. Soc., pl. 16).

Seventh Century.

Uncials and *Minuscule.*

The St. Chad's Gospels in library of Lichfield Cathedral (Palæograph. Soc., pl. 20, 21, 35).

Ninth Century.

Capitals and *Minuscules*.

Paris Lib., Bible of Charles the Bald.

There is scarcely anything more difficult to judge than the true age of square capital MSS. or of pure uncials. Even the rustic capitals, like the first Vatican Vergil, No. 3225, are extremely rare. The letters in this MS. are about three-sixteenths of an inch high.

Texts in use in Western Europe before the Age of Charlemagne.

Lombardic. The national hand of Italy. Founded on the old Roman cursive, it does not attain to any great beauty until the tenth or eleventh century. Examples may be seen in Palæographical Society, pl. 95, and in the excellent lithographs published by the monks of Monte Cassino (*Paleografia artistica di Monte Cassino*, Longobardo-Cassinese, tav. xxxiv., etc.). A very fine example occurs in pl. xv., dated 1087–88. Its characteristic letters are *a*, *e*, *g*, *t*.

Visigothic. The national hand of Spain. Also founded on the old Roman cursive. It becomes an established hand in the eighth century, and lasts until the twelfth. Examples occur in Ewald and Lœwe, *Exempla Scripturæ Visigoticæ*, Heidelberg, 1883. It was at first very rude and illegible, but afterwards became even handsome. A fine example exists in the British Museum (Palæo-

graph. Soc., pl. 48). Its characteristic letters are
g, *s*, *t*.

Merovingian. The national hand of France.
A hand made up chiefly of loops and angles in a
cramped, irregular way. Its derivation the same
as the preceding. In the seventh century it is all
but illegible. In the eighth it is much better,
and almost easy to read.

Celtic. The national hand of Ireland. It is
founded on the demi-uncial Roman, borrowed as
to type from MSS. taken to Ireland by missionaries. It is bold, clear, and often beautiful, lending itself to some of the most astonishing feats
of penmanship ever produced.

Such are the chief varieties of writing found in
the MSS. produced before the great revival of the
arts and learning which took place during the
reign of Charles the Great (Karl der Grosse),
known familiarly as Charlemagne.

Wattenbach (*Schriftwesen, etc.*) says that uncials date from the second century A.D. From
examples still extant of the fifth and following
centuries, it seems that while the Roman capitals
were not uncommon, in Celtic MSS. the form
generally adopted was the uncial. It was the
form also usually chosen for ornamentation or
imitation in those Visigothic, Merovingian, or
Lombardic MSS., which made such remarkable
use of fishes, birds, beasts, and plants for the
construction of initial letters and principal words,
of which we see so many examples in the elabo-
rately illustrated Catalogue of the library at Laon

by Ed. Fleury, and in that of Cambray, by M. Durieux. Most of these pre-Carolingian designs are barbarous in the extreme, dreadfully clumsy in execution, but they evince considerable ingenuity and a strong predilection for symbolism.

Before concluding this chapter perhaps something should be said concerning the shape of books, though this is a matter somewhat outside the scope of our proper subject. Yet, as the brief digression will afford an opportunity for the explanation of certain terms used in MSS., we will avail ourselves of it.

The ancient form of writing upon skins and papyrus was that of the roll. The Hebrew, Arabic, or Greek terms for this do not concern us, but its Latin name was *volumen*, "something rolled," and from this we obtain our word volume. Such words as " explicit liber primus," etc., which we often find in early MSS., refer to this roll-form ; *explicare* in Latin meaning to unroll ; hence, apropos of a chapter or book, to finish. When transferred to the square form, or codex, it simply means, " here ends book first," etc.

The modern book shape first came into use with the beginning of the Christian era under the name of codex. Here it will be necessary to explain that *caudex*, *codex*, in Latin, meant a block of wood, and had its humorous by-senses among the Roman dramatists, as the word block has among ourselves, such as blockhead.[1] So *caudicalis provincia* was a jocular expression for the occupation of wood-splitting.

[1] Terence, *Heautont.*, 5. 1, 4.

Whether the word had originally any connection
with *cauda*, "a tail," is not here worth considering,
as, if so, it had long lost the connection ; and
when used to mean a book, had only the sense of
a board, or a number of boards from two up-
wards, fastened together by means of rings passed
through holes made in their edges.

Probably the first use was as plain smooth
boards only ; examples of such are still in existence. Then of boards thinly covered with, usually,
black wax. A pair of such tablets, wax-covered,
was a common form of a Roman pocket- or
memorandum-book. It was also used as a means
of conveying messages, the reply being returned
on the same tablets. The method was to write
on the wax with a fine-pointed instrument called
a style, the reverse end of which was flattened.
When the person to whom the message was sent
had read it, he (or she) simply flattened out the
writing, smoothed it level, and then wrote the
reply on the same wax. School-children did
their exercises on these tablets, housewives and
stewards kept their accounts on them, and on
them literary people jotted down their ideas as
they do now in their pocket-books. Extant
examples of these early books, or tablets, are
fairly numerous, and may be seen in most public
museums. A codex of two leaves was called a
diptych ; of three, a triptych, etc. The codex
form was used for legal documents, wills, con-
veyances, and general correspondence. Hence
the Roman postman was called a *tabellarius*, the
tablets containing correspondence being tied with

a thread or ribbon and sealed. This custom of sending letters on tablets survived for some centuries after Augustan times. Wattenbach gives several interesting instances of their medi-æval use.[1]

Of course when the tablet gave place to the codex of skin or paper, the papyrus was too brittle and fragile for practical utility, and examples, as we have seen, were very rare ; but vellum soon became popular. We may mention, in passing, that the papyrus roll gave us a word still in use in diplomatics, the word *protocol*. The first sheet of a papyrus roll was called the πρωτόκολλον. It usually contained the name of place and dàte of manufacture of the papyrus, and was stamped or marked with the name of the government officer who had charge of the department.

In the vellum codex, though each leaf might have only one fold, and thus technically be con-sidered as a folio, the actual shape of it was nearly square, hence its name of *codex quadratus*. When other forms of books, such as octavo, duo-decimo, etc., came into use, it was in consequence of the increased number of foldings. The gather-ings, originally quaternions or quires, became different, and those who undertake to examine MSS. with respect to their completeness have to be familiar with the various methods.[2] This kind of knowledge, however, though useful, is by no means essential to the story of illumination.

---

[1] *Schriftwesen,* 48.
[2] Wattenbach, *Schriftwesen ;* Madan, *Books in Manu-script, etc.*

CHAPTER IV

GREEK AND ROMAN ILLUMINATION

The first miniature painter—The Vatican Vergils—Methods of
painting—Origin of Christian art—The Vienna Genesis—
The Dioscorides—The Byzantine Revival.

IT has been already stated that the earliest recorded miniature painter was a lady named
Lala of Cyzicus in the days of Augustus Cæsar,
days when Cyzicus was to Rome what Brussels is
to Paris, or Brighton to London. All her work,
as far as we know, has perished. It was portraiture on ivory, probably much the same as we
see in the miniature portraiture of the present day.

But this was not illumination. The kind of
painting employed in the two Vatican Vergils
was, however, something approaching it. These
two precious volumes contain relics of Pagan art,
but it is the very art which was the basis and
prototype of so-called Christian art of those
earliest examples found in the catacombs and in
the first liturgical books of Christian times.

The more ancient of the two Vergils referred
to, No. 3225, which Labarte (2nd ed., ii. 158)
thinks to be a century older than the other,
Sir M. D. Wyatt considered as containing "some
of the best and most interesting specimens of

ancient painting which have come down to us. The design is free and the colours applied with good effect, the whole presenting classical art in the period of decline, but before its final debasement." Whereas in the second MS., No. 3867, the style, though still classical, is greatly debased, and probably, in addition to this, by no means among the best work of its time. It is described as rough, inaccurate, and harsh. The method is of the kind called *gouache, i.e.* the colours are applied thickly in successive couches or layers, probably by means of white of egg diluted with fig-tree sap, and finished in the high lights with touches of gold (Palæograph. Soc., pl. 114, 117). This finishing with touches of gold brings the work within the range of illumination. There is, indeed, wanting the additional ornamentation of the initial letter which would bring it fully into the class of mediæval work ; but, such as it is, it may fairly claim to be suggestive of the future art. Indeed, certain points in the MS. 3225— viz. that Zeus is always red and Venus fair, that certain costumes and colours of drapery are specially appropriated—would lead to the supposition that even then there existed a code of rules like those of the Byzantine Guide, and that therefore the art owed its origin to the Greeks.

Between this MS. and the first known Christian book work there may have been many that have now perished, and which, had they remained, would have marked the transition more gradually. But even as they stand there is no appreciable difference between the earliest monuments of

Christian art and those of the period which preceded them. Nor shall we find any break, any distinct start on new principles. It is one continuous series of processes—the gradual change of methods growing out of experience alone—not owing to any change of religion or the adoption of a new set of theological opinions. Of course we shall find that for a very long time the preponderance of illuminated MSS. will be towards liturgical works; and we shall also find that where the contents of the MS. are the same the subjects taken for illustration are also selected according to some fixed and well-known set of rules. We shall see the explanation of this by-and-by.

The first example of a Christian illuminated MS. is one containing portions of the Book of Genesis in Greek preserved in the Imperial Library at Vienna. It is a mere fragment, only twenty-six leaves of purple vellum—that is, bearing the imperial stain—yet it contains eighty-eight pictures. We call them miniatures, but we must remember that by "miniator" a Roman bookseller would not understand what we call a miniaturist; and, as we have said, the word "illuminator" was not then known.

This Vienna Genesis is not introduced among illuminated books, therefore, because of its miniatures—pictures we prefer to call them—but because the text is nearly all written in *gold* and *silver* letters. The pictures, according to the Greek manner, are placed in little square frames. They were executed, no doubt, by a professional painter, not without technical skill and not hampered by monastic restrictions. The symbolism which underlies all early art is here shown in the allegorical figures (such as we shall meet with again in later Byzantine work), which are introduced to interpret the scene. We see the same thing in the catacombs. Being a relic of great importance, this Genesis codex has been often described and examples given of its pictures. Of course, in a little manual like the present we cannot pretend to exhibit the literature of our subject. We can scarcely do more than refer the reader to a single source. In this case perhaps we cannot do better than send the inquirer to the Victoria and Albert Museum at South Kensington.

If we select another MS. of this early period it is the one which may be said to be the oldest existing MS. in which the ornamentation is worthy of as much notice as the pictures. We refer to the Collection of Treatises by Greek physicians on plants, fishing, the chase, and kindred matters in the same library as the Genesis fragment. It goes under the name of "Dioscorides," who was one of the authors, and dates from the beginning of the *sixth* century. The Genesis is a century older. Engravings from the Dioscorides are given in Labarte's *Arts industriels*, *etc.*, pl. 78, and in Louandre's *Arts somptuaires*, *etc.*, i., pl. 2, 3.

Enough has been said on these earlier centuries to show quite clearly the character of the art known as Early Christian. It is simply a continuation of such art as had existed from classical times, and had, in fact, passed from the Greeks, who were artists, to the Romans, who were rarely better than imitators. It is carried on to the period when it again is nourished by Greek ideas in the Later Empire, and once more attains distinction in the splendid revival of art under the Emperor Justinian.

NOTE.—Julius Capitolinus, in his Life of the exquisite Emperor Maximin, junior, mentions that the emperor's mother[1] made him a present of a copy of the poems of Homer, written in golden letters on purple[2] vellum. This is the earliest recorded instance of such a book in Christian times. Its date would be about 235 A.D.

[1] Quædam parens sua.   [2] Purpureos libros.

CHAPTER V

BYZANTINE ILLUMINATION

The rebuilding of the city of Byzantium the beginning of Byzantine art—Justinian's fondness for building and splendour—Description of Paul the Silentiary—Sumptuous garments—The Gospel-book of Hormisdas—Characteristics of Byzantine work—Comparative scarcity of examples—Rigidity of Byzantine rules of art—Periods of Byzantine art—Examples—Monotony and lifelessness of the style.

THE signal event which gave birth to mediæval illumination, or rather to the ideas which were thereby concentrated upon the production of magnificent books, was the rebuilding of the Imperial Palace and the Basilica of Constantine, henceforward to be known as the Church of Sancta Sophia, or the Divine Wisdom, at Byzantium. The Emperor Justinian had been reigning six years when a terrific fire, caused by the conflicts between the various seditions, called Circus factions, of the time, almost entirely destroyed not only his own palace and the great Christian church adjoining it, but the city of Constantinople itself. So important a scheme of reconstruction had probably never been forced upon a government since the great fire in Rome under Nero. Justinian, whose early training had been of the most economical kind, and whose disposition seemed to be rather inclined to parsimony thân extravagance, now came out in his true character. For various reasons he had hitherto studiously concealed his master-passion; but this catastrophe of the fire, which seemed at first so disastrous, was really a stroke of fortune. It afforded the hitherto frugal sovereign the chance he had long waited for of spending without stint the hoarded savings of his two miserly predecessors, and gratifying his own tastes for magnificent architecture and splendour of apparel.

Not only Asia, with its wealth of gold and gems, but all the known world capable of supplying material for the reconstructions, were called upon, and ivory, marbles, mosaics, lamps, censers, candelabra, chalices, ciboria, crosses, furniture, fittings, pictures—in short, everything that his own taste and the experience of four or five of the ablest architects of the time could suggest—administered to the gorgeous, the unspeakable splendour of the new edifices and their furniture.

Paul the Silentiary, an eye-witness of the whole proceeding, has left a description in verse, and the accurate Du Fresne in prose, which enable us easily to trace how the Roman city of Constantine became transformed into the semi-oriental Byzantium of Justinian. During the two centuries which had elapsed since the days of the first Christian emperor many foreign luxuries had found their way into the Eastern capital. Byzantine jewellery and Byzantine silks were already famous. The patterns on the latter were not merely floral or geometrical, but four-footed animals, birds, and scenes from outdoor sports formed part of the embellishment, which, therefore, must have taken the place occupied in later times by the tapestries of Arras and Fontainebleau.

Hitherto the Byzantines had imported their silks from Persia. After the rebuilding of the Basilica, Justinian introduced silk-culture into Greece. The garments ridiculed by Asterius, Bishop of Amasia, in the fourth century, were repeated in the sixth century. "When men," says he, "appear in the streets thus dressed, the passers-by look at them as at painted walls. Their clothes are pictures which little children point out to one another. The saintlier sort wear likenesses of Christ, the Marriage of Galilee . . . and Lazarus raised from the dead."

On the robe of the Empress Theodora—the wife of Justinian, who is shown in one of the mosaics of St. Vitale at Ravenna as presenting rich gifts to that church—there is embroidered work along the border, showing the Adoration of the Magi. *Theodora pia* was one among the many rôles played by that all-accomplished actress; but this seems to have been after her death. Like Lucrezia Borgia, perhaps, she was better than her reputation. With such surroundings liturgical books could not have existed without sharing in the universal luxury of enrichment. And, in point of fact, we still have records of such books. While Justinian reigned in Byzantium it happened that Hormisdas, a native of Frosinone, was Pope of Rome. He was a zealous eradicator of heresy (especially of the Eutychian and Manichæan), and in recognition of his services in this direction the Greek Emperor, with his thanks, sent him a great Gospel-book richly decorated, no doubt, with those splendid Eusebian canons and portraits of the Evangelists, the like of which we see in the Byzantine examples still preserved at Paris, in London, and elsewhere. Plates of beaten gold, studded with gems, formed the covers of the Gospel-book of Hormisdas.

Nor was this sumptuous volume the only, or even a rare, example of its kind. We read that the art of book decoration had become a fashionable craze. No expense was spared in the search for costly materials. Colours were imported from India, Persia, and Spain, including vermilion and ultramarine, while the renowned Byzantine gold ink was manufactured from imported Indian gold. Persian calligraphers had taught its use afresh to the Byzantine scribes.

If, as we may believe, the first object of the Roman miniatores was distinctness combined with beauty, we may now believe that the object of the Byzantine scribes was splendour. The progress had been from mere "cheirography" to calligraphy; now it was from calligraphy to chrysography and arguriography.

This employment of gold and silver inks may be looked upon as the first step in the art of illumination as practised in the Middle Ages. And the preliminary to the use of metallic inks was attention to the tint of the vellum. The pioneers in this career of luxury no doubt had

observed that very white vellum fatigued the eye.
Hence, at first, they tinted or stained it with
saffron, on one side at least, sometimes on both.
Once begun, the tinting of the vellum extended
to other colours. For works of the highest rank
the favourite was a fine purple, the imperial
colour of the Roman and Greek emperors. For
chrysography, or gold-writing, the tint was nearly
what we call crimson. For arguriography, or
silver-writing, it became the bluish hue we call
grape-purple. On the cooled purples vermilion
ink was used instead of, or together with, the
gold or silver. As the usage began with the
Greeks, we may be sure that it came originally
from Asia.

The Emperor Nero, once having heard that an
Olympic Ode of Pindar in letters of gold was
laid up in one of the temples at Athens, desired
that certain verses of his own should be similarly
written and dedicated on the Altar of Jupiter
Capitolinus at Rome. This was an imperial
luxury several times repeated by other princes.

After the official establishment of Christianity
it became a common practice to have the greater
liturgical books executed in the same costly
fashion. And between the time of Constantine
and that of Basil the Macedonian many a burn-
ing homily was directed against the custom,
denounced as a sinful extravagance, which no
doubt it was, but in vain until the fashion had
worn itself out.

It might fairly be expected, this being the case,
that many examples of this kind of codex would

still be in existence.   But owing to war, fire, robbery, and other misfortunes but very few remain.   One of the oldest and finest is the so-called *Codex Argenteus*, or Silver-book, now kept at Upsala, in Sweden, containing portions of the Gospels of the Mæsogothic Bishop Ulfilas. Originally the effect of the stamped or burnished silver on the rich purple of the vellum must have been very splendid, but now the action of the air has blackened it, as it has done in many other instances where silver was used in illumination. Even gold will gather tarnish, and in several such MSS. has turned of a rusty red.   Gold ink was not invariably confined to tinted vellum ; it was often used on the plain ground.   The copy of the Old Testament in Greek, presented by the high priest Eleazar to King Ptolemy Philadelphus, was a roll of fine white vellum, upon which the text was written in letters of gold.

To enter upon the antiquities of Greek palæography would lead us too far from our track in view of the brevity of our present survey.   We therefore with some reluctance turn from this interesting topic to our more immediate subject. We may remark, however, that the great majority of Greek MSS. are written on vellum.   In the eleventh century are found instances of what is called *charta bombycina*, or cotton-paper, appearing more plentifully in the twelfth century, but on the whole vellum is the chief material of Byzantine illuminated books.   Much has been said about the want of life and total lack of variety of treatment in this school of art.   To a very great extent the charge is just, yet it could scarcely be otherwise. The one circumstance which compelled Byzantine work to remain so long as if cast in one unalterable mould, and thus to differ so strangely from that of Western artists, was due to the fact that in very early Christian times the scribes and illuminators were enrolled into a minutely organised corporation originating primarily in monasticism, but by no means confined to the monastic Orders. Lay guilds existed, the regulations and methods of which were rigid beyond modern belief. So that, as a class, Byzantine art has acquired the reputation of a soulless adherence to mechanical rules and precedents, depriving it of originality and even of individuality, and therefore excluding the remotest scintilla of artistic genius. Of the great crowd of examples of ordinary work this may be true, but it certainly is not true of the best, by which it has the right to be judged, as we shall see from the examples referred to by-and-by. Certainly there is one invaluable particular in which Greek MSS. are superior to those of the West, Latin or otherwise. That is, they are much more frequently signed with the names, localities, and dates of the copyists and illuminators.

It will be some help towards our knowledge of this school if we divide its existence into chronological sections or periods.

1. From præ-Christianity to the Age of Justinian, *i.e.* down to the year 535. (Justinian reigned from 526 to 564.)

This period marks the decadence of ancient art, but carries with it the characteristics and methods of the ancient Greek painters.

2. From the Age of Justinian to the Iconoclastic paralysis of art under Leo III. the Isaurian, *i.e.* 564 to 726. (Leo reigned from 717 to 741.)

During this period vast numbers of illuminated liturgical books were destroyed for religious or fanatical reasons, just as in our own Cromwellian times numbers of *Horæ*, Missals, etc., were destroyed as papistical and superstitious.

This Edict of 726 did not absolutely put an end to all art in MSS. It only had the effect of excluding images of God, Christ, and the saints, as in Arabian and Persian MSS., leaving the artist the free use of flowers, plants, and line ornament, after the manner of the Mohammedan arabesques.

3. From Leo III. to the Empress Irene, who restored the worship of images in part, *i.e.* from 741 to 785. (Irene ruled from 780 to 801.)

This was a period of stagnation, though by no means of extinction of art.

4. From Irene to Basil I. the Macedonian, *i.e.* from 801 to 867.

A half-century and more of rapid renaissance to the most brilliant epoch of Byzantine art since the time of Justinian, if not the zenith of the school.

Basil I. was a great builder—building, in fact, was his ruling passion—so that it may be said that he took Justinian for his model both as a ruler and as a patron of the arts. (He reigned from 867 to 886.)

5. From Basil the Macedonian to the Fall of Constantinople, *i.e.* from 886 to 1453.

Allowing for a few flashes of expiring skill in various reigns, this may be considered as a period of gradual but certain decline to a state worse than death, for though the monks of Greek and Russian convents still kept up the execution of MSS., it was only with the driest and most lifeless adhesion to the Manual. This so-called art still exists, but more like a magnetised corpse than a living thing.

Examples of the first period are seldom met with. We have one signal specimen in the British Museum Add. MS. 5111, being two leaves only of a Gospel-book, and containing part of the Eusebian canons, or contents-tables of the Four Gospels, etc. The work is attributed to the time of Justinian himself. It is of the kind already referred to as probably affording the model of work to the early illuminators of France and Ireland, and as being like the Gospel-book of Hormisdas and those brought to England by Augustine in 596. Another example of the same Eusebian canons is found in Roy. MS. 1 E. vi.

Of the fourth period—*i.e.* the ninth century—perhaps the most typical example is the Menologium (a sort of compound of a calendar and lives of the saints), now in the Vatican Library (MS. Gr. 1613). This MS. shows that the revival under Basil the Macedonian was a return not to Roman, but to ancient Greek art, the facial types being of the purest classical character.

In some of them we see the horizontal frown

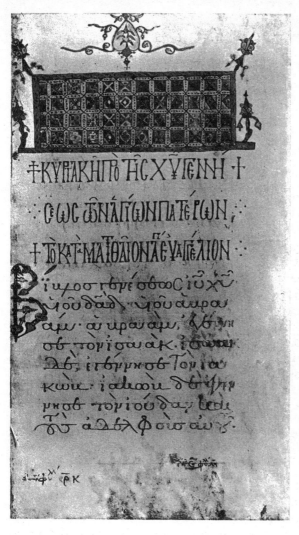

EVANG. GRÆCA

6TH CENT.

Brit. Mus. Add. MS. 5111, fol. 13

EVANG. GRÆCA
9TH CENT.

Brit. Mus. Burney MS. 19, fol. 1 v.

of the Homeric heroes (σύνοφρυς Ὀδυσσεὺς), and of
the Georgian and Armenian races shown in the
features of the Emperor Johannes Ducas. We
have, too, the large Hera-like eye with its mystic
gaze, which, in later Byzantine work, becomes
first a gaze of lofty indifference, as in the portraits
of the emperors and empresses, and lastly a stony
and expressionless stare ; still, if possible, more
stony and glaring when transferred to Celtic and
Carolingian Gospel-books. (See chapter on Carolingian Illumination.)

Of this fourth period we might indeed point to
many examples. One must suffice. It is the
beautiful Greek Psalter, now at Paris (MS., p. 139),
containing lovely examples of antique design, including remarkable personifications or allegorical
figures. In this MS. is one of the most graceful
personifications ever painted, that of *Night*, with
her veil of gauze studded with stars floating overhead. The seven pictures from the Life of David
are among the best ever put into a MS. But
personification is carried to an extreme. Thus the
Red Sea, the Jordan, Rivers, Mountains, Night,
Dawn, etc., are all represented as persons. The
drawings are really beautiful and the illuminated
initials and general ornament in good taste.

For other examples the reader may consult the
British Museum Cat. of Addit. MSS., 1841–5,
p. 87; also Du Sommerard, *Les Arts au Moyen-âge*,
tom. v., 1846, pp. 107, 162–8, and album, 2ᵉ sér.
pl. xxix., 8ᵉ sér. pl. xii.–xvi.

It is noticeable in these Byzantine pictures that
while the figure-painting is often really excellent,

the design skilful, and the pose natural, the landscape, trees, etc., are quite symbolic and fanciful.   The painters seem to have been utterly ignorant of perspective.   Buildings, too, without any regard to relative proportion, are coloured merely as parts of a colour scheme.   They are pink, pale green, yellow, violet, blue, just to please the eye.   That the painter had a system of colour-harmony is plain, but he paid no regard to the facts of city life, unless, indeed, it was the practice of the mediæval Byzantines to paint the outside of their houses in this truly brilliant style. Possibly they did so ; we have similar things in Italy even nowadays.

No doubt the French illuminators of the thirteenth and fourteenth centuries drew from these sources both their perspective and their architectural colouring.   As for ornamental illumination, the principal method of decoration was a square heading,[1] perhaps including a semicircular arch sweeping over several arcades, the corners and wall-space being occupied either with arabesque patterns, showing them to be after the time of Leo III., or with scrolls of line-ornament enriched with acanthus foliages.   Under this the scribe has placed his title.

Other examples have a square frame filled with the latter kind of scrolls and foliages, leaving a sort of open panel in the centre, in which is placed a small scene of sacred history or perhaps of country life.   Sometimes the title, in golden

[1] It has been thought to represent the Greek π, and to mean $\pi\acute{\upsilon}\lambda\eta$, a gate or door.

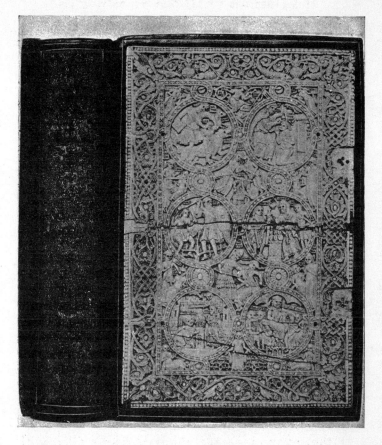

CARVED IVORY COVER
LATIN PSALTER OF MELLISENDA
12TH CENT.

Brit. Mus. Egert. MS. 1139

CODEX AURENS
(GOLDEN GOSPELS OF ATHELSTAN)
C. 835

Brit. Mus. Harl. MS. 2788, fol. 176

letters, is surrounded with medallions containing heads of Christ and the Virgin, apostles, and saints. The peculiar interlacing bands of violet, yellow, rose, blue, etc., which are still often seen in Russian ornament, are also features of these Byzantine MSS.; but most of all is the lavish use of gold. Perhaps the fact most to be remembered about these MSS. is that the painters of them worked in a manner that was absolutely fixed and rigid, the rules of which are laid down in a manual called the *Guide to Painting*, a work which has been translated by M. Didron.

So fixed and unalterable, indeed, is the manner that there is absolutely no difference to indicate relative antiquity between a MS. of the eleventh century and one of the sixteenth or even later, we might almost say, of the present day. In the matter of saint-images this is strictly true.

CHAPTER VI

CELTIC ILLUMINATION

Early liturgical books reflect the ecclesiastical art of their time—
This feature a continuous characteristic of illumination down
to the latest times—Elements of Celtic ornament—Gospels
of St. Chad—Durham Gospels—Contrast of Celtic and
Byzantine—St. Columba—Book of Kells—Details of its
decoration.

IN the earlier centuries of Christianity, when
liturgical books were the chief occupation of
the illuminator, it will need little pointing out to
demonstrate that the page of the illuminated
manuscript, where it contained more than the mere
ornamental initial, was simply a mirror of the
architectural decoration of the church in which
it was intended to be used. Where the church
enrichments consist, as on the Byzantine basilicas,
of panellings, arcades, and tympana of gilded
sculpture in wood or stone, with figures of saints,
the pages of the Gospel-book bear similar designs.
Where, as in the Romanesque, they are rich in
mosaics, and fretted arcades interlacing each
other, so are the illuminated Lives of the Saints,
the Menologia, Psalters, and Gospel-books.
Where, as in the Gothic cathedrals of the West
—of France, Germany, or Italy—the stained
glass is the striking feature of the interior, so

it is with the illumination ; it is a " vitrail "—a
glass-painting on vellum. On this latter point we
shall have more to say when we reach the period
of Gothic illumination.

Incidentally, also, the book reflects the minor
arts in vogue at the period of its execution.
Often in the illumination· we may detect these
popular local industries. We see mosaic enamelling, wood- and stone-carving, and lacquer-work,
and as we approach the Renaissance, even gem-
cutting and the delicate craft of the medallist. In
Venice and the Netherlands we have the local
taste for flower-culture ; in Germany we find
sculpture in wood and stone ; in France the
productions of the enameller and the goldsmith ;
until at length, in the full blaze of the Renaissance itself, we have in almost every land the
same varieties of enrichment practised according
to its own special style of work.

It has been said that the oldest Celtic illuminated
MSS. show no signs of classic, or even Byzantine,
influence, yet the plan or framework of the designs
makes use both of the cross and the arch, as used
in the earliest Byzantine examples. The details,
indeed, are quite different, and manifestly derived
from indigenous sources. It may be, therefore,
that the framework is merely a geometrical co-
incidence which could not well be avoided. The
fact that the basis of pure Irish ornament *is* geometrical, and developed out of the prehistoric and
barbarous art of the savages who preceded the
Celts in Ireland; such art as is used on the carved
shafts of spears, and oars, and staves of honour,

and afterwards on stone crosses and metal-work, may account for the similarity of ideas in ornament developed by old Roman decorators in their mosaic pavements, and may reconcile, in some measure, the varied opinions of different writers who have approached the subject from different points of view. Westwood adhered to the theory of its being purely indigenous. Fleury, on the other hand, in his Catalogue of the MSS. in the Library at Laon, asserts that we owe the knots and interlacements to the influence of the painters, sculptors, and mosaicists of Rome. "These interlacings, cables, etc., there is no Gallo-Roman monument which does not exhibit them, and, only to cite local instances, the cord of four or five strands is seen in the beautiful mosaics discovered in profusion within the last five years (1857–62) at Blanzy, at Bazoches, at Vailly, and at Reims. It was from them that the Franks borrowed their knots and twists and ribbons for their belts and buckles, their rings and bracelets" (pt. i., p. 8).

The elements, therefore, of book ornament, as used by the Celtic penmen, are such as were employed by the prehistoric and sporadic nations in the textile art in plaiting and handweaving, and afterwards transferred to that of metal-work. Terminals of animal, bird, or serpent form afterwards combine with the linear designs. The dog and dragon are common, as may be seen in the archaic vases produced by the Greeks before they came under the influence of ideas from Western Asia.

Among Celtic artists, as among those of later times, the practice of working in various materials was common to the same individual, and Dagæus (d. 586) may compare with Dunstan, Eloy, Tuotilo, and others.

To apply these observations to the style of illumination which now comes under our notice it may be said that if we allow the cross and arch to be copied from the Byzantine MSS. introduced from abroad, the details are undoubtedly supplied by the wickerwork and textile netting familiar to the everyday life of the artist. Assisted by the fertile imagination of bardic lore in snakes, dragons, and other mythic monsters of heroic verse, the illuminator produces a pencilled tapestry of textile fabric or flexile metal-work as marvellous as it is unique. No amount of description can give a true idea of what Celtic work is like; it must be seen to be comprehended. One glance at a facsimile of such a MS. as the Book of Kells or the Lindisfarne Gospels, or those of St. Chad at Lichfield, or wherever, as at St. Gall, such work is to be met with, will supersede the most laboured attempt at description. We must therefore at once refer the reader to the facsimile. When that has been inspected, we may proceed. In the first place it may be noted that with these Occidental MSS. begins the importance and development of the initial, which, indeed, as regards the illumination of Western Europe, is the very root of the matter. It is the development of the initial letter first into the bracket, then into the border, which forms the great distinction of the "Art of Paris," as Dante calls it, from that of Byzantium.   The latter is almost always of a squared or tabular design, traced and painted on a ground of burnished gold.   The former exhausts itself first in fantastic lacertine forms, twisted into the shapes of the commencing letters or words of the writing, to which the suggestion of some Byzantine MS. perhaps occasionally adds a frame.   Next come birds, dogs, dragons, vine-stems, and spirals embedded in couches of colour ; but, whatever its character, always it is the letter that governs and originates the ornament.   Only at the very end of its life, when the border has completely eclipsed the initial, is the idea of origin forgotten.   Then, indeed, we find the border treillages of flower-stem or leafwork starting from meaningless points of the design, or scattered shapelessly at random.

When we meet with work of this sort, we need no further proof that the real art is dead.   We have before us in such a performance—a trade production—a mere object of commerce, valuable so far as it is the result of labour, but not as a work of art.

According to the Abbé Geoghegan,[1] Christianity was known to the people of Ireland in the fourth century.   The Greek Menology asserts that it was carried thither by Simon Zelotes, but this is contradicted by the Roman Breviary and the Martyrologists.   Simeon Metaphrastes attributes it to St. Peter, Vincent of Beauvais to St. James. Unreliable as these traditions may be taken

[1] *Hist. de l'Irlande.*

singly, they nevertheless agree in placing the
conversion of Ireland at a very early date, probably, as Geoghegan says, in the fourth century.
It is certain that about the middle of the sixth
century an Irish prince of distinguished ancestry,
and himself a saint, led a band of missionaries
from Donegal to Iona. It is curious to observe
that the event is almost contemporary with the
renovations of Justinian at Byzantium, and only a
short time before the founding of the famous
Abbey of Monte Cassino by St. Benedict. Before the existence of the Benedictine Order
there was a monastery at Durrow, in Ireland,
and in this monastery the aforesaid prince was
educated. His name was Columba. At least, so
he is called, but whether it be merely in allusion
to his mission—"the Dove"—or really a patro-
nymic, it is hard to say. He was the messenger of
peace to the natives of Iona, and even the name
of the island seems to suggest an allusion to the
Old Testament missionary to the Ninevites, Jonah.
The Irish missionaries called the spot to which
they went *I. columcille*, "the cell of the Dove's
isle," or Columba's cell. It is usually spoken of
as the Monastery of Iona. Columba went on
many other missions, but ultimately returned to
his beloved Iona, where he died in 597, the year
after the arrival of Augustine at Canterbury.

His companions busied themselves with the
transcription of the Gospels for the use of new
converts, after the model of those they had seen
and used at Durrow. It is even traditionally
asserted that Columba himself took part in the

work, and transcribed both a Psalter and a
Gospel-book, moreover, that one of the Iona
Gospel-books written by him is still in existence.
This MS., whether the work of St. Columba or
not, and probably it is not, is the earliest
known monument of Irish calligraphic art. It
is known as the Book of Kells, and there is
no doubt that it is the most amazing specimen
of penmanship ever seen. It is at once the
most ancient, the most perfect, and the most
precious example of Celtic art in existence.
It exhibits the striking peculiarities and features of the style—the bandwork knots and
interlacings, such as may be seen on the
stone crosses which mark the burial-places of
British and Irish chieftains. Witness, for instance, the Carew, or the Nevern Cross, described
in the *Journal of the Archæological Institute*, iii.
71, which might be taken to represent an initial
"I" wrought in stone. There is no foliage, no
plant form at all. It is not, therefore, derivable
from Romanesque, Byzantine, or Oriental ornament. It is indigenous, if not to Ireland, at
least to those prehistoric Aryan tribes of which
the Irish were a branch. Its basis is the art of
weaving, and in some respects resembles the
matting of Polynesia much more closely that the
vine-stems of Sicily or the arabesques of Byzantium. Spirals occur that bewilder the eye, yet
are so faultlessly perfect that only the magnifying-
glass brings out the incredible accuracy of the
drawing. Among them are mythological and
allegorical beasts, snakes, and lizards—thought

to represent demons, like the gargoyles of Gothic architecture—in every conceivable attitude of contortion and agony. There are also doves and fishes, but the latter, being sacred emblems together with the lamb, are seldom made grotesque. It was a monkish legend that the devil could take the shape of any bird or beast, except those of the dove and the lamb.

CHAPTER VII

CELTIC ILLUMINATION—*continued*

The Iona Gospels—Contrast with Roman and Byzantine—Details—Treatment of animal forms—Colour schemes—The Gospel-book of St. Columbanus—That of Mael Brith Mac Durnan—The Lindisfarne Gospels—*Cumdachs*—Other book-shrines.

WE have seen that in both Roman and Byzantine MSS. the titles and beginnings of books were merely distinguished by a lettering in red or gold, rather smaller, in fact, than the ordinary text, but rendered distinct by the means referred to. The handwriting, too, is clear and legible, whether capital, uncial, or minuscule.

In absolute contrast to all this the Iona Gospels have the first page completely covered with ornament. On the next the letters are of an enormous size, followed by a few words, not merely in *uncials*, but in characters varying from half an inch to two inches in height. The page opposite to each Gospel is similarly filled with decoration, separated into four compartments by an ornamented Greek cross. This may, of course, be simply a geometrical device in no way connected with Greece, but, taken in connection with other features, we see in it an indication of contact with

44

Byzantine work and the side of illumination which deals rather with the tabular enrichment of the page than the development of the initial. Further, the writing, though large, is not easily legible, for it is involved, enclaved, and conjointed in a manner sufficiently puzzling to those who see it for the first time.

The plaiting and inlaying are certainly borrowed from local usages, and the survival of the same kind of interlaced plaiting in the Scottish tartans is some evidence of the long familiarity of the Celtic race with the art of weaving. When we remember that some of the early illuminators were also workers in metals, we can understand that penmen like Dagæus, Dunstan, and Eloy had designs at their command producible by either method. So we see, both in the MS. and in the brooch and buckle, the same kind of design. Among the earliest animals brought into this Celtic work we find the dog and the dragon ; the latter both wingless and winged, according to convenience or requirement. The dog is so common in some of the Celto-Lombardic MS., of which examples still exist at Monte Cassino, as almost to create a style; while the dragon survives to the latest period of Gothic art.

Whatever is introduced into a Celtic illumination is at once treated as a matter of ornament. When the human figure appears it is remorselessly subjected to the same rules as the rest of the work ; the hair and beard are spiral coils, the eyes, nostrils, and limbs are symmetrical flourishes. Colour is quite regardless of natural

possibility. The hair and draperies are simply
patterned as compartments of green or blue, or
red or black, as may be required for the *tout
ensemble;* the face remains white. Lightened
tints are preferred to full colours, as pale yellow,
pink, lavender, and light green. A very ludicrous
device is made use of to denote the folds of the
drapery; they are not darkened, there is no light
and shade in Celtic work, but are simply lines of
a strongly contrasting colour. The blue and red
appear to be opaque, and therefore mineral
colours; the rest are thin and transparent.
Nothing can be more wayward than the colouring of the symbolic beasts of the Gospels. In
the Evangeliary of St. Columbanus (not Columba,
but the founder of Luxeuil and Bobbio, who died
in 614) the Lion of St. Mark is an admirable
beast in a suit of green-and-red chain armour in
the form of mascles or lozenges. (See the illustration in Westwood's *Palæographia Sacra Pictoria*
of a figure page from the Gospels of Mael Brith
Mac Durnan for a typical example.)[1]

The only point that might argue the freedom
in Celtic work from Byzantine influence is the
absence of gold, but perhaps this was only
because the earlier Irish illuminators could not
obtain it; we find it later on. In the Book of
Kells and the Lambeth Gospels there is no gold.
The former dates somewhere in the seventh century, not the sixth, as sometimes stated; the
latter, shortly before 927. In the Lindisfarne

---

[1] See also an article by Westwood in *Journ. Archæol.
Inst.*, vii. 17, on "Irish Miniatures."

Gospels (698–721) gold is used. In the Psalter of Ricemarchus, now in Trinity College, Dublin, are traces of silver. It is in connection with these Irish MSS. that decorated and jewelled cases, called *cumdachs,* make their appearance, such as the one attached to the Gospels of St. Moling in the Library of Trinity College, Dublin. These book-shrines are almost exclusively an Irish production. In other countries the idea was to adorn the volume itself with a splendid and costly binding, perhaps including gold, silver, and gems. In Ireland the idea of sacredness was carried out in another way. Instead of decorating the covers of the book itself, it was held, as in such a MS., for instance, as the Book of Durrow, to be too venerable a relic to be meddled with, and a box or case was made for it, on which they spent all their artistic skill. Generally the case is known as a *cumdach;* but one kind, called the *cathach,* was so closed that the book was completely concealed, and it was superstitiously believed that if it were opened some terrible calamity would overtake its possessors. Such was the *cathach* of Tyrconnell. We must remember, however, that in this instance the keepers were not men of book-learning, but hardy warriors who carried the *cathach* into battle as a charm and an incitement to victory.

Of similar shrines, which were made for precious books by both the Greeks and Lombards, the oldest and most famous is that made for Theudelinde, wife of Agilulf, King of the Lombards, and given by her, in 616, together

with the famous iron crown and other relics, to
the Cathedral of Monza, where they are still
to be seen.

The enrichment of the covers of books themselves, as distinct from the use of cases or shrines,
has been usual in almost all ages and styles of
decoration. When we come to speak of Carolingian MSS. we shall find several remarkable
instances.

We must now pass on from this curiously
attractive theme of Celtic calligraphy to its contemporary styles of France, Germany, Spain,
and Italy, only remarking by the way that no
other style of its time had so marked an influence
on the local *scriptoria* into which it was introduced as this same Celtic of Ireland. It is not
only traceable, but easily recognised all along
the Rhine, in Burgundy, the Swiss Cantons, and
Lombardy, until at length overwhelmed by the
general introduction of Romanesque or Byzantine, which was restored and filtered through the
Exarchate and the Lombard schools during the
early days of the new Carolingian Empire.

CHAPTER VIII

SEMI-BARBARIC ILLUMINATION

Visigothic—Merovingian—Lombardic—Extinction of classic art
—Splendid reign of Dagobert—St. Eloy of Noyon—The
Library of Laon—Natural History of Isidore of Seville—
Elements of contemporary art—Details of ornament—Sym-
bolism — Luxeuil and Monte Cassino — Sacramentary of
Gellone—" Prudentius "—" Orosius "—Value of the Sacra-
mentary of Gellone.

TO reach the beginnings of these various de-
generate and illiterate attempts at book-work
we have only to watch the last expiring gleams of
classic art beneath the ruthless footsteps of the
barbarian invaders of the old Roman Empire.

In the sixth century the light of the old civilisation was fast fading away. Perhaps we may look
upon the so-called splendour of the reign of Dagobert in France as the spasmodic scintillations of
its latest moments of existence. The kingdom
of Dagobert, after 631, was almost an empire.
For the seven years preceding his death, in 638,
he ruled from the Elbe and the Saxon frontier to
that of Spain, and from the Atlantic Ocean to the
confines of Hungary. It was during his reign
that we read of the skill in metal-work of the
celebrated St. Eloy of Noyon, the rival of our
own St. Dunstan.

St. Eloy or Eligius (588–659) began his artistic

career as the pupil of Abbo, the goldsmith and
mint-master to Chlothaire II., and rose from the
rank of a goldsmith to that of Bishop of Noyon.
Among his handiwork were crowns, chalices, and
crosiers, and he is reputed to have made the chair
of bronze-gilt now in the National Library at
Paris, called the *fauteuil* of Dagobert, and many
other works, which disappeared either during the
wars of Louis XV. or those of the Revolution of
1789. He founded the Abbey of Solignac, near
Limoges, and it is not improbable that the reputation of this city for metal-work and enamelling
may be dated from his foundation. With such
works as those of Eloy before them, it is difficult
to believe that the wretched and puerile attempts
at ornamental penmanship and illumination which
are shown at Laon and other places as the work
of this period can possibly represent the highest
efforts of the calligrapher. But we must remember that St. Eloy was an extraordinary genius
in his art, and that the bulk of the clergy, not to
mention ordinary workmen, were very ignorant
and ill-taught. Very few, indeed, were men who
could be considered cultured. Gregory of Tours,
the historian, and Venantius Fortunatus, the
hymn-writer, are among the few.

In the Library at Laon, M. Fleury describes a
MS. of the Natural History of Isidore of Seville,
which is looked upon as a work of reference both
as regards art and learning. It was at one time
a very popular book, being a Latin cyclopædia,
dealing with the sciences and general knowledge
of the time ; yet the example referred to by

M. Fleury shows us only a crowd of initials learnedly styled by the Benedictine authors and others "ichthio-morphiques" and "ornithoeides," *i.e.* made up of fishes and birds, and about equal in quality and finish to the efforts of a very ordinary schoolboy.

These initials betray an utter decadence from the beautiful uncials of the fifth and sixth centuries, seen in the St. Germain's Psalter, for example, now in the National Library at Paris. The colours are coarse and badly applied, and even where brightest are utterly unrefined and without taste.

Notwithstanding, however, the apparently total eclipse or extinction of Roman art in Gaul, or, as it must henceforth be called, France, it is claimed by M. Fleury[1] that the interlacements which constitute the principal feature of these earlier Merovingian MSS. are derived from the remains of Roman mosaics found profusely at Blanzy, Bazoches, and Reims. This may be so, but those mosaics would not account for the same features in the Irish work, for the Romans never reached Ireland as occupants or colonists.

Take another example from the Laon collection, the History of Orosius. The first page is a type of the species to which it belongs, and, moreover, a good sample of the earliest efforts of all pictorial art. An ordinary rectangular cross occupies the centre of the page. The centre shows us the Lamb of the Apocalypse and St. John. On the arms are the beasts which typify the Evangelists—their

[1] See later.

emblems, as they are sometimes called. We notice that they are all symbolic, and not intended to be natural imitations of reality. The various animals scattered about the page are all symbolic —all have a mystical interpretation and *raison d'être*. A border-frame, passing behind each extremity of the cross, contains a number of dog-like animals, some plain, others spotted, while the body of the cross itself is occupied with attempts at foliage ornaments. In the left upper corner are the letters "X P I," in the right "I H V," thick foliage springing from the "I" and "V" and falling back over the monogram. In the lower corners are two fishes and two doves, each pair hanging to a penwork chain.

The emblem of John, on the upper extremity of the cross, is an eagle-headed and winged man holding a book; its opposite one of Lucas at foot is a singularly conceived anthropoid and winged ox, also with a book. On the left Marcus, whose head is indescribable; and on the right Matthew, with human head, the rest of the figures being as before. The eye in all the figures is a most remarkable feature. Both in the pictures and the initials of this MS. the outline has been drawn in black ink, and the colours yellow, red, brown, and green applied afterwards.

As the new masters of the West were not so much interested in the artistic remains of the mangled civilisation they were endeavouring to destroy as in mastery and military success, it was left for the monasteries and the church to see to the welfare of books and monuments.

In the seventh century it was the monasteries that saved almost all we know of the preceding centuries. During the turmoil of the period from the fifth to the eighth century we find certain quiet corners where learning and the arts still breathed, grew, and dwelt in security. Lérins, founded by St. Honoratus of Arles ; Luxeuil by Columbanus, Bobbio his last retreat ; and, above all, Monte Cassino, the great pattern of monasticism, the Rule of whose founder was destined to become the basis of all later Orders, were each of them steadily labouring to rescue the civilisation daily threatened by the ravage of war, and to preserve it for the benefit of the ignorant hordes who, because of their ignorance, now only aimed at its entire destruction. We have seen how these monks and clerics, with more goodwill than ability, did their best to adorn the books which came into their hands. It is a poor show, but there is no better. It is absolutely our only record of how civilisation managed to struggle through the storm.

Let us, then, be thankful even for the Laon "Orosius," for the Sacramentary of Gellone, and the Mozarabic Liturgies of Puy. They are among the links between ancient and mediæval art.

As already stated, the handwriting of Merovingian MSS. is mainly an adaptation of the Roman uncial, as it is in Irish and Lombardic, or, we might say, everywhere else. Abbreviations are still uncommon. Where minuscules are used, the writing is not quite so legible as in the larger

hands, but we are not met by the singular diffi-
culties of some of the Lombardic texts.

A few solitary texts of the earliest time are in
capitals, such as the really handsome "Prudentius"
of the Paris National Library, where the entire
text of the great Christian poet is boldly inscribed
in the centre of a large white page of vellum, like
a series of separate inscriptions. The first few
words are "rubrished" in the antique manner.
The MS. is supposed to date previous to the year
527. A little later than this St. Columbanus
founded the monastery of Luxeuil, and later still,
viz. in 616, that of Bobbio.

If we turn to the Visigothic area, including the
South of France and the entire peninsula of Spain,
our first and typical example is the celebrated Sacramentary of Gellone. This MS. dates, it is said,
from the eighth century. It is written throughout in Visigothic uncials, though executed in the
South of France. Its ornamentation is frankly
barbaric. The colours used are yellow, red, and
green. The great initials are double lined, and
the interlinear space filled in with a flat tint of
colour and lines of red dots, as in the Book of
Kells occasionally follow the contours. Here, also,
are the fish- or bird-form letters as in the Laon
"Orosius." Now and then occurs a tiny scene—
perhaps a fight between two grotesque brutes,
neither fish, nor fowl, nor beast known to the
naturalist, but a horrible compound of the worst
qualities of each. The human figure, when it
occurs, is childishly shapeless. But the design
and treatment, nevertheless, bear witness to a

lively imagination and considerable knowledge of Christian symbolism. It is these mental qualities which, in spite of the manifest absence of manual skill, render the Gellone Evangeliary one of the most precious monuments of its time. Of the rest of the MSS. of this wretched period we will say nothing.

"Non ragioniam di lor', ma guard' e passa."

We are glad to hurry on for another century or so, remembering that the leading idea now is the development of the initial letter.

CHAPTER IX

DEVELOPMENT OF THE INITIAL

The initial and initial paragraph the main object of decoration in Celtic illumination—Study of the letter L as an example —The I of " In principio " and the B of " Beatus Vir."

FROM the moment when the initial was placed beneath the miniature the object of the whole design was not to give prominence to the initial but to the picture. Until then, that is, whilst the initial remains above or beside or outside the picture, it is the initial we must watch for style and development. And therefore we seize on one letter among those of the latter part of the eighth century, because of the frequency of its occurrence in the Gospel-book or Evangeliary, one of the commonest books of the time. This the letter L of " Liber Generationis," etc., the commencing words of St. Matthew. This passage is always made of importance, and on the initial and arrangement of the words the artist expends his best efforts.

Properly I should here display pictorially the series of which I speak. It would certainly be the quickest way of explaining the matter. But as this is out of the question for many reasons, and as the present little guide aims rather at showing the way than marching through it, the reader must be content to take its advice about where to look for examples which it cannot reproduce.

Regarding the letter L as an index of time and style, first we may take the Irish L of the Book of Kells on p. 17, pt. 1, of Miss Stokes' *Early Christian Art in Ireland*. Note first the form of the letter, then the way it is filled up with ornament. Compare this, which dates from the seventh century, with a similar L in the Ada-Codex in the Town Library at Trèves, No. 22. A black and white copy of this is given in taf. 6 of Lamprecht Initial Ornamentik. This carries up the work to the second half of the eighth century. Next, say the L in the Town Archives at Cologne, No. 147. This belongs to the second half of the ninth century. The chief departure here is towards the knotted band work which figures so largely afterwards both in German and Italian book ornament, the form is still unchanged. But with the tenth century comes change of form as well as of mode of filling, as for example taf. 19 of Lamprecht, in which there is a complete alteration of treatment. The student may take for similar comparison also the I of " In principio " of St. John's Gospel, and the B of the first psalm in the Psalter, and carry the comparison on to the end of the fourteenth century, by referring to the MSS. in the British Museum and other public libraries, or in the numerous illustrated works to be found in those collections.

CHAPTER X

FIRST ENGLISH STYLES

Transition from Iona to Lindisfarne—Influence of Frankish art—The "Opus Anglicum"—The Winchester school and its characteristics—Whence obtained—Method of painting —Examples—Where found and described.

THE succession of the school of Iona shows us in the first examples of English illumination the type exemplified in the Book of Kells, modified, but not very much, by its transference to Lindisfarne.

Whatever doubt may be felt as to the influence of Byzantine or Romanesque models on pure Irish work, such as the Book of Kells, there can be none as regards the Lindisfarne Gospels. In the first place we have gold both in the lettering and ornament. This MS., known also as the Durham Book (Brit. Mus., Nero D. iv.), was the work of Abbat Eadfrith, of Lindisfarne. It has been often described, as it is really a most precious example of eighth-century art in this country. No other MS. of its time is to be found in any continental scriptorium to be compared with it. It is not a collection of clumsy inartistic attempts at ornamental writing, but high-class, effective work, which should be seen and studied by every student of illumination.

From its style of execution, its details of portraiture, and other features, it may be looked upon as one of the earliest links between the two extremes of Oriental and Occidental Art.

Another MS. in the British Museum (Vesp. A. 1), which combines the Roman method of painting as in the Vergils with the pen-work of these Anglo-Celtic Gospel-books, may also repay careful examination.

It is very possible that the celebrated *scriptoria* of York and Jarrow may have been furnished with both MSS. and copyists from Rome, yet there can be little doubt that the intercourse with Durham would be quite as active. Nor is it less probable that similar intercourse would keep them *en rapport* with Oxford, St. Alban's, Westminster, Glastonbury, and other *scriptoria*, so that in the eighth century England stood with respect to art second to no other country in the Christian world.

During the ninth century active intercourse with the Frankish Empire enriched English churches and religious houses, especially Winchester, with examples of Byzantine and Roman models, which Charlemagne had introduced into his own palatine schools. From such secondary models as the Sacramentaries and Evangeliaries executed at Tours, Soissons, Metz, and other busy centres of production, English illuminators succeeded in forming a distinctive style of their own. In the French or, rather, Frankish MSS., while the richness of the gold and the beauty and delicacy of the colouring are in themselves most charming, and while certain features may in general be recognised as no doubt suggestive, there is nothing which quite predicts the remarkable treatment which characterises the English work. "Opus Anglicum" was its distinctive title. The term, indeed, was applied to all English artistic productions more or less—embroidery among the rest. The women of England, says William of Poitiers, were famous for their needlework, the men excelled in metal-work and jewellery. But it was the illuminated Service Books that have perpetuated the term.

From the Lindisfarne Gospels to the Winchester Benedictionals is a far cry—but Art is long and time is fleeting, hence many pages of intervening description must be omitted. We may, however, refer the reader to Westwood's *Palæographia Sacra Pictoria*, the Palæographical Society's publications, and other works, for enlightenment on this period. On the Rouen and Devonshire Benedictionals much interesting information may be found in vol. 24 of the *Archæologia* and in the recent volume of the Bradshaw Society concerning them.

The work is peculiar ; and if we consider the treatment of foliage apart from the colour, we cannot but notice its similarity to the ivory carving observable in the consular diptychs. Ivory carving was then a popular artistic occupation. The foliage is graceful, the composition well-balanced, and the colour mostly bright body colour applied in the Greek manner. The fault of the heads is that they are too small for the figure, and of the draperies that the folds are overdone with too much fluttering detail.   The gilding differs from the Byzantine in not being laid on the vellum in the form of burnished leaf, but painted on like the colours, not only in the figures but in the frame-work and ornaments.

The British Museum contains several characteristic examples, but, as has been said, the very finest are those at Rouen and in the library of the Duke of Devonshire.

Perhaps no genuine example exists earlier than the Golden Charter of King Edgar of true Winchester illumination, executed forty years after the accession of Athelstan, whose Coronation Book (Brit. Mus., Tib. A. 2) is most probably not English at all, but Carolingian of the finest type.   Many other *scriptoria* in England in the tenth century were equally busy with Winchester, but none could vie with the royal city in the production of illuminated books.

CHAPTER XI

CAROLINGIAN ILLUMINATION

Why so-called—Works to be consulted—The Library of St. Gall—Rise and progress of Carolingian art—Account of various MSS.—Features of the style—Gospels of St. Sernin —The Ada-Codex—Centres of production—Other splendid examples—The Alcuin Bible—The Gospel of St. Médard of Soissons.

ONCE more crossing the Channel let us now inquire what has been doing among the Franks since the Gellone Sacramentary, especially in the schools instituted by the Emperor Charles the Great. Materials for this inquiry are most abundant. One of the more important works on the subject is the lucid monograph of Dr. Rahn, of Zurich, on the Golden Psalter of Folchard at St. Gall, which deals more or less with the whole question of Carolingian art, while M. Léop. Delisle's brochure on the Evangeliary of St. Vaast of Arras gives us a copious account of the Franco-Saxon branch of it. Apart, however, from these sources of information, we have not a few original MSS. still extant, which, of course, more vividly speak for themselves, and only require pointing out to the student.

The clearest method of study being to take things in the order of their creation, so in order

to understand the " character of savage grandeur
and naïve originality" which has been attributed
to this style, it will be best to take up these MSS.
chronologically.   At the same time, if anyone
merely wishes to know what the style is like at
its best, Dr. Rahn must be his guide, as the Golden
Psalter which he has selected for study is as
splendid an example as perhaps may be found in
the whole career of the art.   We have noticed
how the Irish missionary-artists carried their
work to their continental settlements, how they
planted their schools in Burgundy, Switzerland,
and Lombardy.   Of all their depositories, however, numerous as they are elsewhere, none is
richer in the relics of their work than the celebrated abbey which takes its name of St. Gall
from that disciple of St. Columbanus, who in 614
founded his little cell beside the Steinach, about
nine miles south of the Lake of Constance.   Under
Charles Martel the cell had become a monastery,
which he endowed as a Benedictine abbey.   In
830 was founded its magnificent library of MSS.
The library still exists, and at the present moment
gives shelf-room to 1,800 MSS. and more than
41,700 printed books.   Besides this, another, called
the Town Library, founded in the sixteenth century, and containing 500 MSS. and 60,400 printed
books, gives this upland, busy, modern manu-
facturing Swiss town no mean importance as a
centre of literary culture.   Physically it is probably
the highest town in Europe, its street-level being
very nearly 2,200 feet above that of the sea.   Its
libraries and museums are rich storehouses of

mediæval treasures.   The architect raves over its
monastic buildings; the scholar and palæographer
gloat over its books and MSS.   In the libraries
of St. Gall are some of the masterpieces of Irish,
Saxon, and Carolingian art, and its great Benedictine abbey under Grimald from 841, *i.e.* during
the later Carolingian period, possessed one of the
most active *scriptoria* in Europe.   To begin with
the beginning, however, we must leave St. Gall,
and, passing by some less important MSS., go
back to the year 781 and the city of Toulouse.
In that year, and in the Abbey of St. Sernin
(Saturninus) in that city, was finished a wonderful
and truly splendid manuscript of the Gospels as
a present to the Emperor and his wife Hildegardis.
This is our first example.   It now is to be seen in
the National Library, Paris (Nouv. acqu. Lat.
1203).

Next comes the Evangeliary of Abbat Angilbert
of Centula (now St. Riquier), near Abbeville,
Charlemagne's son-in-law.   This MS., executed
about the year 793, is still preserved in the Town
Library of Abbeville.   In the same rank, but somewhat finer in execution, comes a third Evangeliary, that of St. Médard of Soissons, now in the
National Library, Paris (No. 8850, Lat.).

In these three MSS., reproductions from which
are to be found in various modern works on art,
the writing and ornamentation are the parts into
which the artist puts his best work, not the figure
drawing.   Although in the St. Sernin MS. there
is, in the Christ-figure, a distinct attempt at
portraiture quite different from the coils and pen-

flourishes which make up the Gospel-figures in
the Irish and Merovingian MSS.   Here the in-
spiration is clearly Greek, not Irish.   The figure
is draped in green* and violet—seated on an
embroidered cushion before a low castellated wall.
The hair is light, and the chin beardless.   The
design shows a decided likeness to the consular
ivory diptychs, and the painting follows the
Eastern methods.   In the details of ornament
only are Irish features.   Thus we trace in this
MS. the sources of Carolingian art.   The MS.
being dated, is important as affording a means
of comparison with other undated work.   It was
presented to St. Sernin on the occasion of the
visit of the Emperor and Empress with their son,
the amiable Louis "le Debonaire,"[1] just after the
latter had been made King of Aquitaine.   Godeschalk, the writer of it, on the last two leaves tells
us that it took him seven years to accomplish.
It is written throughout in gold and silver letters
on purple vellum, and is, moreover, ornamented
with borders, pictures, portraits, and panellings.
At first it was kept in a *cumdach* of silver, set
with precious stones, but that has disappeared.

The Golden Gospels of St. Médard, like the
Centula MS., are similar, but betoken an advance
in both taste and execution.   The figures are still
rude and deformed, but the artist shows a laudable desire, an ambition, in fact, to imitate the
work of better artists than himself.   Nevertheless,
the calligraphy and borderwork are the best parts
of his performance.   In this MS. the use of silver

[1] Mod. Fr. "Debonnaire."

betrays a tendency to prodigality.   In design, the influence of the artists who built the new church of San Vitale at Ravenna, a church which became the model for the Abbey of St. Médard itself, is quite manifest, yet perhaps need not be traced further than Soissons or Pavia.   In certain of the illustrations, as, for instance, the " Fountain of Life," there is at once a likeness and a variation as compared with the same symbol in the Evangeliary of St. Sernin.   They are both too intricate to describe, but of both it may be said that they show an intimate acquaintance with early Christian symbolism.   The ivory carving and architecture of Ravenna have evidently been known to the director of these frames and backgrounds.   In the year which saw the completion of Godeschalk's Gospels, Alcuin was at Parma, but when the St. Médard's Gospels were written he was Abbot of St. Martin's at Tours.   It was the presence of Alcuin at the Court of Charlemagne that accounts for the prevalence of the Saxon character in the new and beautiful handwriting we now call Carolingian.   It was the presence of Paul Warnefrid that accounts for much of the classic and most of the Lombardic features, both of the writing and the illumination.   Many other scholars assisted these two in the various centres in which Alcuin established branches of the palatine schools.   The intercourse with Italy and England was constant, and led to the frequent interchange of books, and community of methods and models.   Another fine MS. of the same period (c. 780) is the Golden Ada-Codex of St. Mesmin or Maximin, of Trèves.

In 1794 this MS. was taken from Trèves to Mainz;
in 1815 it was transferred to Aix-le-Chapelle, and
is now back again at Trèves.   The externals of
the Ada-Codex are very costly, its binding being a
late Gothic pendant to the cover of the Echternach
Evangeliary at Gotha.   In the centre of the fore-
cover there is a magnificent topaz,[1] with several
imperial figures.   Inside, the work is a handsome
example of the early Carolingian.[2]   It contains
the four Gospels written by order of the "Mother
and Lady Ada," sister of Charles the Great,
Abbess of St. Mesmin.   Next we have in the
British Museum another grand example of the
style as modified by English or Saxon influence.
Also the Zurich Bible, of the same date, executed
at Tours—and the Bamberg Bible, said to be a copy
of the Alcuin Bible of the same school.   Then follow
the Drogo Sacramentary, presented by the Emperor to his natural son Drogo, Archbishop of
Metz (826–855), perhaps illuminated at Metz, but
of the same school as those above mentioned.

In our own National Library, again, we have the
Athelstan Gospels (Harl. 2788), also in all probability executed at Metz.   At Paris (Nat. Lib.,
Theol. Lat. 266) is the Evangeliary of Lothaire—
a most beautiful example of gold-writing and
ornament.   So we might enumerate a score of
splendid MSS., and classify them into their various
minor schools.   But such is not our object.   All
we want here is a general but clear idea of the
style as a whole.

[1] Or sardonyx (Lamprecht says topaz.)
[2] A photograph of the cover is sold by F. Linz of Trèves.

To characterise it broadly by the names of its most important elements we should call it a Lombard-Saxon style—the interlacing bands and knots and other minor features and the main character of the writing being of Saxon origin, the classical foliages and manner of painting the figures and certain ideas of design Lombardic, strengthened by direct contact with the sources of the latter style. Whatever variations there may be, they can generally be accounted for according to locality and centre of production.   We have instanced a few examples of the earlier time as showing the principal features of the style.   Under the Emperor Charles the Great's grandson, Charles the Bald, Carolingian illumination reached its highest point of excellence, and the MSS. executed for him or his contemporaries accordingly give a correct idea of what Carolingian illuminators considered as good work.   The chief centres were still Tours and Metz—the latter a branch of the former, but gradually developing distinct features of its own ; and among the productions of these schools there still remain precious—we might say priceless— examples, such as the Vivien Bible of the Paris Library, so-called because presented by Count Vivien, Abbat of St. Martin's of Tours, to Charles the Bald in 850.[1]   It contains a fine picture of the presentation with *beardless* figures.   It has also a number of exceedingly splendid initials showing strong Byzantine influence— capitals of columns of classic origin and traces of Merovingian in letter forms and ornamental details.   It is

[1] Plate in t. 1 of Louandre.

like the Evangeliary of Lothaire, already mentioned, a most sumptuous example rich in silver
and gold—the latter having a grand portrait of
Lothaire seated on his throne.   Both MSS. are
in the National Library at Paris, the Vivien,
No. 1 (Theol. Lat.), the Lothaire, No. 266.   But the
one example to which we would call the reader's
attention, though among the earlier productions
of the period, as not only most readily accessible,
but most precious to the English student, is the
celebrated Alcuin Bible in the British Museum
(Add. MS. 10546).   This venerable MS. is a copy
of the Vulgate revised by Alcuin himself, and
said to be exactly similar to the one at Bamberg.
Biblical revision was perhaps the most important
of his many literary occupations, and this volume
is reasonably believed to be the actual copy prepared for presentation to Charlemagne under the
reviser's own superintendence, possibly, in part
at least, the work of his own hand.   It is a
large folio, finely written in a neat minuscule,
mainly Saxon hand, with uncial initials in two
columns.   The miniatures, including their architectural details, are in the Roman manner, the
ornaments partly Byzantine, partly Celtic.   The
great similarity of design between different manuscripts is strikingly exemplified by a comparison
of three borders from (a) the Evangeliary of St.
Vaast of Arras, fol. 28 v. (see Delisle); (b) the
Evangel. in National Library, Paris, anc. fds. Lat.
257 (see Louandre), and Evangeliary No. 309
Bibl. de Cambrai (see Durieux).

Indeed, comparisons of this kind are very instructive frequently as suggestive of *provenance*, as each working centre would have its own set of models and designs. Of course, comparison of the MSS. themselves is out of the question, but the comparisons can often be effected by the student's having Louandre, Durieux, Fleury, Labarte, etc., by his side during the examination of any given period. The limits of our little book forbid our speaking of other examples of this splendid style, but we cannot conclude without noticing that in the opinion of M. Ferdinand Denis, the Golden Gospels of St. Médard of Soissons is the most beautiful Carolingian MSS. extant.

CHAPTER XII

MONASTIC ILLUMINATION

Introductory—Monasteries and their work from the sixth to
the ninth century—The claustral schools—Alcuin—
Warnefrid and Theodulf—Clerics and monastics—The
Golden Age of monasticism—The Order of St. Benedict
—Cistercian houses—Other Orders—Progress of writing in
Carolingian times—Division of labour.

IN the sixth century the monasteries, such as
they were, necessarily kept themselves very
quiet and unobtrusive. They were situated usually
in out-of-the-way corners, solitudes apart from
civilisation, or, at least, apart from the busy
haunts of men. In the eighth century there is
a marked difference. The Capitular of Aix-la-
Chapelle, of 789, required that minor schools
should be attached *to all monasteries and cathedral
churches* without exception, and that children of
all ranks, *both noble and servile*, should be received
into them. Also that the larger monasteries
should open major schools in which the seven
sciences of mathematics, astronomy, arithmetic,
music, rhetoric, dialectics, and geography, were
to be taught—and this in two ways. There were
to be two sorts of schools—interior or *claustral,*
intended for monastics only, and exterior or
canonical, intended for secular students. These

schools were under separate scholastics or masters, and lay students were received in the exterior schools as freely and fully as in the public schools of the present time.   Mabillon[1] gives a list of some twenty-seven monastic and cathedral schools, by no means confined to great or wealthy cities, but well distributed throughout the Empire.

In the time of Charlemagne those most in repute were Tours, St. Gall, Fulda, Reims, and Hirsfeld.

We have given the names of Alcuin and Paul Warnefrid as the chief promoters of the Carolingian Revival, but we should not omit that of Theodulf, of Orleans, the indefatigable school inspector of the time.   He it was who assisted the artistic side of the movement by his ingenious contrivances as a writer and illustrator of school books.   Undoubtedly it was from his suggestions that we so often find in mediæval scientific treatises of the driest kind those graphic and wonderful tabulations and edifices, labelled and turreted, which make Aristotle, Priscian, and Marcianus Capella, not only comprehensible, but attractive. Theodulf composed in simple and easy Latin verse—somewhat after the style of the *Propria quæ maribus* of our own childhood—the description of a supposed tree of science, which he had drawn and painted, on the trunk and branches of which were the figures and names of the seven liberal arts.   At the foot sat Grammar—the basis of all learning—holding on her hand a lengthy rod (ominous for the tender student).   On the right

[1] Præfat. in iv. Sæcul. 184.

Rhetoric stretched forth her hand. On the left was Dialectic. Philosophy sat on the summit; the rest being disposed according to their relative importance. The whole was explained in the *Carmina de septem artibus*, in which the bishop, who was one of the famous poets of the age, strove in flowery language to render these dry-as-dust studies acceptable to the youthful understanding. Theodulf was a great scholar, and assisted Alcuin in the revision of the Bible, one copy of which he himself had written whilst still Abbat of Fleury, about 790. At the beginning of this Bible is a poem in golden letters on purple, and a preface in prose, also in golden letters, giving a synopsis of the several books. The text differs somewhat from the Alcuin Bible, as it is that of Jerome before Alcuin's revision. This MS. is now at Paris. Another Bible executed to the order of Theodulf is now in the Town Library at Puy.

It seems incredible, after the efforts made by Charlemagne and his ministers for the maintenance of learning and the arts, that there should ever be any risk of a return to barbarism, but it is a fact that the dissolution of the Empire proved in certain localities the suspension of prosperity. Fortunately the monastics—especially the Benedictines—and the canons of the cathedrals still kept up the practice of copying books; but almost all the South of France, Languedoc, and Provence, always conservative, remained more or less illiterate. They produced poets and jongleurs, but seldom artists or scholars. And even in the

North, where the capitular schools were most flourishing—as Paris, Reims, and Chartres—the general tendency was towards relapse. In High Germany it was even worse. In spite of all efforts of the clergy by the extension of secular schools, the laity preferred the excitement of chase and camp to the quiet humdrum of the schoolroom. Religion seemed to be regarded rather as a profession than a principle, quite right in its place, *i.e.* the Church and the monastery, but unsuited for active life. The wealthy land-owners, therefore, did not cease to endow religious houses or to build churches, but they left book-learning to the clerics. Accordingly the clerics and the monastics flourished exceedingly.

From the beginning of the tenth century to the beginning of the thirteenth was the Golden Age of monasticism. The Order of St. Benedict scattered its foundations thickly over France and Western Germany, while its reformed colonies of Cluny, Citeaux, Clairvaux, and the Chartreuse again spread their settlements in all directions. Thus we find Cluny established in 910, Grammont in 1076, the Chartreuse in 1080, Citeaux in 1098, Savigny in 1105, Tiron in 1109, Austin Canons in 1038, Premonstrants in 1120, Crutched Friars in 1169. In England, from 1100, scarcely a year passed by without the establishment of some fresh foundation. During the thirty-five years of the reign of Henry I. more than 150 religious houses were founded. And even during the disastrous reign of Stephen, in less than twenty years, no fewer than 100 houses of various Orders were established.   The twelfth century in England was especially the age of monasteries.

It is true that not very much in the way of original literature, except theological treatises, can be assigned to the three centuries referred to, but the unwearied labours of the copyist and illuminator did much to preserve the works which previous centuries had created.   Of course, in so long a period changes were many and great.   So great, indeed, that between a MS. of 850 and another of 1200 scarcely is there a common feature.

From 850 to 1000 in France the Carolingian minuscule, from the first so clear and beautiful, remained with scarce a stroke of alteration.   But immediately after the opening of the eleventh century a series of rapid changes set in, and by the beginning of the twelfth a new hand, perfectly clear and regular, but quite different from the Carolingian, had been formed, which lasted until it was superseded by the Gothic, while a system of contractions adopted because of the scarcity of parchment creates a fresh need for study apart from the peculiarities of personal habits.   Side by side, too, with this there grows up a non-professional hand—the so-called cursive or running hand of the ordinary writer—in many cases, especially in deeds and other brief compositions, all but utterly illegible, except to the professional palæographer.   Occasionally these autographs are of the highest importance and intensely interesting, as, for instance, when in an English MS. we come across a note in the handwriting of Ordericus (Vitalis) or Matthew Paris.

From 900 to 1200 the vast majority of MSS., illuminated and otherwise, were the work of monastics. Every house of any note had its room set apart for writing. The larger monasteries sometimes utilised the cloisters of the churches themselves, in recesses of which they had desks or tables placed for the copyist. Usually, however, they had a large common room called the *scriptorium,* where either the copyist and illuminator worked separately and each on his own account, or where a number of copyists awaited with pen and parchment the dictation by one of the fraternity of some work of which a number of copies had to be made. "No admittance except on business" was the rule of this chamber. There, under the direction of the *armarius,* the expert writers did their work.

Sometimes a single monk executed the book from first to last by himself. He prepared the vellum, ruled it with the fine metal point, copied the text, painted the illuminations, put on the gilding, and even added the binding. Generally, however, the labour was divided—one monk scraped and polished the parchment; another ruled it; another wrote the text, leaving spaces for initials and miniatures; another put in the initials and did the gilding and flourishing with borders, etc.; and another painted the miniatures. This in the monasteries was done in the case of large and important MSS., and afterwards, when illuminating became a lay-craft, subdivision of labour was the common practice. Binding was usually done in a special apartment, and by one specially skilled therein.

The *scriptorium* was looked upon as a sort of sacred place, and the work of copying often considered as a labour of piety and love—entered upon with devout prayer, and solemnly blessed by the superior, especially in cases where the books to be written were Bibles, or connected with the services of the house, the Lives of the Saints, or Treatises on Theology.

Very frivolous or absurd indeed are sometimes the inducements to copyists to do gratuitous work of this kind, such as that every letter transcribed paid for one sin of the copyist, and it is said that a certain monk—a heavy sinner—only owed his salvation to the fact that the number of letters in a Bible which he copied exceeded by a single unit the sum total of his sins.

CHAPTER XIII

MONASTIC ILLUMINATION—*continued*

The copyists—Gratuitous labour—Last words of copyists—
Disputes between Cluny and Citeaux — The Abbey of
Cluny: its grandeur and influences—Use of gold and
purple vellum—The more influential abbeys and their work
in France, Germany, and the Netherlands.

OF course, only really expert calligraphers were
employed on great and important works.
In the monastery all such labour was gratuitous,
that is, the copyist received no pecuniary remun-
eration, only his food and lodging. Yet even this
had to be provided for. Hence the frequent
requests for donations from the laity.

To give a volume to a monastery did not always
mean actually to present the book, but to stand
the expense of its production in the monastery
itself. In the case of specially distinguished penmen, their entertainment in a monastery was
sometimes an expensive business. It was only
in later times, however, when lay-artists were
invited to reside in the monastery to do their
work that money was paid for their services.
Very often we find notices at the end of volumes
that "So-and-so" had ordered the book to be
written and illuminated at his expense, and an

invocation for the gratitude of the reader and remembrance in his prayers is added, sometimes with the date to the very hour when the book was finished.

The copyist's last words after his task was completed are often very full of weariness—sometimes pious, sometimes hankering after fleshly lusts, occasionally quite too dreadful to repeat. "May Christ recompense for ever him who caused this book to be written." At the end of a Life of St. Sebastian : "Illustrious martyr, remember the monk Gondacus who in this slender volume has included the story of thy glorious miracles. May thy merits assist me to penetrate the heavenly kingdom, and may thy holy prayers aid me as they have aided so many others who have owed to them the ineffable enjoyments both of body and soul." Wailly quotes the following : "Dextram scriptoris benedicat mater honoris " ("May the mother of honour bless the writer's right hand"). A very common ending is "Qui scripsit scribat semper cum Domino vivat " ("He who wrote, let him write ; may he ever live with the Lord "). Another : "Explicit expliceat. Bibere scriptor eat" ("It is finished. Let it be finished, and let the writer go out for a drink "). Another ending is "Vinum scriptori reddatur de meliori " ("Let wine of the best be given to the writer "). And again : "Vinum reddatur scriptori, non teneatur " ("Let wine be given to the writer ; let it not be withheld "). Here is the recompense wished for by a French monk : "Detur pro penâ scriptori pulcra puella" ("Let a pretty girl be given to

the writer for his pains," or "as a penance ").
The monks enjoyed puns, as "bibere," a com-
mon pun on "vivere." One writer groans thus :
"Scribere qui nescit, nullum putat esse laborem "
("Whoso knows not how to write, thinks it is no
trouble ").

As time goes on, after the tenth century, it is
noticeable that the more beautiful a manuscript
becomes in its writing the less accurate becomes
its Latinity. And so the monks who once were
noted for learning, gradually lose their grip on
Latin. The manuscripts executed in Benedictine
abbeys became inaccurate — almost illiterate.
Faults of ignorance of words ; misrendering of
proper names ; blundering in the inept introduction of marginal notes and confounding such notes
with the text, showing that the heart of the
copyist was not in his work nor his head capable
of performing it. His hand is simply a machine,
which when it goes wrong does so without re-
morse and without shame. So in the greater
houses, men were appointed whose sole business
was to supervise the copyists—in fact, to supply
the brains, while the scribe furnished the manipulation of the pen. Even they, however, did not
always succeed to perfection, as very few of them
were too well furnished with scholarship. There
were not many Alcuins or Theodulfs in the
twelfth century. What they did usually keep free
from serious error were the books used in their
own services. It was the aim, particularly among
the Cistercian houses, to have their liturgical texts
absolutely without fault. In respect of illumina-

tion, there was a great quarrel between the Abbey of Citeaux and that of Cluny. The great Abbey of Clugny (or Cluny) in ancient Burgundy was founded in 910, and in the course of a century or so obtained a degree of splendour, influence, and prosperity unrivalled by any other mediæval foundation. It possessed enormous wealth and covered Western Europe with its affiliated settlements. Under Peter the Venerable, when the controversy began, it was the chief monastic centre of the Christian world. The words of Pope Urban II., when addressing the community, were : " Ye are the light of the world."

The grand Basilica at Cluny was completed in 1131, and, until the erection of St. Peter's at Rome, was the largest church in Christendom, and even then was only ten feet shorter than the Roman edifice. The building is a masterpiece of architectural beauty and massiveness, being with its narthex added by Abbat Roland de Hainaut, no less in length than 555 feet. The splendour of the church, its gorgeous tombs and mausoleums, its huge coronals for lights of brass, silver, and gold—the grand candelabrum before the altar, with its settings of crystal and beryl—the mural painting of the cupola, and the general luxury and magnificence of the whole constituted an unpardonable sin in the eyes of the stern and self-denying Cistercians. Hence arose long disputes between the abbats of the two houses about tithes and other matters. Among the other matters were included questions of candlesticks and bindings and gildings of books. The two houses were long at variance on the right definition of luxury in living, and this variance may to this day be observed in their separate and distinct styles, both of architecture and the ornamentation of books. The use of gold was still continued in the older Benedictine abbeys, but was long forbidden in the Cistercian, almost all the ornament of the latter being confined to pen-drawing and the use of coloured inks. The employment of gold for the text of manuscripts so common in the ninth century became rare in the eleventh. Only here and there do we hear of such volumes. Where the gold lettering still lingers, it is confined to the first page or two, and the same may be said of the purple vellum. A certain monk, Adémar, who died at Jerusalem in 1034, wrote a Life of St. Martial of Limoges entirely in letters of gold ; but it was quite an exceptional volume. Another example occurs in an Evangeliary, which was probably a copy of a ninth-century model, as at first glance it might be assigned to that age, but on closer examination it is found that in one of the borders is a medallion bearing the name of the Emperor Otho, showing that it cannot be later than the latter part of the tenth century. It is now in the National Library at Paris.

Before speaking of Othonian illumination it may be well to refer to that of the Netherlands in these earlier centuries.

The most ancient writings known in this district were charters and other documents, and the pious effusion of the occupants of the monasteries, such as St. Amand, Lobbes, Stavelot, etc.

It was the revival of art and literature under Charlemagne that was the beginning of artistic calligraphy, then followed the production of books outside the monasteries, classical authors, chronicles, and mirrors of various sciences. In the eleventh century we find monastic books and others of which the ornamentation is sometimes even splendid, such as Psalters, Evangeliaries, Bibles, and Missals, glowing with gold and colours. Already the Abbeys of Stavelot and Liége were high-class centres of production. St. Martin's of Tournay had a famous scriptorium also, noted for the beauty of its writing and its grand initial letters. Immediately following St. Martin's, the Abbeys of Gembloux, St. Bavon at Ghent, and others, produced or acquired MSS. of the most sumptuous kind, and before the thirteenth century the Netherlands had established quite a distinguished reputation.

In a later chapter we shall deal with the development of its remarkable schools, whose work eventually took rank, not only among the most artistic, but the most prolific in Europe.

CHAPTER XIV

OTHONIAN ILLUMINATION

Departure from Carolingian—Bird and serpent—Common use
of dracontine forms in letter-ornament—Influence of metal-
work on the forms of scroll-ornament—The vine-stem and its
developments—Introduction of Greek taste and fashion into
Germany—Cistercian illumination—The Othonian period—
Influence of women as patronesses and practitioners—German
princesses — The Empress Adelheid of Burgundy — The
Empress Theophano—Henry II. and the Empress Cunegunda—Bamberg—Examples of Othonian art.

PERHAPS the first departure towards a new
style arising out of the elements of Carolingian illumination is in the combination of the
bird and serpent used for letter forms and continued into coils of vine-stem and foliage in combination with golden panelled frames or pilasters.
The monsters thus produced seem to be a revival
of the dracontine forms of the semi-barbarous
Celtic and early Frankish arts. But the difference
in elegance and refinement of drawing and beauty
of colouring is very great indeed. Other animal
forms are also made use of, nor is the human
figure altogether absent. Sometimes entire letters
are made up of the latter in various attitudes.
Little scenes illustrative of the subject which the

BIBLIA SACRA
12TH CENT. (LATE)

Brit. Mus. Harl. MS. 2799, fol. 185 v.

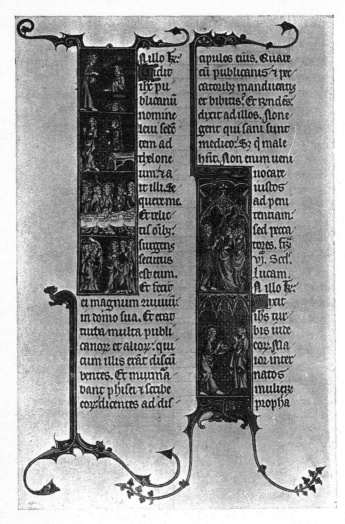

EVANGELIA (PARIS USE)

C. 1275

Brit. Mus. Add. MS. 17341, fol. 120 v.

initial commences are often placed within it, as, for instance, in the B of the first psalm.[1]

Many twelfth-century initials look like designs in metal-work placed on the panelled grounds of coloured enamels. But the rapid development of the vine-stem coils out of the stemless foliages of the Carolingian and Winchester styles is one of the wonders of the early German revival after the accession of the Emperor Otho I. A still greater improvement takes place after the marriage of his son Otho II. to the Princess Theophano, daughter of Romanus II., attributable, no doubt, to a fresh accession of artistic enthusiasm from the home of the new Empress. In point of elegance of design, beauty of curve, adaptation of every part to its share in the composition, nothing could be finer than the initial letters of the Othonian period of illumination. The year 963 introduced Greek fashions and Greek artists into Germany, the results of which are at once traceable in the increased splendour of monastic illumination in that country. The details of Greek ornament become the fillings of the frames and panels of the large initials.

The Cistercian illuminators, or rather calligraphers, while they constantly repudiate the golden splendour and monstrous follies of their rivals, absolutely excel in this same ornamental draughtsmanship. What, for example, could be finer than the pen-drawing of the great Arnstein

[1] A characteristic Othonian Evangeliary of the eleventh century, executed at the Abbey of Stavelot, may be seen in the Royal Library at Brussels.

Bible in the British Museum (Harl. 2800)?   The
ornament is mostly in a red ink, with flat-coloured
blue, green, or yellow backgrounds, but it is
not to be surpassed.   No, the interlacements and
coils, foliages and panels of the twelfth century
are absolutely among the finest examples of ornamental lettering ever conceived.   Illuminating
seemed at this epoch to be more and more closely
following the details of contemporary architecture,
and so paving the way to the next great variety
of the art, which is looked upon by some writers
as the real beginning of mediæval illumination.

It must be admitted, however, that the excellence limits itself to the ornament.   The human
figure is wretchedly incorrect—even barbarous.
It may be asked why is this?   How is it that
while the decorative portion of an illuminated
book is beautiful in the highest degree, both in
line and colour, and yet occasionally the artist
seems not to have the remotest idea of the true
shape of hands and feet or any part of the human
body?   Of course the usual explanation offered
is that monastic education did not permit the
study of the nude, and hence the monkish ignorance of figure drawing.   But that is scarcely an
excuse for the monstrous hands and feet and exaggerated facial expression of the miniatures.
The Italian monk Angelico, in spite of his
monastic limitations, succeeded in a most graceful rendering of the figure, and a charming delicacy in the forms of the hands.   As in some
instances the artist does reach a fair standard, it
must be admitted that where he does not is

owing to actual inability in himself and not in his system. The three emperors who give the name of Othonian to the period immediately succeeding the Carolingian ruled Germany, and had much to do with the ruling of Italy, from 936, when Otho I., called the Great, succeeded Henry the Fowler about five years before the death of Athelstan, whose sister Eadgyth [1] was Otho's first wife. His mother Mathilda was the patroness of the cloister-schools for women, working in them personally. She herself taught her servants and maids the art of reading. Her daughter Mathilda, the famous Abbess of Quedlinburg, in 969 persuaded the Abbat Wittikind of Corvey to write the History of the Saxon Kings, Henry her father, and Otho her brother (now in the Royal Library at Dresden).   Hazecha, the Treasurymistress of Quedlinburg, also employed the monks of Corvey, with whose beautiful initial drawing she was greatly pleased, to illuminate her own Life of St. Christopher. The beautiful but imperious Princess Hedwig, another of Otho's sisters, read Virgil with Ekkehard of St. Gall, and taught the child Burchard Greek, while Otho's niece Gerberga, Abbess of Gandersheim, was the instructress of the celebrated Hrosvita, "the oldest German poetess." And this reminds us that at this time the women-cloisters of Germany and the Netherlands were among the most active centres of learning and book-production.   The great monument of feminine erudition

[1] The chroniclers are rather confused as to the name of this Princess.

and artistic skill, called the " Hortus Deliciarum,"
was of a somewhat later time, but other examples
still exist, among them the beautiful Niedermünster
Gospels of the Abbess Uota, now at Munich.   A
wood-cut by Albert Dürer prefixed to the first
edition of Hrosvita's works (Nürnberg, 1501)
represents the nun Hrosvita kneeling before the
Emperor and beside the Archbishop Wilhelm of
Mainz presenting her book.[1]   As to the literary
labours of Hrosvita, this is not the place to discuss them.   She is simply an incidental figure in
our view of the brilliant Court of the Othos.   A
MS. of her works 500 years after her death was
found among the dust of the cloister-library at
St. Emmeram of Regensburg by Conrad Celtis,
and, as we have seen, printed for the first time
in 1501.   Thus she stands out as an illustration
of the fact often alluded to, of the importance of
feminine foundations in the monastic scheme.

Her picturesque story of the romantic adven-
tures of Adelheid of Burgundy, her marriage in
947 to King Lothaire of Italy, her widowhood
and perils, her misfortunes and eventual marriage
to the Emperor Otho, reads more like a chapter
from the *Morte d'Arthur* or the *Arabian Nights*
than a veracious history of real people.   The
Empress Adelheid was, indeed, a remarkable
woman, and the nun of Gandersheim is full of
her praises.   In her younger days she had been
a zealous patron and protectress of the Abbey of

---

[1] It is thought, however, by some that the figure behind
is that of the Abbess—not the Archbishop. See Dürer Soc.
Portfolio for 1900.

Cluny, which stood on her native land of Burgundy, and her sympathies remained always with the religious houses. In this respect, indeed, she was a worthy successor of the pious Mathilda and her daughters. She died in her seventy-first year in her Abbey of Selz in Elsass, leaving a memory rich in benefits to the monastics, especially those of Cluny, and venerated as the patroness of many an illuminated volume of poems or theology, not to mention the liturgical books executed at her expense for use in her various foundations. The tenth century seems to have been an age of illustrious women. No sooner do we leave the story of Adelheid than we enter upon that of the young wife of Otho II., the Empress Theophano, daughter of the Greek Emperor, Romanus II. When little more than a child she was married to the son of Adelheid, he himself being in his twentieth year in the year 972, and in the city of Rome. The young Greek Princess who had been reared amid the luxury and splendour of the Eastern capital at once became the fashion—the manners of her Byzantine household became those of her Roman court, and were transplanted to her German home at Bamberg. Artists, limners, copyists, musicians, scholars, formed part of her retinue, and at once the German Court became the rival of those of England, Byzantium, Cordova, and Rome.

It was, indeed, a Renaissance, an awakening in literature, art, and social life. Nor did its glory fade until eclipsed by the succeeding rivalries of France and Italy. Theophano survived her husband, who died in 983, and proved herself a capable Regent during the infancy of her son Otho III. She, however, did not live to see his early death, nor indeed to see that of the aged Adelheid, who survived her eight years, and died in the same year (999) as Otho's aunt, Matilda, Abbess of Quedlinburg.

The death of Otho III. in 1002 did not affect materially the steady advance of monastic art. Bamberg, St. Gall, Corvey, Luxeuil, Bobbio, Monte Cassino continued their accustomed labours. Under the Capetian Kings the French foundations maintained the reputations they had won during the Carolingian times, while others were added from time to time throughout the Rhineland, Limousin, and the South of France, where the Romanesque or Byzantine tastes had not yet penetrated, and whose work therefore remained distinct from that of Italy and the German Empire.

Henry II. and the Empress Cunigunda made Bamberg the great centre of German art, and it is to Bamberg, St. Gall, Luxeuil, Monte Cassino, and Magdeburg that we have to look for the finest productions of the eleventh century. Among the earlier works of the Othonian period we may mention the famous Gospel-book executed for the minister of Otho II., Egbert, Archbishop of Trèves, and known as the Codex Egberti. It was written in 980 at Reichenau on the Lake of Constance (or Bodensee, as it is locally known) by two monks, Kerald and Heribert, whose dwarfish figures appear beneath that of the archbishop on the frontispiece. It contains fifty-seven illuminations and several folios of violet parchment with golden ornaments and lettering. But its pictures are rather remarkable, mostly the figures are too short and the limbs and extremities badly drawn, but in some of the statelier personages the error is reversed and they are too tall—this seems to be owing to Greek influence, while the Byzantine taste shows itself in the treatment of the border-foliages. Beasts are unnatural—demons and swine are alike, both in form and colour (Pub. Lib., Trèves).

An Evangeliary, formerly in the Cathedral Treasury at Bamberg, but now in the Royal Library at Munich (Cimel. 58), is a good example of the kind of work that at first glance appears to be actually Carolingian both in the figures, attitudes, and treatment of drapery, but which on closer examination proves to be really due to the reign of Otho II. In this MS. the beginning of St. Matthew contains four medallions—two of Henry I. (the Fowler), one of Otho I., his son, and another of his grandson, Otho II. (Nat. Lib., Paris, Lat. 8851).

A still more notable MS. is kept in the Munich Library (Cimel. 58), containing a two-paged picture of tributary cities bringing gifts to the Emperor Otho III. In the painting in this MS., notwithstanding the exaggerated solemnity of expression, the faces are well drawn and the features carefully modelled. The painting is in the Greek manner, as is also the general character of the draperies. The small, ill-drawn feet are by no means comparable with the heads.

The Imperial crown is square, like those of the Magi in the Bremen MS. now in the Library of Brussels, or like that of Baldwin as Emperor of Constantinople. In the several enthronements which occur among the Imperial miniatures at Munich there are important and significant differences which might not be noticed unless pointed out.

The changes in the shape and treatment of the orb, for instance, mean more than a mere advance in enrichment, or an improvement in artistic skill. The difference indicates a change in political usage. In the miniature of Charles it does not occur at all; in that of Otho III. it is a mere symbol; in that of Henry II. it is the actual emblem of sovereignty presented by the Pope to the Emperor, to be held by the latter in token of his investiture.

It was Selden's opinion that the orb, surmounted by the cross, never appears in western art until the time of Henry II. Thus it is here one of the many seemingly insignificant details which, in the miniature art of the Middle Ages, contribute to the elucidation of History.

CHAPTER XV

FRANCONIAN ILLUMINATION

The later Saxon schools—Bernward of Hildesheim—Tuotilo
and Hartmut of St. Gallen—Portrait of Henry II. in MS. 40
at Munich—Netherlandish and other work compared—
Alleged deterioration of work under the Franconian
Emperors not true—Bad character of the eleventh century
as to art—Example to the contrary.

THE MS. just referred to (Munich, Cimel. 58)
brings us most probably to the time of the
third. Otho, but it is really with his father's
marriage to the Princess Theophano that the
great revival in the arts began, and the names of
St. Bruno of Cologne and Augsburg, Gerbert,
Bernward of Hildesheim, Tuotilo, Salomon,
Hartmut, Folchard, and Sintramn of St. Gallen,
are, as it were, points of light and centres of
expanding circles of artistic skill. Bruno and
Gerbert are too well known to need any further
remark. Bernward of Hildesheim, made bishop
there in 992 by Theophano, and tutor to her son
Otho III., "excelled no less in the mechanical
than in the liberal arts. He was an excellent
penman, a good painter, and as a household
manager was unequalled." Such is Tangmar's
tribute to his pupil's character. He was, indeed,

an enthusiast in painting, mosaic, and metal-work, and used to collect all the objects of art he could lay hands on, to form a museum or studio for the instruction of a class of art students and work-men.   The collection was formed mainly out of the numerous presents brought to the young Emperor from foreign, and especially Greek and Oriental, princes, and contained many examples of beautiful metal-work and Greek illumination. His own Cathedral of Hildesheim was supplied with jewelled service-books, in part at least the work of his own hand.   The chalices and incense-burners and the massive golden corona or cande-labrum of the cathedral were also the productions of his own workshops.   The mural paintings, too, were executed by himself.   His handiwork, so lovingly described by his old schoolmaster Tangmar, may still be seen in Hildesheim, where visitors to that quaint old Saxon city are told that the bronze gates of the cathedral and the jewelled crucifix were placed there by the vener-able bishop himself in 1015, while in the cathedral-close rises a column adorned with bronze reliefs from the Life of Christ, authoritatively declared to be the work of his own hands—let us say they came out of his own workshops, in the year 1022, nearly a thousand years ago.   St. Bernward was canonised by Celestine III. in 1194.   His sarco-phagus is in the crypt of the Basilica of St. Michael at Hildesheim.   Of Tuotilo, the pupil of Moengall (or Marcellus), it is said that he was physically almost a giant ; just the man, says his biographer, that you would choose for a wrestler.

He was a good speaker, had a fine musical voice, was a capital carver in wood, and an accomplished illuminator. Like most of the earlier monks of St. Gallen, he was a clever musician, equally skilful with the trumpet and the harp. And the charm about it all was that he was always cheerful and in excellent spirits, and in consequence a general favourite. Nor is this all. Besides being teacher of music in the upper school to the sons of the nobility, he was classical tutor, and could preach both in Latin and Greek. His chief accomplishments, however, were music and painting, and on these his reputation mainly rests. He composed songs, which, like an Irish bard, he sang to the harp—the popular instrument of this Irish foundation. Being thus multifariously accomplished (he was, by the way, an excellent boxer), he was much in request, and by the permission of his abbot travelled to distant places. One of his celebrated sculptures was the image of the Blessed Virgin for the cathedral at Metz, said to be quite a masterpiece. Nay, he was even a mathematician and astronomer, and constructed an astrolabe or orrery, which showed the courses of the planets.

This allusion to the astrolabe reminds us that it was Abbat Hartmut of St. Gallen, who was also an accomplished illuminator, who constructed a large map of the world—one of the extremely few that until that time the world had ever seen.

St. Gallen and its artists, however, must not be permitted to monopolise our attention too long. The reader must for the rest refer to Dr. Rahn and the writers whom he quotes. Sometimes it

is said that the illuminations of the eleventh century are proofs of the rapid decline of art, and
to demonstrate the fact that they are frankly
hideous, some writers bring forward instances
such as the miniatures of a Missal, especially a
Crucifixion, said to be at Paris,[1] and a MS. at
Berlin said to have been executed in the earlier
days of the Franconian dynasty (1034-1125) containing another Crucifixion, which, though not
quite so horrible as the one just referred to, is
sufficiently bad.   These miniatures are irredeem-
ably barbaric and not in any sense typical of the
age.   Such examples, in fact, can be found in any
age and in any country.   Were they really representative of the best art of the time, there might
be an excuse for their reproduction, but they are
not, and therefore no reliance can be placed on
their evidence.

In the miniatures of MSS. executed for the
Othos and Henrys of the early Saxon dynasty the
worst they can be charged with, as compared
with the periods before and after them, is slavish
imitation.   The portrait of Henry II. (Saint
Henry, husband of Cunegunda) in MS. 40 at
Munich is by no means barbaric—it is more Greek
than anything else—but it is down to the smallest
element of composition a direct imitation of the
similar portrait of Charles the Bald in the
Emmeram Gospels.   It is not a copy, for there
is a significant difference in the attitudes of the
emperors.   Henry holds a sceptre in his right
hand and an orb in his left, like Otho III. in the

[1] *Le Livre, etc.*, par M. P. Louisy, Paris, 1886, 8°, p. 79.

miniature already described, whereas Charles is
empty handed.   Then both on the Emperor's
head and on the smaller figures the crowns are
different—the panelling of the Imperial canopy is
different, and, of course, there is a different inscription.   Lastly, it may be said that some of the
differences are improvements.   Another change is
characteristic—Charles was beardless, Henry has
a pointed beard.

It is true this is an example belonging to the
very brightest years of the Othonian revival. But
to pass over other Saxon MSS., there are extant
examples from Evroul (when Roger de Warenne,
son of the great Earl of Surrey, practised as a
scribe and illuminator on his retirement to that
monastery), St. Martin's of Tournay, St. Amand,
Benedictbeuern, Lobbes, and Weissobrunn could all
boast accomplished calligraphers. The last establishment produced the celebrated Diemudis, who,
though a woman, was distinguished by a most
extraordinary activity and skill.

Nor are these all that could be named, for by
no means least among them we may quote Monte
Cassino, many of whose elegant productions have
been published by the present occupants of the
monastery.   Then the Greek miniaturists of the
eleventh century are once more to the front.   The
famous Slav Evangeliary of Ostromir (1056-67)
shows us a MS. probably executed for a governor of
Novgorod, which contains by no means despicable
work, whether in the figures of the evangelists or
the ornamental borders.   Of course, in Greek
MSS. we know pretty well what to expect ; fairly

good ornament, rich details of embroidery, etc., wilfulness of colour in architecture, mannerism in the attitudes and faces, but good, clever technic and bright gold.

Lastly, there is the celebrated Evangeliary given to San Benedetto of Mantua by the Countess Matilda now in the Vatican, enriched with little miniatures from the Life of the Virgin, which Lanzi declares surpass everything else he ever saw of the same period.

The Poitevin MS. at Poitiers, a biographical compilation of saints in honour of St. Radegonde, though nothing wonderful, is worth recording as a transitional example just before the close of the century. As an example of the latter part of a continual deterioration, it should be worse than anything preceding. Yet it is not so. It is certainly heavy and rather dull, and the drawing far from excellent, but it is also, on the other hand, far from "frankly horrible." In introducing examples of other schools into this chapter the writer's object has solely been to vindicate the illuminators of the eleventh century from the sweeping charge sometimes made against them of absolute deterioration. Of the school directly under our notice, the charge is certainly not true, and the wretched stuff cited in support of it can only be looked upon as accidental salvages of no artistic value whatever.

In proof that the book-work of the eleventh century was not all worthless, we may refer to just one example. It is a MS. consisting of but a few fragments executed at Luxeuil under Abbat

Gerard II.   The remains are such as to cause regret for the loss of the rest.   On one page Christ is shown seated on a rich *sella* covered with an embroidered cushion in the manner of the consular diptychs.   He is clothed in a pale yellow tunic, over which is worn a purple pallium with a white border.   He is beardless, and his brown hair is kept close to the head and neck, and falls over the shoulders.   The feet are nude and by no means ill-drawn.   Surrounding the head is a cruciform nimbus enclosed in a circle—both cross and circle being pale green, the latter outlined with red.   The chief fault of the head is the excessive length of the nose and the wide stare of the eyes.   The right arm is raised somewhat as in the St. Sernin Evangeliary, but with the palm outwards, and much superior in drawing.

The whole figure is painted on, or at least surrounded by, a golden background—so far indicating the Byzantine origin of the design.   It is enclosed in a cusped aureola formed of several coloured bands of green, violet, and rose.   This shows German taste.   Eight circlets or medallions surround this figure of Christ, four of which contain the symbols of the evangelists ; the other four—Isaiah, Daniel, Ezechiel, and Jeremiah.   All hold portions of the band which connects them, and on which appears a series of inscriptions in Latin.   These consist of passages from the Vulgate.

The whole picture is placed in a square frame consisting of bands of various colours and gold outlined in red.   The inner ground is chiefly blue, and the names of the prophets and evangelists are painted on it in white Roman capitals. Taken altogether it is a very splendid page, but even this is surpassed in gorgeous richness of ornament by the miniature of St. Mark. And the borders of other pages in this Luxeuil fragment are full of ornament, giving the impression that the work was imitated from that of the goldsmith and enameller. The figures and symbols of the evangelists in these early Gospel texts are fully explained after St. Jerome by Alcuin, whose revision of the Vulgate forms the text of the Durham Book already referred to.

The "Manual" shortly to be mentioned differs somewhat in its explanation of these symbols. The curious combination called the "Tetra morph" is a compound of the four attributes or symbols into a single figure, to signify that the four evangelists give only one gospel, and ought not to be separated. It occurs frequently in Greek, but only seldom in Latin or Western iconography.[1]

[1] On this figure see *Annales Archéologiques*, tom. 8, p. 206, etc.

CHAPTER XVI

ARTISTIC EDUCATION IN THE CLOISTER

The "Manual"—Its discovery—Its origin and contents—
Didron's translation—The "Compendium" of Theophilus
—Its contents—English version by Hendrie—Benedictine
and Cistercian illumination—How they differ—Character of
monastic architects and artists.

ABOUT the twelfth century comes forward the
mention of a certain manual minutely detail-
ing every process of painting, and laying down
rules for the due composition and arrangement of
every subject to be represented in the sacred
history and other books connected with divine
service. How long such a manual had been in
use is unknown, but it is thought that something
of the kind must have existed from the time,
at least, of Justinian, perhaps earlier. The
manual here referred to was found by M. Didron
at Sphigmenou, on Mt. Athos. This little
monastery is said to have been founded by
the Empress Pulcheria, sister of the Emperor
Theodosius the Younger. She died in the year
453. Theodosius, it may be remembered, was
himself an admirable penman and illuminator,
so much so as to have acquired the cognomen of
Kalligráphos.

The monastery is built in a narrow valley by the seaside, between three little hills, and as it were "squeezed" in, and hence its name (in Greek σφιγμένος), which describes its situation exactly. It is occupied by about thirty unusually neat and orderly monks, who are justly proud of the few relics and curiosities which they exhibit to visitors. It was at Sphigmenou that Curzon saw the piece of *ancient* jewellery set with diamonds and a Russian or Bulgarian MS. of the Gospels.

The book which M. Didron found there is the copy of an older MS. which, it is said, was copied by Dionysius, one of the monks, from the works of the once celebrated master, Manuel Panselinos of Thessalonica, who was the Giotto of the Byzantine school and flourished in the twelfth century. If by works the monk meant literary, it is most likely that it was the transcript of a still older document. If by works Dionysius meant paintings, it is a manual of his practice. One of his pupils, in order to propagate the art of painting which he had learnt at Thessalonica, writes down the series of subjects to be taken from the Bible, so as to epitomise the divine scheme of salvation, and describes the manner in which the events of the Old Testament, and the miracles and parables of the New, ought to be represented. He mentions the scrolls and inscriptions (such as we noticed in the Gospels of Luxeuil) belonging to each of the prophets and evangelists, with the names and characteristics of the principal saints in the order of the menologium or martyrology, and then goes on to direct how the subjects should be arranged on the walls and cupolas of the churches.

The Manual of Dionysius is an abstract of this wide scheme, but is still very comprehensive. The copy of it seen by Didron was one belonging to a monk of Sphigmenou named Joasaph, who was himself a painter. It was "loaded with notes added by himself and his master, which in course of time would be incorporated, according to immemorial custom, in the text." In this way, indeed, the Manual has grown to what it is at present. A transcript of it may probably be found in every monastery belonging to the Greek Church. Another monk named Macarios, also a painter, had a fine copy of it laid open in his atelier, and his pupils read from it in turn, whilst the rest painted according to its directions. For the scheme itself we must refer the reader to the second volume of Didron's *Christian Iconography*, p. 193. Unfortunately the transcriber did not think it of sufficient importance or relevancy to copy the first part, as being purely technical and dealing merely with the art of painting. The scheme, therefore, only contains the part relating expressly to iconography. It is to be regretted, too, that this part also has been in some places considerably abridged, as dealing with Greek art and martyrology more copiously than, it was thought by the translator, would be interesting to English readers. There are numerous good and reliable introductory works dealing with early Christian art, besides the greater treatises to which the student who wants to pursue this line of research shall be directed later on. But there is another of these original manuals to which we must call attention, as especially dealing with the practice of monastic artists in the twelfth and following centuries.

The one to which we now refer is quite distinct from the Greek Manual which we just mentioned, and by way of contrast may be called the Latin Manual as being originally composed in that language. Moreover, as the Greek Manual formed the guide and *vade mecum* of all the painters of the Greek Church, so this Latin one became the indispensable monitor in all Latin foundations. Its origin was German, and said to be the compilation of a Benedictine monk who is variously spoken of as Rutgerius, Rugerius, Rotkerius, etc., and assigned by different editors and critics to either the eleventh, twelfth, or thirteenth centuries. Probably we shall not be far wrong in placing him about the middle of the twelfth. The treatise is known as *Diversarum Artium Schedula*, and the compiler of it calls himself simply *Theophilus presbiter humilis*, which, of course, records nothing but his personal modesty.

It was at first attributed to Tuotilo of St. Gallen. This opinion was put forward by Lessing, but it had no foundation whatever beyond the fact of Tuotilo's well-known versatility.[1] Besides, Tuotilo lived in the ninth century. But really the question of attributions does not concern us here. It

---

[1] Tuotilo was renowned throughout all Germany as painter, architect, preacher, professor, musician, calligrapher, Latinist, Hellenist, sculptor, and astronomer.

matters little who he was outside the Treatise,
and certainly we shall not discuss the question
further.   It is with the Treatise that we are con-
cerned.   We shall simply call the author Theophilus, and his work the Compendium.   Let us
turn to it at once.

The Compendium, which is thus known to contain the working methods of all the monastic
illuminators, mosaicists, glass painters, enamellers,
and so forth, throughout Germany, Lombardy,
and France, consists of three books, containing
altogether one hundred and ninety-five chapters
of definite and special instructions in artistic
matters.   Book I., comprising forty chapters,
treats of the preparation, mixture, and use of
colours for wall-painting, panel, and parchment,
i.e. for the decoration of churches, furniture, and
books.   It contains some most curious and valuable instructions for the employment of gold,
silver, and other metals in the decoration of
MSS. ; how it should be applied ; whether in leaf
or as an ink ; how raised and burnished, down to
the minutest details of practice ; how colours are
to be tempered (*i.e.* mixed) ; what *media* or tem-
perings are best for each colour, according to
the surface to which it is to be applied.   Such is
the Compendium.   We need not, therefore, wonder at its popularity and the estimation in which
it was held.

Thirty-one chapters on glass, glass painting,
enamelling, etc., form a second book, and the
third and last book contains some hundred and
twenty-four chapters on gold and silver work—

the art of the goldsmith—in cups, chalices, vases, candelabra, shrines, and so on. It is the first book that is of most interest to us, and had we space we would have liked to quote from its pages. But as it is we can only refer the reader to the work itself. It is to be met with in various forms and editions. First, we recommend the English translation by Robert Hendrie. The oldest MS. of the work is one of the twelfth century in the Library at Wolfenbüttel. The next is in the Imperial Library at Vienna. Fragments of other copies exist in several other public libraries, but the completest copy known is that in the Harl.[1] Collection of the British Museum used by Hendrie as the basis of his translation (8°, 1847).

It was, as we have said, in the eleventh and twelfth centuries especially that the great abbeys were founded. And it cannot be too clearly stated that the principal abbatial churches—those most splendid monuments of architecture whose structure and dimensions are still the admiration of the most cultured critics, and in which all the rules of art were so marvellously applied—were the work of simple monks. The great Church of St. Benignus at Dijon (so often spoken of by writers on Burgundian art) was built in 1001, under Abbat William, assisted by a young monk named Hunaldus. The period between 1031 and 1060 saw the creation of the grand abbatial Church of St. Remi at Reims. In the words of the Comte de Montalembert : " From the very

[1] Harl. MS. 3915.

beginning of the Monastic Orders St. Benedict had provided in his Rule that there should be artists in the monasteries. He had imposed on the exercise of their art only one condition—humility." Hence it is that all we know of the author of the Compendium from himself is "humilis presbiter Theophilus." For the same reason Tuotilo and Folchard and Sintramn and the rest are never anxious to put their names upon their work. For the same reason the occurrence of an artist's name in a monastic MS. is quite exceptional and unexpected. The foresight of St. Benedict "was accomplished and his law faithfully fulfilled." The Benedictine monasteries soon possessed not only libraries but ateliers, where architecture, painting, mosaic, sculpture, metal-chasing, calligraphy, ivory carving, gem-setting, book-binding, and all the branches of ornamentation were studied and practised with equal care and success, without interfering in the least with the exact and austere discipline of the foundation. The teaching of these various arts formed an essential part of monastic education. "The greatest and most saintly abbeys were precisely those most renowned for their zeal in the culture of Art. St. Gallen in Germany, Monte Cassino in Italy, Cluny in France, were for centuries the mother-cities of Christian Art." And after the establishment of the reformed colony at Citeaux, the Cistercian Order became the one above all others which has left the most perfect edifices, and if the Cistercian illumination may not claim the splendour of some contemporary examples, it often excels them in soundness of design and severe correctness of execution.

In saying that all this kind of work was executed by monks, we are speaking literally. The monks were not only the architects, but also the masons, and even the hodmen of their edifices. Nor were the superiors in this respect different from their humble followers. Whilst ordinary monks were often the architects-in-chief of the constructions, the abbats voluntarily accepted the rôle of labourers. During the building of the Abbey of Bec, in 1033, the founder and first abbat, grand-seigneur though he was, worked as a common mason's labourer, carrying on his back the lime, sand, and stones necessary for the builder. This was Herluin. Another Norman noble, Hugh, Abbat of Selby in Yorkshire, when, in 1096, he rebuilt in stone the whole of that important monastery, putting on the labourer's blouse, mixed with the other masons and shared their labours. Monks, illustrious by birth, distinguished themselves by sharing the most menial occupations. It is related of Roger de Warenne that when he retired to Evroul, he took up quite a serious rôle of this kind in cleaning the shoes of the brethren, and performing other offices which a mere cottager would have probably considered degrading.

Occasionally in our school histories we come across the mention of a man like Dunstan, of whom it is related as a wonderful thing that he was at the same time a metal worker, architect, and calligrapher ; but monastic biographies abound in such instances. We have already quoted several. "The same man was frequently," says Montalembert, "architect, goldsmith, bell-founder, miniaturist, musician, calligrapher, organ builder, without ceasing to be theologian, preacher, litterateur, sometimes even bishop, or intimate counsellor of princes.[1]

[1] "L'Art et les Moines," *Ann. Archéologiques*, t. vi. p. 121, etc.

CHAPTER XVII

THE RISE OF GOTHIC ILLUMINATION

Germany the chief power in Europe in the twelfth century—
Rise of Italian influence—The Emmeram MSS.—Corona-
tion of Henry II.—The Apocalypse—The "Hortus Deli-
ciarum"—Romanesque—MS. of Henry the Lion—The
Niedermünster Gospels—Description of the MS.—Rise of
Gothic—Uncertainty of its origin—The spirit of the age.

IN the chapter on Othonian art we saw how the
ornamentation of books was drawn away from
the great French centres, and began to take a
new departure from the various leading cities of
Germany, such as Bamberg, which the Othos had
made their capital. Whilst the decline, which
was the inevitable consequence of a personal
government like that of Charlemagne, took
place in France, it was but natural that the new
artistic movement at Bamberg should become the
fashion, and Germany predominant in art, as
she was in politics. In the twelfth century the
German Empire was the principal power in
Europe. France, Italy, England, and Spain
were all more or less secondary. Italy, however,
was already on the alert. She was initiating
certain movements in social life that must soon
withdraw the cultivation of all the arts from the
control of the monasteries. At the same time

the love of learning and personal accomplishments of the second and third Othos and (St.) Henry II. soon prepared the Imperial Court to become as brilliant as classical scholarship and artistic skill of the highest class could make it.

The wave of Byzantine influence which had passed over Germany by the time of Henry II. had immensely benefited the Germans. We notice it especially in the miniatures of the Gospel-books. The technic is much more masterly, the painting really methodical in soundly worked body-colour with a delicate sense of harmony, and showing no longer that coarse handling and slovenliness of execution that marks some of the Carolingian miniatures. In the figure a sense of proportion has been gained, the tendency, perhaps, being rather to excessive tallness, as compared with the thick-set proportions of the Carolingian work. Again, expression is improved—the faces are more intellectual—not beautiful but strong, and quite superior to the utterly expressionless faces of the Carolingian type.

Take, for example, that fine Missal now at Munich (Cimel. 60—Lat. 4456), in which St. Henry, who is bearded, receives his crown from a bearded Christ, his arms being upheld by two bishops, Ulrich of Augsburg and Emmeram of Regensburg, the two great saints of Bavaria. We know these to be the personages represented, because two inscriptions tell us so. To the one supporting the King's right hand : " Huius VODALRICVS cor regis signet et actus." To the other: "EMMERANVS ei faveat solamine dulci." The Christ is seated on a rainbow within a cusped aureola or "amande" of several bands of different colours, on the central one being inscribed in a mixture of Greek and Latin characters —one of the new fashions brought in by the Greek revival:

> "Clemens XPE tuo longum da vivere $\overline{\text{XPIC}}$ to:
> Ut tibi devotus non perdat temporis usus."

Some writers have thought this to be a picture of the Emperor's apotheosis, and that the crown is that of Life or Immortality; but such is certainly not the import of the above verses.

> "O gentle Christ give to thy Christ long to live
> That devoted to Thee he may not lose the use of time."

Besides, two angels on either side Christ precipitately bestow on the Emperor the spear and sword of a temporal sovereignty. Round the Emperor are the words: "Ecce coronatur divinitus atque beatur. Rex pius Heinricus proavorum stirp(e) polosus," all which can scarcely refer to anything but his German Empire.

The expression, "give to thy Christ," is an allusion to the Hebrew usage of calling the king the "anointed" or the "Christ."

Besides the interest possessed by this MS. as a monument of the art of its own time, it has a special value resting in the fact that its illuminations were copied from the famous Emmeram Golden Gospels of Charles the Bald, written by Linthard and Berenger, and sent as a present to Regensburg. Another illumination in it, representing the enthronement of the Emperor, is extremely interesting as showing how the later artist renders the work of the earlier one.   The general composition is precisely the same, the lower figures in the same attitudes and bearing the same insignia.   But in the details of costume, and in the significant position of the Emperor, there are alterations.   In the miniature of the Emmeram Gospels the two angels above are simply winged messengers of the usual biblical type ; in the Missal they are cloaked and crowned and bear horns in their hands.   In the older MS. the two crowned figures with horns on either side wear simple mural crowns ; in the later one they are regal like those of the Emperor.   The details also of the canopies are different.   But the remarkable difference is that while Charles the Bald is beardless and bears nothing in his hands, merely sitting as if addressing an assembly, Henry II. holds in his right hand a sceptre and in his left an orb and cross.   Here is a distinctly new feature with a meaning.   Here are the symbols of authority in the Emperor's own hands, and not merely in those of his attendants.[1]   These two MSS. are worthy of careful study.

In another Missal in the library at Bamberg is a miniature of the Emperor presenting the book to the Virgin.   In the great Evangeliary presented by the Emperor Henry II. to the Cathedral of Bamberg there is a grand picture of the Emperor and his consort the famous saint Cunegunda being crowned by Christ, with SS. Peter and Paul stand-

[1] See p. 92.

ing at the sides. Here also, as in the Carolingian MS. already mentioned, are the nations bringing tribute, but not in the same order. Here Germany stands upright between two figures of Gaul and Rome, while six others appear simply as busts (Munich, Cimel. 60. 4456).

The twelfth century was clearly much given to symbolism and allegory, as shown in apocalyptic commentaries and similar works. A very remarkable "Apocalypse" is that in the library of the Marquis d'Astorga. The latter is remarkably rich in pictures, which have been described by M. A. Bachelin of Paris. The drawing in these pictures reminds one of the bas-reliefs of the campaigns of Hadrian and Trajan and other work of the early Roman centuries. One hundred and ten miniatures of uncommon interest constitute the illustrations, many of which are perfect curiosities of symbolism, depicting not only the four figures of the evangelists, but the mysteries of the seals and vials, serpents, beasts, etc., on yellow, red, green, blue, and brown backgrounds. The draperies in some of the miniatures show Byzantine teaching, but with the grandiose style of the early Roman times. The MS. it might be compared with of the twelfth century is the "Hortus Deliciarum" of the Abbess Herrade. This latter MS., which unfortunately was burnt with many other treasures during the siege of Strassburg by the Germans in 1870, was a veritable treasury of mediæval customs, furniture, and costumes, illustrating a medley of encyclopædic information for the use of the nuns and secular students of the

Abbey of Hohenburg in Alsace. The good abbess called her book a "Garden of Delights."

It is known that it dated from 1159, as that date and also the date of 1175 occurred in its pages. We do not know whether the authoress was also the illuminatrix, but at any rate she directed the illumination. Their style is of the same type as that of the Apocalypse just spoken of, somewhat monumental as figures of the Liberal Arts, allegorical figures of the virtues and vices, and the syrens as symbols of sensual temptation. There was a figure of the Church riding upon a beast with the four heads of the evangel-symbols—the sun and moon in chariots as in the classical mythology, and scenes of warfare, marriage festivities, banquets, everything indeed depicting the life of contemporary persons.[1] The drawing and treatment generally is of no very skilful kind—the colouring bright and in body-colour. Draperies as usual much folded and fluttering, and the heads generally of the calm expression of the later French school, but the action sometimes very spirited.

The title began thus : "Incipit hortus deliciarum, in quo collectis floribus scripturarum assidue jucundetur turmula adolescentularum." In the *Rhytmus* came the lines :—

> "Salve cohors virginum
> Hohenburgensium
> Albens quasi lilium
> Amans dei filium

[1] For a copious and exhaustive account of the "Hortus," see "Het Gildeboek," Utrecht, 1877, v. 1. Also Engelhardt, Herrad v. H., etc., 8°, with atlas of twelve plates, 1818.

Herrat devotissima
Tua fidelissima
Mater et ancillula
Cantat tibi cantica

Sic et liber utilis
Tibi delectabilis
Et non cesses volvere
Hanc in tuo pectore."

In the Netherlands, which mostly at this time lay within the boundary of Lotharingia or Lorraine, the style of illumination was much the same as in other German districts. Gospel-books and Psalters, however, exhibit features somewhat akin to English work.

In the eleventh and twelfth centuries the continental methods prevail in more solid painting and less pen-work.

Of the twelfth-century work of Germany examples are exceedingly numerous, stretching over every province from West to East, as Westphalia, the Palatinate, Burgundy, Switzerland and Bavaria, extending even into Bohemia. An Evangeliary in the University Library at Prag agrees altogether with those of Germany.

Towards the middle of the twelfth century, with the accession of the House of Hohenstauffen (1138, etc.), arose a new style, since called Romanesque, of which many examples are to be found in various libraries. It is not very easy to select the most typical examples, but one good and typical MS. is found in a Gospel-book at Carlsruhe, which contains some capital miniatures of this most thoroughly German style.

Under Frederick Barbarossa, as under the Caroling Emperors and the Othos, we may note a wave of new life, especially in Saxony. A contrast as regards artistic ability to the "Hortus Deliciarum" is the Gospel-book executed for Henry the Lion at the convent of Helmershausen, once in the Cathedral Library at Prag, and bought by King George of Hanover.[1] In the page of the Eusebian Canons we see features which take us across the plains of Lombardy to the doors of S. Michele of Pavia, and to the churches of Venice. The columns rest on crouching animals. Allegorical figures are introduced striving with each other as in the later Gothic illuminations. A half-nude figure of Faith vanquishes the champion of Paganism. On the dedication page sits the Madonna with SS. John Baptist and Bartholomew, and below them the patron saints of Brunswick, Blaize, and Egidius leading forth the Duke and his wife, Mathilda. It may indeed be called a splendid book. Among the rest of the pictures, some of them within richly decorated borders, occurs the usual representation of the Duke and his Duchess receiving crowns. The figures are well drawn, even elegant, the draperies good, and the colouring skilful.

One of the many characteristic MSS. of this period to be seen in continental libraries is the "Mater Verborum" of the monk Conrad, of Scheyern in Bavaria, a noted scribe, illuminator, goldsmith, and grammarian. The subject is one

[1] See F. Culemann in *Neue hannov. Zeitung*, 1861, Nos. 22-4.

that scarcely gives promise of lending itself to pictorial illustration, but after the successful attempts of Theodulf we may be prepared for anything in the way of diagram and symbol. Imagine a dictionary in which not only actual objects are pictorially represented, but also abstract terms. Music, philosophy, virtues and vices illustrated by historical instances—sacred subjects treated in the manner of the glass painters which is so commonly found in German and French work of this period.

Of twelfth-century illumination in general it may be said that it shows a marked effort towards true artistic design and subtle beauty of linear outline. Some of the noblest curve-drawing, with rich and massive grouping of foliages, is to be found in the ornamental initials and digni-fied border designs presented on the later ex-amples of the century, and it is very interesting to observe the rapid pace at which the climax is reached in mere calligraphic ornament after the opening of the Gothic period. Initials become smaller but exquisitely drawn, and reasonable expression takes the place of the senseless stare or grotesque exaggeration of attitude and feature which detract from the artistic value of all pre-ceding efforts. To conclude our list of German illuminations of purely monastic production, we will bring forward one more example of women's work, which whether as regards its curious illus-trations of symbolism, or its richly foliaged geo-metrical backgrounds and borders, is one of the most interesting MSS. in any collection. It is the

Evangeliary of the Abbess Uota, or perhaps, rather, Tuota of Niedermünster, a lady of the House of the Counts of Falckenstein (1177–80); or of Utta, abbess from 1009 to 1012, but more probably the former.   Another, Tutta, ruled the abbey from 920 to 934, and still another 1239–42.   This precious MS., which Cahier has very fully described as the "Manuscrit du Niedermuenster de Ratisbonne," is now in the Royal Library at Munich (Cimel. 35).   Some writers, in speaking of it, have classed it among the MSS. of the eleventh century, but it is too refined and too well done for that period, and, indeed, that it belongs to the *latter part* of the twelfth is almost proved from the work itself.   Perhaps it was the profusion of inscriptions or legends placed all over the miniatures that gave the idea of its belonging to the eleventh century.   In this respect the MS. certainly resembles the Evangeliary of Luxeuil already described.   The miniature of the Crucifixion is very remarkable. Besides the figure of Christ showing a return to the primitive Syriac idea,[1] instead of the figures as usual of Mary and John, here are given allegorical figures of Life and Death.   (Cf. Fest. in exaltatione sce crucis.   Ad Laudes, 14th Sept.).   Perhaps the best commentary on these old figures is the " Biblia Pauperum," as it is commonly called, or as it should be called, the Bible of the poor preachers.   It also has the old allegories and inscriptions rendered into later forms.

[1] Cf. the Rabula MS. at Vienna.

As for the texts or inscriptions, they would require a commentary to themselves—not to speak of translations and remarks upon the calligraphy. One of these remarkable miniatures may be described, as it depicts the presentation of the volume to the Madonna. Our Lady in the centre of the design is seated on a Byzantine *sedile* with the infant Jesus on her knees. She is crowned, and has the nimbus, and appears as if intended to represent the glory of the Church. Her hand is raised as in the act of teaching. Christ, also, has the nimbus, but with the cross upon it, and raises his hand in the attitude of benediction. In the tympanum of the semicircle over the Madonna, written in letters of gold on purple, surrounded by the word "Sancta" in ordinary ink, is the monogram of Maria, having a small sun and moon above it, and other inscriptions, partly Latin, partly Greek. Below the Madonna, on the left, stands the abbess, her knees slightly bent, holding up her book, and clothed in the costume of her Order, but coloured, no doubt, simply for artistic reasons. Thus she wears a blue veil and a claret-coloured robe. In the reversed semicircle before her is another monogram, Uota or Tuota, a name which perhaps may be translated Uta, Utta, Ida, etc. It has been said already who she is likely to have been. It does not follow, of course, that she herself wrote or illuminated the book she is presenting, but judging from similar instances, as *e.g.* Herrade of Landsberg and Hrosvita of Gandersheim, she may have done so.

Still the work looks technically too masterly for anyone not a trained artist to have done. In the corners are small quadretti, containing busts of the four cardinal virtues :—Prudence, Justice, Temperance, and Fortitude ; and in circlets in the centre of each border are Faith, Hope, and Charity, the latter twice, at top and bottom. A number of extraordinary beasts fill up little niches in the design, which may possibly be also symbolical, but possibly also nothing but artistic fancies. The other miniatures we must pass over. Nevertheless those representing the four evangelists are worth examination ;[1] the ornamentation being especially rich and elaborate. Let us now turn our attention to a new element—a new spirit we might term it—which was manifesting itself in Italy and France. We cannot too strongly insist upon the fact that whatever appears in illumination has appeared first in architecture and its auxilliary arts. Now we have to see how this fact begins to change almost entirely the character of the ornamentation of books. During the latter part of the twelfth century, when precisely we cannot say, nor where, a new form of architecture began to show itself. This new style, laying aside both the classic cornice and the Romanesque arch, makes use of a new vertical principle of construction, called in French the *ogive* or arch, composed of two sections only, instead of the whole semicircle. By some fatality, of which no exact explanation can be given, English writers have

[1] For more about them, see Cahier, *Mélanges d'Archéologie, etc.*

given this new style the name of Gothic.   Scores of cathedrals throughout Europe are called Gothic cathedrals, whereas in all probability, if we exclude Sweden, there is only one really Gothic building in the world, that is the Tomb of Theodoric at Ravenna, and none of the so-called Gothic cathedrals are in the least like it. As to the invention itself, it has been claimed by almost every nationality in Europe.   There can be no doubt that accidentally, or otherwise, the pointed arch had been used often enough without any idea of its adoption as a principle of construction even in ancient buildings.   The famous gate at Mycœne is one instance.   This is not the place to discuss the question, so we let it pass. We could point out long and elaborate arguments intended to prove that it originated in England— that it originated in France — in Germany.[1] Possibly they may all be right in a sense, for most probably the origin was not in any particular locality, but in the religious spirit of the time.   It was a general revival of the Church itself that was its cause.   If any special locality has more reason on its side than another, it is probably France, but as we say, that is not an essential point.   It must suffice us here that it arose, and that by the end of the twelfth century it was a fact.   And the remarkable part about it is that it was by the influence of lay artists and especially of the freemasons that it became the accepted architecture of Christendom.

[1] Not to mention *theories,* which are endless.

Book II

CHAPTER I

THE GOLDEN AGE OF ILLUMINATION

The Gothic spirit—A "zeitgeist" not the invention of a single
artist nor of a single country—The thirteenth century the
beginning of the new style—Contrast between North and
South, between East and West, marked in the character of
artistic leaf-work—Gradual development of Gothic foliage—
The bud of the thirteenth century, the leaf of the fourteenth,
and the flower of the fifteenth—The Freemasons—Illumination transferred from the monastery to the lay workshop—
The Psalter of St. Louis—Characteristics of French Gothic
illumination—Rise of the miniature as a distinct feature—
Guilds—Lay artists.

WE have now reached the parting of the
ways. The study of Nature is fast super-
seding the dogmas of the monastic code, and
what some writers have characterised as the
hieratic is giving way to the naturalistic treatment
of art. Like the pointed architecture itself, it is
an outcome of the spirit of the age. Exactly
when it begins we cannot say. As in the physical
sciences, our limits are necessarily somewhat
arbitrary to suit our convenience in classification.
We take the beginning of the thirteenth century
as a convenient dividing line between old and new.
We accept it as the boundary between the artistic

sway of the East and South—and that of the
West and North—between the lifeless fetters of
prescription and the living freedom of invention.
The contrast between the two is very strongly
marked. The soft and curling foliages of the
sunny South are for a season giving way to the
hard and thorny leafage of the wintry North. It
would seem as if pointed architecture began with
the hard and frozen winter of its existence, and if
it had been the plan or design of one individual
we might have accepted this peculiarity as part of
the scheme, and all that followed as a natural
consequence and development. But it is curious
that as a system worked out by many minds
pointed architecture should thus begin. First
come thorns and cusps and lanceolate forms without foliage. Then, not perfect leaves, but buds.
In due time the bud opens, at first into the profile
coil, and by-and-by into the full-spread leaf.
Then comes the flower, and finally the fruit.
After that, rottenness and decay. It is curious
that this should actually take place through a
course of centuries. That it should be reflected
in book illumination is simply the usual order of
things—the fact has been frequently observed,
and as it is curious, we call attention to it. But,
as we have • said, the great change itself was
brought about by the influence of lay artists, and
chiefly by the freemasons.

Who and what the freemasons were everybody
is supposed to know, but on inquiry we find very
few people indeed know anything definite about
them. Of course we do not refer to the friendly

societies or social guilds that now bear the name, but to the mediæval builders. "Everybody knows," says Batissier,[1] "that the study of the sciences and of literature and the practice of the various branches of art took refuge in the monasteries during the irruptions of the barbarians and the strife of international war. In those retreats, not only painting, sculpture, engraving on metals, and mosaic, but also architecture were cultivated. If the question arose about building a church, it was nearly always an ecclesiastic who furnished the plan and monks who carried out the works under his direction. The brethren in travelling from convent to convent naturally exercised a reciprocal influence over each other. We conceive, then, that the abbeys of any given Order would put in vogue the same style, and that the art would be modified under certain points of view, in the same manner in each country.

"It is certain, moreover, that outside the cloisters there were also troops of workmen not monastics, who laboured under the direction of the latter.

"Masons were associated among them in the same way as other trade corporations. It was the same with these corporations in the South as with the communes—the *débris* of the Roman organisation ; they took refuge in the Church, and had arrived at a condition of public life and independence, when order was established between the commune, the Seignory, and the Church.

[1] *Hist. de l'Art Monumental,* p. 466, Paris, 1845, l. 8°.

"During the twelfth and thirteenth centuries these corporations were organised into recognised fraternities having their own statutes, but there is abundant evidence of their having a much earlier existence.

"A great number of masons were trained in Italy, and came from Lombardy, which in the tenth century even was an active centre of civilisation. Italy had its corporations of masons called *maestri comaccini*, enjoying exclusive privileges, who, having passed the different degrees of apprenticeship, became 'accepted'[1] masons, and had the right of exercising their profession wherever they might be. The sovereigns of different countries granted them special privileges, and the popes protected them in all Catholic countries where they might travel. Thus the lodges grew and prospered. The Greek artists who had fled from Constantinople during the various Iconoclast persecutions had got themselves enrolled in the ranks of the freemasons, and taught their fellow-masons their Byzantine methods.

"Speedily these corporations spread through France, England, and Germany, where they were employed almost exclusively by the religious Orders, in building their churches and conventual buildings."

While, therefore, the general plan and rules of construction were common to all members of the fraternity, the details were almost entirely left, under regulations, to the individual taste of certain members of each band of workmen, who,

---

[1] German "angenommen."

being all qualified artists, were quite capable of putting in execution, and with masterly skill, any such minutiæ of ornament as might be left to their discretion.[1] Local illuminators would thus speedily get hold of every novelty, and the page of the Psalter or Bible would become, as a French writer has explained it, a *vitrail sur velin*. If not indeed exclusively following the stained glass, they copied the mural decorations, and so we find the backgrounds of the miniatures, whether fitted into the initials or placed separately in framed mouldings, faithfully reproducing the imbrications, *carrelages*, panellings, and diapers of these mural enrichments.

To select an example of Gothic illumination which shall exemplify the earliest features of the

---

[1] Governor Pownall ("Observations on the Origin and Progress of Gothic Architecture, and on the Corporation of Freemasons," *Archæologia*, 1788, vol. 9, pp. 110-126) was of opinion that "the Collegium or Corporation of Freemasons, were the first formers of Gothic architecture into a regular and scientific order by applying the models and proportions of timber framework to building in stone," and that this method "came into use and application about the close of the twelfth or commencement of the thirteenth century."

See also Gould (R. F.), *History of Freemasonry*, vol. i. p. 259, note. "Without going so far as to agree with Governor Pownall that the Freemasons invented Gothic, it may be reasonably contended that without them it could not have been brought to perfection, and without Gothic they would not have stood in the peculiar and prominent position that they did, that there was mutual indebtedness, and while without Freemasons there would have been no Gothic . . . without Gothic the Freemasons would have formed but a very ordinary community of trades unionists."

pointed style is not an easy matter, notwithstanding the number of thirteenth-century MSS. which
still exist in public collections. In the National
Library at Paris are several such MSS. One that
decidedly marks the change from the German
work hitherto in vogue is the Psalter of St. Louis
(Nat. Lib., Paris., Lat. 10525), which contains
nearly eighty small, delicately executed miniatures.
It was completed about 1250. Its noticeable features are a vastly improved dexterity in draughtsmanship, which displays a refined certainty of
touch, enabling the artist to express his intention
with unhesitating freedom. The drawing thus
produced in outline is filled in with flat tints of
body-colour, without gradation or any attempt at
brush-work shading. Whatever finishing in this
respect might be thought necessary was added
with the pen. Nothing could show more clearly
that it is simply and frankly imitative of stained
glass. As in the glass the black outline is left
for definition. No colour is used on hands or
faces except a slight touch of red on the cheeks
and lips. The prevailing colours are rich blue
and bright scarlet. Perhaps the illuminator would
have been better advised had he neglected some
of the harder features of this kind of work. Not
considering that the limits of the glass painter
did not apply to his vellum, he fettered himself
unnecessarily, and instead of a picture he has only
succeeded in producing a surface enamel, or a
mere reticulation of surface-patterns. This very
defect has by some writers been held up to
admiration as the true perfection of all illumina-

tion. Its flatness was applauded because it had to be shut up in a book, and was therefore the only appropriate way of making a picture for such a purpose. But whoever would dream that because a picture, painted in due perspective and proper light and shade, was to be shut up in a book that the figures represented in relief would actually be crushed. Such reasoning is most puerile. The supposed parallel case of a carpet or hearth-rug representing groups of flowers—even if the latter ever did deceive the domestic cat—does not in the least affect the most childish conception of a picture in a book. We see it in a scene in light and shade, we enjoy and admire its reliefs, but at the same time we know it is a picture, and that it is quite flat. The two tests of knowledge never interfere with each other. To suppose they do is to suppose a case of imbecility that even a lunatic must laugh to scorn. So far, therefore, we think the illuminator mistaken in slavishly copying the limitations of the glass-painter. It is no very great knowledge of nature that is shown in these drawings. There is a good example of the method of study followed by thirteenth-century artists in the sketch-book of a French mason named Villars de Honnecourt, still kept in the National Library at Paris.[1] In this book the artist has made drawings, as he says, from the life—some are views, others drawings of objects of art; one represents a lion of the mediæval heraldic type, yet the artist assures us

[1] It has been published as the Album of V. de H., Paris, 1858.

it is from the life. But there is no real accuracy, everything is done with reference to some canon. It is, however, quite free from the Byzantine influence, though by no means free from a certain tincture of symbolism. The nude is rarely attempted, but when it is it is certainly less ugly than in Carolingian and Romanesque. To return to the Psalter —the style of the figures is rather graceful, attitudes are gentle and modest, though the inclination of head and body are such as to suggest a sort of undulatory movement in walking that is scarcely natural. The forms are slender, and the limbs occasionally beyond the owner's control —sometimes even deformed. The feet are small and weak—now and then over-twisted. The hands more delicate than formerly, especially when open. Faces are gently oval and sometimes expressive.

Sometimes the "histories" are placed in initial letters, the grounds of which, when not of burnished gold, consist of imitations of mural *carrelages*, chequers, etc., or rich enamelled patterns imitative of engraved traceries on metal. In other cases they are placed in frame-mouldings, consisting of a bar or beading of gold supporting an inner bar of coloured and polished wood or enamel work—the polish being represented by a fine line of white along the centre. For illustrations of this precious volume the reader may refer to Labarte, *Hist. des Arts industriels,* album, pl. 92 (Paris, 1864).

Now that the monasteries had ceased to be the exclusive nurseries of art and literature, the masters of the different arts and crafts usually belonged to the middle classes of the towns, where at first each art or craft had its own fraternity, and as the idea of trade-association grew, the crafts most nearly related would form a guild or corporation. All who joined these corporations bound themselves to work only as the ruler of the guild permitted. Nor were outsiders allowed to compete with them in their own branches, so exclusive was the protection of the guild.

Each confraternity had its altar in some particular church, whose patron saint became the protector of the guild. And indeed the constitution of the guild included even political rights and obligations —military service among the rest, like other feudal institutions. Each town had its own special corporations, which thus led to the formation of separate schools of art ; while travelling apprenticeships gave the opportunity to all of acquiring knowledge not accessible at home. Members were accustomed to travel and to attach themselves to the service of various princes, receiving appointments as "varlets" or "escripvains" or "enlumineurs," which sometimes obliged them to resign their membership. Occasionally they became political agents and even ambassadors.

It will be remembered that, some pages back, we noticed the fact that in Western illumination generally the design of the page depended upon the initial letter, or that at least the initial was the principal object of it. In the thirteenth century, although the initial had very much diminished in size, the same principle still prevailed. The letter itself was formed of some fabulous long-necked and long-tailed animal or bird, mostly a dragon as conceived by the mediæval artist. The head framed more or less on that of the mastiff or lion, or both; the legs of a bird of prey; the body and tail of a serpent; wings of heraldic construction to suit the form of the letter. While the body of this unspeakable beast formed the body of the letter, the tail was indefinitely extended to sweep down the margin of the text and round the base of it, so as to form a border, while not unfrequently slender branches would spring from it to form coils here and there ending in a kind of flower-bud, the extremity of the tail forming a similar coil. Very soon, however, the animal form was abandoned, and the letter made simply as a decorated initial or capital. If possible, one of its limbs was made to sweep up and down the "margin" and along the bottom or top as before. Where the interior is not occupied by a "history," we find coiled stems ending in profile leaves or buds.

At the same time the text has diminished in size, sometimes down to dimensions no greater than those of an ordinary printed book of to-day, but often beautiful and regular as the clearest printing. Such a book is the Bible written by a certain William of Devon, now in the British Museum (Roy. MS. 1 D. 1). A description of this beautiful MS. may be seen in *Bibliographica*, vol. i. p. 394, written by Sir E. M. Thompson. Here, though the writing is that of an Englishman, the style is completely French.

Another MS. deserving of study is a richly illuminated Bible now in the Burney Collection of our National Library (No. 3). Another, which, owing to its being recommended for study by the late John Ruskin, was once known as the Ruskin Book, is Add. MS. 17341, which contains many fine initials with border and bracket foliages similar to those of the Evangeliary of the Sainte Chapelle, now in the National Library, Paris (MS. Lat. 17326). Both the MSS. show the contemporary peculiarity of presenting Bible characters, excepting divine personages, apostles, and evangelists in ordinary local costume. Paris, of course, is the city where most, and perhaps the best, of these MSS. are preserved ; but those named above, in London, are also among the finest known examples.

CHAPTER II

RISE OF NATIONAL STYLES

The fourteenth century the true Golden Age of Gothic illumination—France the cradle of other national styles—Netherlandish, Italian, German, etc.—Distinction of schools—
Difficulty of assigning the *provenance* of MSS.—The reason
for it—MS. in Fitzwilliam Museum, Cambridge—The Padua
Missal—Artists' names—Whence obtained.

THOUGH the thirteenth century is the epoch
of the Gothic renaissance, it is the fourteenth
to which really belongs the title of the Golden
Age. The style of work remains precisely the
same, only it grows. It changes from the bud to
the leaf. It casts off the severity and much of the
restraint of its earlier character. To the grace
of youth it adds beauty, the beauty of adolescence.
To fourteenth-century illumination we can give
no higher praise than that it is beautiful. Not,
indeed, because of its deliberate limitations, but
in spite of them. For after ages have taught us
that if in pure ornament and resplendent decorative completeness the pages of the fourteenth
century cannot be surpassed, in miniature histori-
ation it must take a second place. The skilled
illuminators of the later schools are the masters
of the mere picture. For surely no judge of art

could possibly assert that the miniatures of the
Grunani Breviary or of the Brera Graduals as
miniatures are inferior to those of the Psalter of
St. Louis, the Berry Bible, or the Prayer-book
of Margaret of Bavaria.   Yet these are typical
MSS. of the highest rank.   Hence we say that
while the illumination of the Golden Age of the
art was beautiful, it was not absolutely perfect.
It is not to be taken by modern students as the
only possible model or basis simply because it
was the best of its kind.   There is no such
despotism in art.   To those who think it the only
possible form of book decoration, let it be so by
all means, but we may as well hope to clothe our
soldiers in chain or plate armour, and send the
élite of our nobility on another crusade to Jerusalem, or satisfy our universities with the *quod
libets* and *quiddities* of the *trivium* and *quadrivium*,
as hope to make popular to the England of the
twentieth century the artistic tastes of the fourteenth.   We indulge in no such dreams.   If we
are to have illuminated books, our own age must
invent them.   The illuminators of the Bibles,
Romances, Mirrors, and Chronicles of the fourteenth century no doubt did their best, and we
honour and praise them for it.   We think their
work among the loveliest gratifications of the
eye that can be imagined.   But the eye is very
catholic—it has immense capacities for enjoyment.
The window of the soul opens on illimitable pros-
pects, and if the soul be satisfied for the time,
it is not necessarily repleted for ever.   Golden
ages are cyclical, and it may be that the glory of

the books of the future shall surpass all the glories
of the past.

By 1350 France had absorbed all the antece-
dent varieties of illumination. From France,
therefore, spring all the succeeding styles now
considered national.

And as is most natural, these styles develop by
proximity—the nearest to French being Netherlandish. The next, as a result of immediate
intercourse, Italian. Then German, Spanish, and
the rest, as intercourse gave opportunity. It is
not always an easy matter to say offhand whether
a MS. is French or Flemish. In the earlier days
it is not easy to say whether it be French or
English, or even whether French or Italian. But
the distinctness comes later on.

In the fifteenth century the Italian, German,
French, and English are quite distinct varieties.
Towards the sixteenth the Netherlandish is quite
as distinct. But the styles of Spain, Bohemia,
Hungary, Poland, though possessing features
which identify them to an experienced eye, are
to the ordinary spectator merely sub-varieties of
Netherlandish, Italian, or German.

With regard to the distinctions of schools or
local centres within the same country, the evidence of probable origin has to be corroborated
by historic fact. It is not safe without further
proof than that afforded by general features to
affirm that this or that MS. was executed at
Paris, Dijon, Amiens, or Limoges in France ; or
at Ghent, Bruges, or elsewhere in Flanders ; or
whether a MS. be Rhenish or Saxon, Bavarian

or Westphalian, in Germany ; Bolognese, Florentine, Siennese, Milanese, or Neapolitan in Italy ;
or executed at Westminster, St. Albans, Exeter,
or elsewhere in England. Nevertheless the
special characteristics of all these schools are
quite. distinguishable. In the attempt to distinguish them, although the diagnosis may be
perfectly accurate, the actual facts may be otherwise accounted for. Hence the danger to which
even the experienced connoisseur is liable. For
example, certain MSS. are written in a fine
Bolognese hand, which it is proved were actually
executed in Flanders ; others that one would feel
sure were Netherlandish, were illuminated in
Spain. Some very fine typical Flemish miniatures were painted in Italy ; certain Florentine
miniatures were the work of artists residing in
Rome. Milanese illumination is quite distinguishable from Neapolitan, and Venetian from both,
yet the school is not proof of the *provenance*.

Illuminators, like other craftsmen, travelled
from city to city, and princes employed men, who
resided in their patrons' palaces, who yet had
learned their art many leagues away. How often
we find the names of artists with the words Dalle-
magna, il Tedesco, le Poitevin, Veronese, Franco,
Crovata, etc., employed in Italian houses, indicating the place of their nativity. So that even when
we know every feature of the work we have
much to learn ere we can say with truth that
it was executed in such and such a city. We
must take into account details which are liable
to escape the ordinary observer, such as quality

of vellum or paper, choice of pigments, mode of application, and other particulars quite distinct from style of ornament or varieties of form in foliage. In the Fitzwilliam Library at Cambridge is an Italian MS., the characteristics of whose ornamentation are unequivocally French, but whose mode of treatment shows not only that it is Italian but that it is Milanese, but whether executed in Milan or not is more than anyone can affirm. In the British Museum is a magnificent service-book called the Padua Missal, but the probability is that the Paduan artist who painted its splendid pages, painted them at Venice. That it was executed for Sta. Justina, at Padua, is no proof that the work was done in that city.

In monastic times we have seen why the artist rarely signed his name. After the thirteenth century the lay artist had no such scruples, and hence we often find particulars of origin and purpose which explain all we wish to know. But if the MSS. themselves do not contain the particulars, very often the account-books of cathedrals and other establishments for which the books were illuminated, give the details of price and purpose, and add the names of the artists. The household expense books, guild books, municipal records, and the journals of the painters themselves are fertile sources of information. And if we seek with sufficient diligence these will probably be the means by which it may eventually be found.

CHAPTER III

Ivy-leaf and chequered backgrounds—Occasional introduction
of plain burnished gold—Reign of Charles VI. of France—
The Dukes of Orleans, Berry, and Burgundy; their prodigality
and fine taste for MSS.—Christine de Pisan and her works
—Description of her "Mutation of Fortune" in the Paris
Library—The "Roman de la Rose" and "Cité des Dames"
—Details of the French style of illumination—Burgundian
MSS., Harl. 4431—Roy. 15 E. 6—The Talbot Romances
—Gradual approach to Flemish on the one hand and Italian
on the other.

IN addition to the expanding ivy leaf which
forms the chief feature of fourteenth-century
book-ornament, we find the miniaturist as a further
improvement adding delicate colour in the faces.
Also that instead of the invariable lozenging or
diapering of the background he occasionally makes
a background of plain burnished gold. And as if
to prove that his predecessors were really hampered
with the restrictions imposed by their imitations of
painted glass, he begins to try his best to paint
up his miniatures into real pictures with high
lights on draperies and shading upon the folds.
A certain amount of flatness, however, still remains,
but it scarcely seems to have been the intention
or aim of the painter. There is a similar flatness

in the work of all the early schools of painting, which had no reference whatever to the destination of the picture. See, for instance, the Origny Treasure Book in the Print Room at Berlin (MS. 38), and the Life of St. Denis in the National Library at Paris (Nos. 2090–2), both MSS. dating somewhere about 1315. The drapery shading in the latter MS. is no longer the work of the pen, but brush-work in proper colour. The Westreenen Missal in the Museum at the Hague, which dates about 1365, though not a French MS., is an example of the fact that by the middle of the century the tradition of pen-work outline and flat-colouring had become pretty nearly obsolete.

The reign of the afflicted Charles VI. of France, disastrous in the extreme to the material welfare of his own subjects, full of untold misery to the poor, and of oppression to the growing community of artisans and traders, was nevertheless, as regards literature and the arts, a period of progress and even splendour. The King's incapacity, by affording his uncles and brothers opportunities for fingering the revenues during the self-appointed and irresponsible regencies, enabled them to gratify their magnificent tastes in the purchasing of costly furniture and the ordering of splendid books. Louis of Orleans, usually credited with the worst of this prodigality, was by no means singular in his conduct. His uncle, the Duke of Berry, while daily earning the execrations of the tax-payers by his unscrupulous employment of the public money, was constantly enriching his library, and both he and his brothers and nephews were in the habit of sending priceless volumes, illuminated by the best artists, as wedding and birthday gifts, to each other, or their wives or acquaintances. We talk, and justly, of the fine taste and noble love of literature of Jean de Berry. His contemporaries, at least those beneath his own rank, looked upon him as a tyrant and plunderer. His disastrous administration of Languedoc was described as "one long fête where the excess of expenditure was rivalled only by the excess of scandal." If the *marmousets* could have hanged him they would. In default they hanged his treasurer.

All this maladministration was very wrong, but we cannot afford to burn the MSS. in consequence, for the Bible, the "Grandes Heures," and other books once possessed by the wicked Duke, are among the most precious relics of any age. Add to them the beautiful volumes of poetry and romance composing the contemporary literature of the fourteenth and fifteenth centuries, and we have treasures that we dare not relinquish.

By the beginning of the fifteenth century pure French illumination was losing its own characteristics and acquiring others. In the North, in Flanders and Brabant, Franche-Comté and the Burgundian Dukedom generally, it was becoming that peculiar kind of French which had received the name of Burgundian. It can scarcely be said to be Flemish enough to rank as Netherlandish, yet neither can it stand side by side with "French of Paris."

Let us look at a few examples. There is the

Book of Offices in the Library of St. Geneviève at Paris (Bibl. Lat. 66), also the St. Augustine in the same library. Also a small crowd of volumes in the Royal Library at Brussels, another in the National Library at Paris. One of the richest examples known is the "Psalter of the Convent of Salem," in the University Library at Heidelberg. Other grand MSS. are the two volumes of the "Mutacion de Fortune" of Christine de Pisan and the "Cité des Dames" of the same authoress. The volume of her poems, etc., in the British Museum, is a marvellously fine work (Harl. 4431). The greater part of this volume is in the earlier or "Berry" style, *i.e.* the fine pensprays of ivy leaf of burnished gold. But the first grand border is altogether transitional, consisting of the pen-sprays of golden ivy leaf alternating with sprays of natural flowers. This innovation, it has been said, was due to the school of van Eyck, but as no proof is forthcoming that J. van Eyck ever worked on illuminating we may be content to say that it arose about 1413, and that probably it came from Bruges. It is the beginning of the Burgundian style. But the ornamental leafage is different from ordinary Brugeois, inasmuch as it is "pearled" along the central veins, and is not symmetrical. The pearling is perhaps a suggestion from glass painting. It was very early adapted in German foliage work. On the first fly-leaf are several signatures, including the name and device of Louis Gruthuse : "Plus est en vous Gruthuse." The miniatures still remain French

PSALTERM. ET OFFICIA
14TH CENT.

Brit. Mus. Harl. MS. 2897, fol. 184

HEURES, ETC.
14TH CENT.
Brit. Mus. Harl. MS. 2952, fol. 21

with mostly panelled backgrounds, some with landscape. It is evidently a transitional document.

The works of Christine de Pisan, the popular— one may fairly say fashionable—authoress, were perhaps among the best known and most widely read while Caxton was setting up his press at Westminster, as she was among the most welcome guests at the Courts of Charles VI. and Philip of Burgundy. She was the daughter of a distinguished Venetian savant, Thomas de Pisan, who had come at the invitation of Charles le Sage to Paris as "Astrologue du Roi." At the age of fifteen Christine, who was as beautiful as she was accomplished, became the wife of a Picard gentleman named Estienne Castel. Two years afterwards the death of the King brought trouble upon her father, and with it sickness and despondency. Then followed sorrow upon sorrow. Whilst she was herself still burdened with the cares of early motherhood her father died, and within nine years from her marriage the sudden death from contagion, of her husband, to whom she was most fondly attached, left her a widow with two little children dependent upon her, and with only what she herself could earn as a means of livelihood. She was not yet twenty-six years old. To assuage her misery she betook herself to study and the composition of essays and poetry. Her works speedily brought her the recognition of distinguished personages ; her children were provided for, and she herself soon acquired both fortune and reputation. Charles VI. allowed her a pension, and she composed for his Queen, Isabella of Bavaria, several important treatises. Among her numerous compositions were "Les cens Histoires de Troyes" in verse, "Le Chemin de longue estude," "La Mutacion de Fortune," and a Life of Charles V., the latter composed at the request of Philip the Good of Burgundy. But the work which sets off her wit and learning to the best advantage was an allegorical essay on Womanhood, which she called "Le Trésor de la Cité des Dames." Altogether her works include fifteen books and about sixty smaller writings, which she dedicated to the King and Queen of France, the Dukes of Burgundy and Orleans, and the princesses and princes of the Court.

One beautifully illuminated copy of the Mutation of Fortune in two volumes is a curious example of its title, for one volume of it is in the National Library at Paris (fonds fr. 603) and the other in the Royal Library at Munich. In the former we have her portrait. In a blue gown she sits at her writing-desk busy at her work. On her head is the muslin-draped and high-peaked "hennin." Beside her a table covered with a green cloth and laden with crimson and violet-bound books and an inkstand. Her chair has a high back, and the floor is of the usual kind seen in illuminations ; that is, as if composed of a parquetry of coloured woodwork or of tiles of various kinds of marble. On the sill of the Gothic-latticed window, through which we catch a glimpse of the blue sky, stands a vase of flowers. Not perhaps an ideal lady's boudoir, but still an apartment of taste, and an altogether charming little picture. In the second miniature of the Munich volume Christine is standing in a chamber—in the same costume as above described. The pictures on the walls are—a fortress, a watchman, two knights, a prince with crown and sceptre, seated on his throne, surrounded by courtiers; a duel; and a martyr having his head struck off. Just such mediæval subjects as we may expect in a fifteenth-century mansion.

In a copy of the "Cité des Dames" at Munich is another portrait of Christine. The book is an Apology for the feminine sex, and it is well thought out. It appears that the conversation of the time was not always free from rather severe sarcasm concerning the ladies. We learn from Du Verdier that the continuator of the Romance of the Rose narrowly escaped most condign chastisement from some of the insulted sex at the French Court for the base insinuations in his poem against the character of women. Christine herself heartily disapproved of the Romance of the Rose, and wrote a sharp criticism upon it. Her "Cité des Dames" is an elaborate confutation of the opinion that women are naturally more immoral and less capable of noble studies or high intellectual attainments than men. In her introduction she says: "I reflected why men are so unanimous in attributing wickedness to women. I examined my own life and those of other women to learn why we should be worse than men, since we also were created by God. I was sitting ashamed with bowed head and eyes blinded with

tears, resting my chin on my hands in my elbow-
chair, when a dazzling beam of Light flashed
before me, which came not from the sun, for it
was late in the evening.   I glanced up and saw
standing before me three female figures wearing
crowns of gold, and with radiant countenances.
I crossed myself, whereupon one of the three
addressed me.   'Fear not, dear daughter, for
we will counsel and help thee.   The aphorisms of
the Philosophers are not Articles of Faith, but
simply the mists of error and self-deception.'"
The three ladies or goddesses are Fame, Prudence,
and Justice, and they command Christine under
the supervision of Reason (or Commonsense) to
build a city for the noblest and best of her own
sex.   So the city was begun, and the elect, alle-
gorically, let into it.   In varied ranks following
one another came goddesses and saintly women,
Christian and heathen women—among them walks
as leader the Queen of the Amazons.   "Queen"
Ceres, who taught the art and practice of agri-
culture.   Queen Isis, who first led mankind to
the cultivation of plants.   Arachne, who invented
the arts of dyeing, weaving, flax-growing, and
spinning.   Damphile, who discovered how to
breed silkworms.   Queen Tomyris, who van-
quished Cyrus.   The noble Sulpicia, who shared
her husband's exile, and many others, among
whom may be seen Dame Sarah, the wife of
Abraham, Penelope, Ruth, and the Saints Kathar-
ine, Margaret, Lucia, and Dorothea.   In the first
miniature on the left sits Christine with a coif
upon her head and a great book on her lap ; on

her left hand is the plan of her new city, while opposite stand the three ladies already spoken of as her advisers, furnished with building tools and giving her their advice. On the right she appears again in elegant costume with hewn stones and a trowel assisted by two workmen who are busily at work. Before her is an unfinished wall and several completed towers. In two other miniatures the gradual progress and entire completion of the city are shown, and in the foreground of each Christine and her three patronesses as before. Other examples deserving of extended notice are the Shrewsbury Romances (Roy. 15 E. 6) and Augustine, Cité de Dieu (Roy. 14 D. 1), two great folios, the former most interesting for its miniatures—the latter as a fair example of the rougher kind of Lille work, bold in design, good drawing. The choice of colours includes marone, blue, green, and gold. The ornaments, as usual, consist of sprays of ivy leaf and grounds filled in with treillages of natural flowers, among which are the daisy, viola tricolor, thistle, cornbottle, and wild stock. Fruits and vegetables also, as grapes, field peas, and strawberries. The miniatures include a few rather coarse grisailles.

A little volume (Harl. 2936) contains exquisitely drawn Brugeois scrolls in monochrome on grounds of the same colour or plain gold or black. Lastly we may mention "Les Heures de la Dame de Saluces," otherwise called the "Yemeniz Hours," in the British Museum (Add. 27967), a large octavo, as an example of transitional

Burgundian. Here the secondary borders have mostly the penwork ivy leaf with Brugeois corners and with strawberries, etc., in the midst of the sprays. Among the foliages grotesque figures frequently appear. The principal pages, however, are more like Harl. 4431, yet without the ivy-leaf tendrils. The miniatures are still Gothic, but richer and deeper in colour than ordinary French work. It would appear that two different artists were employed—one decidedly French, the other Netherlandish, and of a more individual character, still with French accessories. Every page has a border of some kind. Among the flowers the thistle is peculiar in having a golden cup next the down. The work generally resembles, in some parts, 4431 Harl.; in others, and perhaps more strongly, 15 E. 6. The colours are chiefly blue, scarlet, rose-pink, green, and gold.

We have now pretty nearly worked our way into Flemish illumination. The after-history of French as developed through the influence of Italy on the schools of Paris and Tours must have a chapter to itself.

CHAPTER IV

ENGLISH ILLUMINATION FROM THE TENTH TO THE FIFTEENTH CENTURY

IN a former chapter we left our native schools of illumination at work on such MSS. as the Devonshire and Rouen Benedictionals, and with the reputation of being the best schools of the kind in Christendom. Mention also is made elsewhere in dealing with monastic art of the usages of the *scriptoria*. Such usages, of course, could only obtain in houses where scribes themselves were to be had. Hence we should discover, were it not otherwise known, that writing and illumination, even in the monastic age, were not confined absolutely to the cloister.

With respect to the secular scribes, who sometimes worked in the monastery, sometimes at their own homes, in those days when the monastic orders still did most of the book-production, there were three classes of specialists. These were the *Librarii* or ordinary copyists ; the *Notarii* or law-scribes, whose business lay in copying deeds, charters, and such-like instruments, and taking notes in the courts ; and *Paginators* or *Illuminatores*. It sometimes happened, as we have said, that in some monastery or other, no monastic was found qualified to undertake any of these duties. It then fell to the prior or abbat to seek the assistance of professional outsiders. The paging and rubrication, putting in initials in the spaces left by the common scribe, and, if needed, the addition of pictures or marginal drawings and ornaments, caricatures, heraldic illustrations, etc., were the proper work of the illuminator, but it often happened that the same man had to do the whole work from the commencement to the finish. The Chronicon Trudonense tells us : "Graduale unum propria manu formavit, purgavit, pinxit, sulcabit, scripsit, illuminavit, musiceque notavit syllabatim." Several of our old English chronicles, of which the MSS. exist in the British Museum and elsewhere, seem to be of this description.

Reference has been made to the *scriptoria* at Winchester, *i.e.* at St. Swithun's and the New Minster. It is the latter foundation which is usually referred to in speaking of Winchester work. The Monastery of the Holy Trinity or the New Minster was founded in the first year of his reign by King Edward, son of Alfred, no doubt in obedience to his father's wish, if not absolutely in the terms of his will. Its first charter is dated 900 (for 901) and the second in 903. In the latter document the abbey is spoken of as dedicated to the Holy Trinity, the Blessed Virgin Mary, and to St. Peter, and is amply endowed under the Augustinian Rule. In 965, not without trouble and resistance, it was converted into a Benedictine abbey. In 968 Ethelgar, who had been trained at Glastonbury and Abingdon, became abbat, and from this time the New Minster became famous for both discipline and the production of MSS. As we walk along the High Street of Winchester now we find the story in moss-grown stones or other memorials how, among other methods, William the Norman punished the monks for their English warlike proclivities by walling them up nearly close to their church with the walls of his royal palace. In the old time, when the two monasteries stood side by side—St. Swithun's is close behind the New Minster—" so closely packed together," says the old chronicler,[1] " were the two communities of St. Swithun and St. Peter that between the foundation of their respective buildings there was barely room for a man to pass along. The choral service of one monastery conflicted with that of the other, so that both were spoiled, and the ringing of their bells together produced a horrid discord." The result of this was, first the above-mentioned hemming in of the younger establishment and eventually its migration to another site in Hyde Meadow. Here while the monastic

[1] Dugdale, *Monasticon.*

buildings suffered much through fires and other
disasters, the Rule remained until 1538, when it
was surrendered into the King's hands, and the
abbat, prior, and nineteen monks, the last survivors
of this once-famous foundation, were pensioned.

The scriptorium at St. Alban's, to which the
fame of book production in the Middle Ages very
largely reverted, was not founded until nearly
three centuries after the foundation of that abbey.
The library began with twenty-eight notable
volumes, and eight Psalters, a book of collects,
another of epistles, and *Evangelia legenda per
annum*, two Gospel-books bound in gold and silver
and set with gems, together with other necessary
volumes for ordinary use. Almost every succeeding abbat contributed something to the library
shelves. Geoffrey, the sixteenth abbat, a Norman
who once had a school at Dunstable, and who was
both a popular and liberal ruler, enriched the library
with a Missal bound in gold, another incompar-
ably illuminated and beautifully written, and also
a Psalter richly illuminated, a Benedictional, and
others. His successor, Ralph Gubiun, also gave
a number of MSS. Robert de Gosham, the next
abbat, gave " very many " books, which he had
caused to be written and sumptuously bound for
the purpose. And Abbat Simon, who followed in
1166, created the office of historiographer to the
abbey, repaired and enlarged the scriptorium, and
kept two or three of the cleverest writers constantly employed in transcription, and ordained
that for the future every abbat should main-
tain at least one suitable and capable scribe.

PSALTERIUM CUM CANTICIS

A.D. 1240

Brit. Mus. Roy. MS. 2, A. xxii, fol. 14

EPISTRE AU ROY RICH. 2

C. 1375

Brit. Mus. Roy. MS. 20 B. vi, fol. 1

Among the many choice MSS. added by Abbat
Simon was a beautiful copy of the Bible specially
written with the greatest care and exactness.   In
addition he presented the library with all his own
precious collection.   Another liberal benefactor
was John de Cell, a man of vast learning in
grammar and poetry, and also a practitioner in
medicine. Being unfit for household management,
he committed the secular affairs of the abbey to
his prior Reymund, by whose zeal many noble
and valuable books were transcribed for the
library.   And so grew in magnitude and importance the great collection which supplied
Roger of Wendover and Matthew Paris with
materials for their famous histories.   St. Alban's,
indeed, was at one period perhaps the most noted
of all the English centres of book production.
To dilate on other centres, such as Westminster,
Exeter, Worcester, Norwich, or York, would lead
us too far afield for a mere handbook like the
present.   Enough has been said to give a good
idea of what our English abbats and priors were
in the habit of doing for art and letters.

Since 980 a considerable quantity of transcription and illumination must have been produced,
notwithstanding disquiet, turbulence, and war.
At Westminster the traditions of illumination
seem to have followed the methods of the earlier
Winchester school.   But in the twelfth century
English work shows, on the whole, a greater
likeness to the contemporary work of Germany.
Of Westminster work an example occurs among
the Royal MSS. (2 A. 22).   The subject is the

Psalter, and the text is the handsome style of penmanship known as English Gothic of the latter part of the twelfth century. It would appear from the frequent occurrence of this particular service-book that it held the place of the later Book of Hours, and so we may expect a great similarity among different copies, both in the selection of the illustrations and their mode of treatment. It was usual in all such volumes to prefix to the text a series of subjects from the Old and New Testaments and the Lives of the Saints. Here we have them from the Life of the Virgin and from the Life of David, by no means unworthy samples of the school. One represents the Virgin and Child seated on a seat of the Germano-Byzantine type beneath an arch and within a square frame-border. The border seems first to have been flatly painted in two colours, pale blue and pale red ochre, and on this a foliage scroll of recurring forms in a bold dull red outline finely relieved with white. This is more or less repeated as the form of border to the other illuminations. Outside the whole is a characteristic slender frame of bright green in two tints. The arch overhead has two bands of vermilion, with white edge-reliefs and a central band of blue, again in two tints, with pairs of black cross-bars every half-inch or so resting on the capitals of the two pillars which form the sides of the scene. These pillars have each a green abacus at the top of each capital and scarlet bead below. Each pillar is of dappled red, marble-like porphyry, with plinths of scarlet and blue. Tiers of differently coloured steps

separated by bands of scarlet, green, etc., form
the seat. The Virgin wears the hood, cape, and
robe of the Benedictine nun, but coloured grey,
chocolate, and blue respectively. An under gar-
ment of pale amber completes her dress. The
infant wears an amber tunic, wrapped in a scarlet
robe. A very common embroidery of the drapery
consists of little stars or triads of white studs.
This also is a characteristic of German and early
Netherlandish illumination. There is a rich gold
brocade border to the blue robe of the Virgin. Both
mother and child have round nimbuses, the former
in plain circular bands of russet and orange, the
latter consisting of bands of pale blue surmounted
by a scarlet cross. Two lumps of green glass or
metal hang from the arch. The background is a
plate of gold. The flesh tones are livid, being of
a pale greenish ochre tint. One other of the
illuminations of this exceedingly interesting MS.
may be mentioned, viz. the David playing his
harp. He also wears three garments—a tunic of
white shaded with pale blue, then another of
lavender or lilac and having rich brocaded
borders, and, lastly, a pallium or robe of pale
chocolate lined with ermine; orange-coloured
hose. The throne, like the previous one, is of
several colours—slate-blue, green, orange, and
white, with a buff cushion. Here is a back to
the throne of a deep blue, with a background, as
before, of bright flat gold. The white moulding
is shaded with pale green, with bluish slate
corners. The outer border is of the pale red
ochre or pink, so common in later work in contrast

with deep blue. An outer frame or edging of
green completes the page. The harp is not gilded,
but of a drab hue, with two quatrefoil studs or
orifices in the frame, relieved as usual with fine
edges of white. Compare this MS. with one in
the Library at Lambeth.

The English illumination of the thirteenth century is so like that of France that it is often
difficult to determine its real nationality. There
is occasionally some feature which we know from
other sources to be English, or some circumstance
in the history of the MS. which fixes its origin,
as, for example, in the Additional MS. 24686,
known as the Tenison Psalter. Sir E. M. Thompson also describes this MS. in the *Bibliographica*,
i. 397. But it was previously described at some
length by Sir Edward Bond in the *Fine Arts
Quarterly Review*. The Psalter, which has had
a somewhat eventful history, is one of the best
examples of English thirteenth-century illumination. At least, this may be said of the early
portion of it, for while it is illuminated throughout, only the first gathering is in the earlier
manner. The peculiar value to the student lies
in the fact that although quite in the same style
as contemporary French work, it is the work of
an English illuminator. The colouring, however,
is not confined, as in somewhat earlier examples,
to blue and dull pale rose or paled red ochre and
gold. It gives us scarlet, crimson-lake, green,
and brown, besides the blue and pink and bright
gold which suggests some German influences.
The line fillings are somewhat peculiar as

having silver tracery, on the blue, side by side with golden tracery on the crimson. The full ivy leaf appears in the long branch work of the borders, and some of the initials still retain the bird or dragon forms in their construction. The compound bar-frame, gold and traceried colour side by side, is however already taking the place of the mere sweeping tail or branch. But perhaps the best indication of English design is the presence of a number of grotesque animals, with birds and occasional humorous scenes disposed, not in framed miniatures, but simply among the stems and coils of the foliage. This is a form of illustration much appreciated by English illuminators at all times, though it appears also in much continental work. Among other English MSS. which display this taste we may point out Arund. 83, which among many other treatises and curious compositions, such as the "Turris Sapientiæ" and a valuable calendar, in which are notes on the Arundels of Wemme, contains a psalter with anthems, etc., and hence is known as the Arundel Psalter. Its date is probably between 1330 and 1380.

The drolleries are very funny, and the other illuminations very instructive and curious. Some of them contain really good pen-drawing—refined, expressive, and graceful, but above all typical of English draughtsmanship. In a little scene of the adoration of the Magi (folio 125) the kings are costumed like our Henry III., as we find him in sculpture, wall paintings, etc. Over a very expressive picture of the three living and the

three dead occur the lines, each over a figure:
" Ich am afert Lo wet ich se Methinketh hit beth
deueles thre. Ich wes welfair Such scheltou be
For godes loue be wer by me " (folio 128).[1] The
three living in this illumination are three fashionable ladies—no doubt princesses, for they wear
crowns. Generally they are men, as at Lutter-
worth in the sculptures over the door, and in
the famous fresco of Gozzoli at Pisa. The subject
occurs sometimes in Books of Hours.

Many MSS. of this period and later have
hunting scenes, shooting practice, and games.

In MS. 264, Misc., Bodl. Lib., Oxford, there are
such scenes, one being a game at " Blind Man's
Buff," or as literally here " Hoodman Blind," for
the latter actually wear a hood drawn down over
his head and shoulders, and three girls are having
a fine game with him. The goldfinch or linnet
looking on from the border seems to enjoy the
fun. Another fine source of similar things is the
Louterell Psalter in the British Museum. In
this also are some richly diapered backgrounds
and exquisite border bands. This MS. dates
about 1340. But the gem of English fourteenth-
century illumination is the Royal MS. (2 C. 7)
called Queen Mary's Psalter, not as being painted
for her, since it had been painted nearly two
centuries before she ever saw it. But in the
year (?) 1553, being about to be sent abroad, it was

---

[1] " I am afraid. Lo, what I see
Methinketh it be devils three.
I was well fair. Such shalt thou be.
For love of God beware by me."

stopped by a customs officer and presented to
Queen Mary Tudor. It is bound in what appears
to be the binding put on it by the Queen
—*i.e.* crimson velvet embroidered on each cover
with a large pomegranate, and having gilt corner
protections and (once upon a time) golden clasps.
The clasps are gone, but the plates remain
riveted on the covers, engraven with the Tudor
badges. The MS. contains 320 large octavo
leaves, the first fifty-six being taken up with
illuminated illustrations of biblical history from
the Creation to the death of Solomon. These
pictures are arranged in pairs one over the other,
and to each one is given a description in French,
taken sometimes from the canonical text, sometimes from an apocryphal one. The drawings are
really exquisite, they are so fine, so delicately yet
so cleverly sketched. They are not coloured in
full body - colours, but just suggestively, the
draperies being washed over in thin tints, the
folds well defined, but lightly shaded. Next
after these subjects follows the Psalter with
miniatures of New Testament scenes and figures
of saints accompanied with most beautiful initials
and ornaments, illuminated by a thoroughly practised hand, for the artist of this volume was by
no means a novice at his work. A good example
of it is given in *Bibliographica*, pl. 7 [23], which
forms the frontispiece to vol. i., and one or two
outlines in the folio catalogue of the Arundel MSS.

Arund. MS. 84 is also a good example of
thirteenth-century illumination to a rather un-
promising subject, being a Latin translation of

Euclid from the Arabic by Athelard of Bath.
It is illustrated with diagrams.

Speaking of fourteenth-century illumination
brings us to notice a very striking change which
takes place in the reign of Richard II. in the
character of English illumination. In the British
Museum (Roy. 20 B. 6) is a MS. entitled an
Epistle to Richard II., written, it is said, in Paris,
in which the illuminations and foliages are purely
French, but which are the type of all the English
work of the same date. Take, for example, the
MS. already spoken of (Roy. 2 A. 22), produced in
the scriptorium at Westminster Abbey. Compare
with it a Bible written for the use of Salisbury,
and dated 1254. Then add the Tenison Psalter,
the Arundel Psalter, illuminated 1310-20. If
these MSS. be compared, however, with Lansd.
451, or Roy. 1 E. 9, the least accustomed eye
must notice the entire and almost startling change
in the luxuriance and character of the flowers and
foliages which constitute the initial and border
decorations. It is not merely a development.
There are additional features, but that these
features are added, as usual, from France, is
contradicted by reference to Roy. 20 B. 6, mentioned above. The new features are not French.
The question is, where did they come from?

CHAPTER V

THE SOURCES OF ENGLISH FIFTEENTH-CENTURY
ILLUMINATION

Attributed to the Netherlands—Not altogether French—The home of Anne of Bohemia, Richard II.'s queen—Court of Charles IV. at Prag—Bohemian Art—John of Luxembourg, King of Bohemia—The Golden Bull of Charles IV.— Marriage of Richard II.—The transformation of English work owing to this marriage and the arrival of Bohemian artists in England—Influence of Queen Anne on English Art and Literature—Depression caused by her death— Examination of Roy. MS. 1 E. 9, and 2 A. 18—The Grandison Hours—Other MSS.—Introduction of Flemish work by Edward IV.

IT has been suggested by a high authority that the immediate sources of the third period of English illumination were Netherlandish, but probable as this seems at first sight, there is another explanation which seems to the present writer to be a better one. As already pointed out, the influence on English work before 1377, notwithstanding political conditions, are distinctly French. After this date, though the artistic relation with France is not broken off, yet long before 1390 we find this new influence which is not French, and for which we have no special evidence that it is Netherlandish. If we go, however, a little farther afield, we shall find it. In the new work is a softer kind of foliage and a greater variety of sweet colour, and both these characteristics are found in a school of illumination that was being formed under the auspices of the Emperor Charles IV. at Prag in Bohemia. The artists in that capital who executed the famous Golden Bull and commenced the grand Wenzel Bible were a select band of Frenchmen and Italians ; the combined result of whose designs and labours was this very mixture of Gothic ivy leaf and thorn with the softer Othonian and Roman foliages and a new scheme of colour. Charles IV., son of that famous John of Luxembourg, the blind king of Bohemia, who perished at Crécy, was himself King of Bohemia as well as Emperor, and a man of brilliant personal accomplishments and cultivated tastes in literature and art.

Becoming Emperor the very next year after his succession to the throne of Bohemia, he fixed his residence at Prag, where he began the building of the new city, and founded a university on the model of that of Paris, where he had studied, and whence he had married his first wife, Blanche, daughter of Charles, Count of Valois. His university soon attracted some thousands of students, and with them no small crowd of literary men and artists, both from France and Italy. The great fact, however, to remember about Charles IV. is the Golden Bull, the masterly scheme by which all matters concerning the election to the Empire were in future to be settled. All the Constitutions were written in a book called, from the *bulla* or seal of gold which was appended to it, the Golden Bull, of which the text was drawn up either at Metz or Nuremberg in 1356, and many copies distributed throughout the Empire.   It is further affirmed that the absolute original is at Frankfort.   But the splendid copy made by order of the Emperor Wenzel in 1400 is still preserved in the Imperial Library at Vienna.   And as it is an example of the style of illumination practised in Prag during the reign of Charles IV., we may call it Bohemian.   It is true that the foliages are a little more luxuriant in this Wenzel-book than in the earliest examples of the style seen in England, but the twenty years which had elapsed would easily account for this difference.   As compared, however, with either French or Netherlandish, the new English style shows a much greater similarity to the work then being done in Lower Bavaria.   In these soft curling foliages and the fresh carnations of the flesh-tints of the Prag and Nuremberg illuminators we may trace the actual source of the remarkable transformation seen in English illumination after the marriage of Richard II.

Charles IV. was four times married.   His successor, Wenzel, whose ghastly dissipations can only be regarded as the terrible proofs of insanity, was the child of his third wife.   His fourth wife, the beautiful daughter of the Duke of Pomerania and Stettin, had four children, of whom Sigismund, the eldest, afterwards succeeded Wenzel as emperor, and Anne, the third, came to England as the wife of Richard II.   The magnificence of her equipage and the crowd of persons who formed her retinue are noticed by contemporary writers, and the effect upon English manners was instantaneous. Her beauty, sweetness of manners, and culture rendered her at once not merely the idol of her husband, who, says Walsingham, "could scarcely bear her to be out of his sight," but universally beloved by all the English nation.

To her the first English writer on heraldry, John of Guildford dedicated his book, and the artists who came with her from her luxurious home at Prag would naturally become the leaders of taste in their adopted country. After a while, indeed, the numbers of countrymen of the Queen were looked upon as the cause of extortions practised on the English people in order to supply the money lavished on these foreigners. More than once is this grievance referred to. In an old MS. in the Harley Library (2261), containing a fifteenth-century translation of Higden's Polychronicon, these foreigners are made responsible for at least one fashionable extravagance : "Anne qwene of Ynglonde dyede in this year (1393) at Schene the vii[th] day of the monethe of Janius, on the day of Pentecoste : the dethe of whom the Kynge sorowede insomoche that he causede the maner there to be pullede downe, & wolde not comme in eny place by oon yere folowynge where sche hade be, the churche excepte ; whiche was beryede in the churche of Westmonastery, in the feste of seynte Anne nexte folowynge, with grete honoure & solennite. That qwene Anne purchased of the pope that the feste of Seynte Anne scholde be

solenniysed in Ynglonde.   The dethe of this qwene
Anne induced grete hevynesse to noble men & to
commune peple also, for sche causede noo lytelle
profite to the realme.   But mony abusions comme
from Boemia into Englonde with this qwene, and
specially schoone with longe pykes, insomoche
that they cowthe not go untylle that thei were
tyede to theire legges, usenge that tyme cheynes
of silvyr at the pykes of theire schoone."

It is a fact that the Bohemian manner of illumination, with its three-lobed and vari-coloured
foliages, became the fashion in every English
centre of illumination.   In the preceding remarks
we have endeavoured to account for it.   That the
same style went from Prag to Nuremberg may
be only the natural *result* of its being carried in
the marriage and retinue of the Princess Margaret,
Anne's half-sister, who became the wife of the
Burggrave John.

Quite a similar MS. to those executed in the
reign of Richard II. in England and those of
Bohemia is the Wilhelm van Oransse of Wolfram
v. Eschenbach, now in the Imperial Library at
Vienna.   A similar, but inferior, work exists in
the Prayer-book written by Josse de Weronar
in the British Museum (Add. 15690). The English
foliages never show quite all the varieties of
colour seen in the continental examples, but the
golden diapers and pounced gold patterns are
quite as elaborate.   See this work, however, in
Arundel 83.   It appears also in the mural paintings of the end of the fourteenth and beginning
of the fifteenth centuries.   No doubt the English

art of the fourteenth century is of French origin
—so mainly is that of Bohemia—for Charles IV.
was brought up at the Court of France. Further
than this, we think we are justified in tracing the
new elements in Bohemian to Italy, and those in
English to Bohemia. The most striking proof is
not only the foliages, but the change from the
long, colourless faces of French miniatures to the
plump and ruddy countenances seen, for example,
in the Lancastrian MSS. in the Record Office and
in Harl. 7026[1] of the British Museum. Of course,
this suggestion of source is not put forward as a
dead certainty, but it affords this probability that
as the style suddenly arose during the lifetime of
Anne of Bohemia—and she was the acknowledged
leader of fashion—so her tastes in respect of
illuminated books and heraldic decoration would
become those of her new subjects. Let us examine
this fifteenth-century English work, and for this
purpose let us take the great illuminated Bible
in the Royal Library, 1 E. 9. It is an enormous
folio, and rather unwieldly, but a most interesting
example of the new style. Its initials are large,
richly illuminated in gold and attractive colours.
It has well-executed histories within the initials,
and boldly designed border frames, elegantly
adorned with foliages and conventional or idealised
flowers. Perhaps the most noticeable feature is
the beautiful, decorative foliage work in the limbs
of the letters—itself a South German peculiarity
—then the alternation of colours without interrupt-
ing the design, the profusion of foliage modelling

---

[1] The Lovell Psalter.

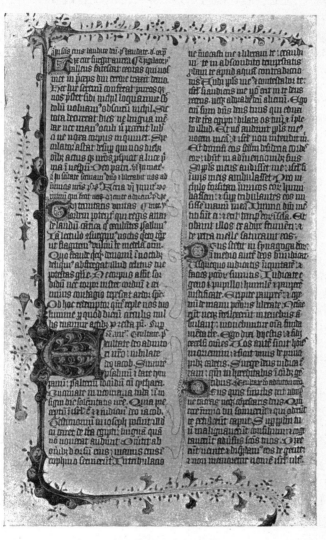

MISSALE (SARUM USE)
14TH CENT. (LATE)

Brit. Mus. Harl. MS. 2785, fol. 194 v.

HORÆ B. MAR. VIRGIS.
15TH CENT. (EARLY)
Brit. Mus. Roy. Ms. 2, A. xviii, fol. 66

in the backgrounds of the letter panels outside the historiations.   The next thing is the bold use of minium side by side even with pure rose-petal colour, pale bright cerulean blue, and bright gold. Lastly, the immense variety of leaf-forms, based on the three, five, and seven-lobed groupings of the typical form.   The coil and spiral are freely used as the groundwork, and the colours alternated as the coils or spirals change from front to back of the leaf.

Backgrounds of miniature histories are treated as in the Bohemian MSS.—Wilhelm v. Oransse, for example—that is, with fine golden tracery-patterns on deep, rich colours.   The figure-painting is vastly improved—the features now being actually painted and modelled as in modern portrait painting, not merely indicated by pen strokes.   The flesh-tints as previously noticed are bright and ruddy.   The principal colours used on the foliages are blue, crimson, of various depths, and bright vermilion, with occasional admission of bright green and paled red ochre.   Very similar to 1 E. 9 is Harl. 1892, and among other MSS. that may be studied with this one is 2 A. 18—a book of Offices, very sweetly illuminated, and full of typical examples of treatment both of architectural design and treillages of foliage.

The Gothic pilasters are filled with the same kind of coiling and spiral leaves and ribbons that are used in 1 E. 9 and Harl. 1892, the backgrounds of the miniatures enriched with fine gold patterns.   The furniture and costumes indicate the later years of the reign of Richard II., being

similar to those shown in the miniatures of Harl.
1319, which relates the story of Richard's misfortunes. A few miniatures of saints accompany
the prayers to them. One of the saints is
peculiar, being the Prior of Bridlington, perhaps
the " Robertus scriba " who copied certain theological treatises for the library, and who lived
in the time of Stephen or Henry II.

In the beautiful initial D is the figure of a lady
praying, the first few words of the prayer being
written on a floating ribbon above her head. A
fine panelling of black and gold forms the background. The lady's costume is that of the end
of the fourteenth century, her head-dress being
somewhat lower than that worn in the time of
Isabella of Bavaria ; in other respects she recalls
the figure of Christine de Pisan in Harl. 4431—
one of the fine MSS. of the French school. As
the psalter or offices was once the property of the
Grandison family, as is shown by the numerous
entries respecting them in the calendar, no doubt
this lady was the first owner of the MS., and
probably the same as shown in the beautiful
miniature of the Annunciation previously given.
Many charming initials follow this one, and
brightly coloured bracket treillages and borders
are given in profusion, introducing every variety
of coloured ideal leaf-form known to the art of
the time. It seems probable from its style and
the costumes that the MS. was executed for the
Lady Margaret, widow of Thomas, the last Lord
Grandison, who died in 1376, and given to her by
Sir John Tuddenham, her second husband. A

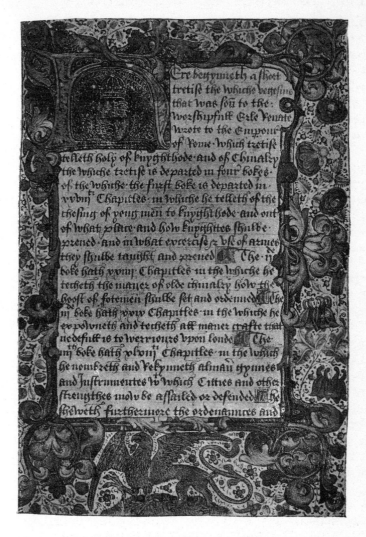

VEGETIUS FOUR BOOKS OF KNIGHTHOOD
(DE RE MILITARI)

15TH CENT.

Brit. Mus. Roy. MS. 18 A. xii, f. 1

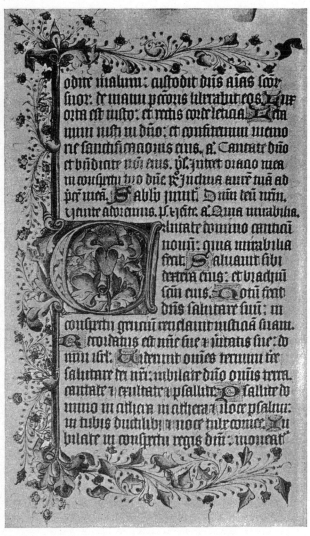

PSALTERIUM

C. 1470

Brit. Mus. Harl. MS. 1719, fol. 73 v.

better model for the modern illuminator could not easily be found.   Other examples may be briefly enumerated, in 2 B. 8, 2 B. 10, 2 B. 1, 2 B. 12 and 13, 18 A. 12, 18 C. 26, Harl. 1719, 1892, etc.   The Psalter 2 B. 8 has the good fortune to be dated, and its purpose and other particulars clearly set forth in a statement at the beginning of the volume.   The gist of this is that it was composed at the instance of the Lady Joan Princess of Wales, mother of Richard II., and that it was executed by Brother John Somour (Seymour), a Franciscan, in 1380.   Thus the illumination of it would probably be done about the time of the young Queen's arrival in England.   The Princess Joan died July 8th, 1385.   The work corresponds with this date.   The Grandison Psalter is perhaps somewhat later than Roy. 2 B. 1, and the rest are later still.

One rather fine example is seen in Arund. MS. 109, a folio called the Melreth Missal, because given by William Melreth, Alderman of London, to the church of St. Lawrence, Old Jewry.   He died in 1446.

For topographical miniature a good example occurs in Roy. 16 F. 2, which contains a grand view of London, including the Tower, but this MS. is probably not of genuine English production.   Nor is Roy. 19 C. 8, though a very interesting example as regards costume and local usages. The genuine English work of which Arund. 109 is a type has received the name of Lancastrian, as falling to the reigns of the three Lancastrian kings—Henry IV., V., and VI.

In the reign of Edward IV. we meet with the introduction of Flemish illumination, which gradually supersedes the native style, and by the time of Henry VII. the latter has almost disappeared. Its final extinction, however, was left for the sixteenth century, when either Flemish or Italian renaissance work entirely took its place. By the time of Queen Elizabeth English illumination was a thing of the past.

CHAPTER VI

ITALIAN ILLUMINATION

Barbaric character of Italian illumination in the twelfth century
—Ravenna and Pavia the earliest centres of revival—The
"Exultet"—La Cava and Monte Cassino—The writers of
early Italian MSS. not Italians—In the early fourteenth cen-
tury the art is French—Peculiarities of Italian foliages—The
Law Books—Poems of Convenevole da Prato, the tutor of
Petrarch—Celebrated patrons—The Laon Boethius—The
Decretals, Institutes, etc.—"Decretum Gratiani," other
collections and MSS.—Statuts du Saint-Esprit—Method of
painting—Don Silvestro—The Rationale of Durandus—
Nicolas of Bologna, etc.—Triumphs of Petrarch—Books at
San Marco, Florence—The Brera Graduals at Milan—Other
Italian collections—Examples of different localities in the
British Museum—Places where the best work was done
—Fine Neapolitan MSS. in the British Museum—The white-
vine style superseded by the classical renaissance.

CONSIDERING the position occupied by the
Roman Empire as the civiliser of Europe, it
is not a little curious and somewhat surprising to
find that in the twelfth century, when German
and French artists were doing such good and
even admirable work, that of Italy was almost
barbaric. A MS. in the Vatican (4922) is shown
as a proof of this. It is not an obscure sort of
book that might have been written by a merely
devout but untrained monk for his own use, but a

171

work of importance executed for no less a personage than the celebrated Countess Matilda. The scribe was Donizo, a monk of the Benedictine Abbey of Canossa. It is of the early or præ-Carolingian type, rather inclined to Byzantine, but with the big hands and aimless expression of all semi-barbaric work. Yet it has a certain delicacy and carefulness. In Rome itself during the ninth century barbarism was at its very lowest point. Only the sea-port towns had any notion of what was being done in other places. Painting was practised, it is true, so was mosaic, but the worst of Oriental carpets would be a masterpiece of elegance beside anything done in Italy. Whatever gleams of artistic intelligence appear, they certainly emanated from Ravenna or Pavia. But as there were no wealthy and peaceful courts, no indolent, high-bred, luxurious courtiers during that dark and troublous period, miniature or illumination had no call for existence. In the twelfth century book-illustration consisted simply of pen-sketching of the most elementary kind. The Lombards alone produced anything like illumination. A sort of roll containing pictures of the various scenes of the Old and New Testaments which represented the leading doctrines of the Church, and which used to hang over the pulpit as the preacher discoursed upon them, is the only representative of the time. Such a roll was called an "Exultet" from its first word, which is the beginning of the line "Exultet jam Angelica turba cælorum" of the hymn for the benediction of the paschal wax tapers on Easter

Eve.   Several of these "Exultets" are still kept
in the Cathedral at Pisa, and in the Barberini
and Minerva Libraries in Rome.[1] Of course the
pictures are upside down to the reader, so as to
be right for the congregation.

Very little progress was made, as we may
imagine, until after the great revival movement
begun by Cimabue, Giotto, and their contemporaries, about the middle of the thirteenth century.
But before taking up any inquiry into Italian
work generally we must not omit reference to the
remarkable MSS. produced at La Cava and
Monte Cassino during the Franco - Lombard
period.   Some idea has already been furnished
in dealing with Celtic MSS. and the foundations
begun by Columbanus and his scholars.   Indeed,
the general character of these Lombard MSS. is
seen in the Franco-Celtic.   The distinguishing
feature, if there be one, is the frequent recur-
rence among the interlacements of the *white dog*.
The La Cava Library, which was one of the
finest in Italy, has been transferred to Naples.
Monte Cassino still continues and maintains not
only a library but a printing press, from which
the learned fathers have issued at least one great
work on the subject of Cassinese palæography.
Of all the præ-Carolingian hands, Lombardic or
Lombardesque was certainly the most peculiar,
and is perhaps the most difficult to read.   One
evidence of this is the diversity of opinion on the
true reading of certain proper names in the

[1] See one in British Mus., Add. MS. 30337, and description of it in *Journ. of the Archæol. Assoc.*, vol. 34, p. 321.

original MS. containing the oldest text of Tacitus which happens to be a Lombard MS. The characters and other examples of the eleventh to the thirteenth century that have been published at Monte Cassino, however, fully illustrate the peculiarities of the handwriting, and give besides several splendid examples of calligraphy.[1]

One of the earliest illuminated Italian MS. which bears a date is a Volume of Letters of St. Bernard, now in the Library of Laon. It is very seldom that the earlier scribes and illuminators who produced Italian MSS. or worked in Italy were Italians. They were usually foreigners and mostly Frenchmen, and the art was looked upon at the beginning of the fourteenth century as a French art. This very decided example of Italian work is already different from the French work of the same period. The profile foliages have already acquired that peculiar trick of sudden change and reversion of curve, showing the other side of a leaf with change of colour, which is a marked characteristic of all fourteenth-century Italian illumination. For examples of it, the Bolognese Law Books, Decretals, and such-like, afford frequent illustration. Before leaving this first-quoted MS., we may say that it points to France rather than to Germany or Lombardy for its general form of design, but the foliages are quite of another kind. Another Laon MS. (352) shows the same treatment of foliage, but in effect

---

[1] The La Cava MSS. have been described by P. Gillaume in an essay published at Naples, 1877, and those of Monte Cassino by A. Caravita, Monte Cassino, 1860–71.

more like what may be considered as the typical Italian style seen in the famous Avignon Bible of the anti-pope, Clement VII. (Robert of Geneva), which dates between 1378 and 1394.[1]

A further example still more powerful in expression and skilful in manipulation is seen in a copy of the Poems of Convenevole da Prato, in the British Museum (Roy. 6 E. 9), executed for King Robert of Naples, a patron of Giotto (1276–1337), which, in comparison with the Laon Letters of St. Bernard of about the same date, is even still more Italian.

Cardinal Stefaneschi, another of Giotto's patrons, was also a promoter of illumination. His Missal, now at Rome in the archives of the Canons of St. Peter's, is a fine example of this style. It dates from 1327 to 1343. The MS. of Boethius at Laon is another. But one of the most masterly, whether as to design or manipulation, is a law book in the Library at Laon (No. 382). This grand folio contains "Glossa Ioannis Andreæ in Clementinas "— "The Gloss or Explanation of Joannes Andreas on the Clementines."

By the way, as illuminated law books, civil and canonical, form so large a section of Italian MSS., it may be well in this place to warn the reader against random explanations sometimes offered in sale catalogues concerning these books, their authors and commentators. For instance, this commentator Joannes Andreas was not, as we have seen it confidently stated (as if it were part

[1] See Humphreys, *Illum. Books of the Middle, Ages,* pl. 16; and Silvestre, *Paléographie Universelle,* pl. 117.

of the actual contemporary title of the MS.),
Bishop of Aleria (Episcopus Aleriersis), but a
jurist of Bologna. The bishop lived a century or
so after the jurist, who had completed his long
career as professor of law at Bologna extending
over forty-five years before the bishop was born.
His chief works are Commentaries on the Clementines (printed in folio at Mayence 1471, and again
at Dijon in 1575), and Commentaries on Five Books
of the Decretals (printed in folio at Mayence in
1455, and at Venice in 1581). While on this topic of
Italian law MSS., it may be useful to state clearly
what they are. By way of contrast to the *Corpus
Juris Canonici*, or Body of Canon Law, the subject
of books dealing with the so-called Decretals, the
other branch, including the Institutes Digest and
Novellæ of Justinian, was entitled *Corpus Juris
Civilis*.

The Decretals, then, which we so often meet
with in public libraries under various names, are
the canons which mainly constitute the Canon
Law. Strictly speaking they are the papal epistolary decrees (decreta), said to have existed from
very early times. In the ninth century a collection
of them was formed, or manufactured, in the name
of the celebrated Isidore of Seville. But with the
donation of Constantine to Pope Sylvester and
many others in the later compilation of Gratian,
these are usually looked upon as spurious and
false. The great and authorised collection was
completed by a simple Benedictine monk of St.
Felix, in Bologna, a native of Chiusi, the ancient
Clusium, in Tuscany, a man so learned in the law

as to have earned the title of "Magister." This
is the work often richly illuminated which goes
by the name of the "Decretum Gratiani."[1] When
glancing over the lovely initials and beautiful
foliages or resplendent ornaments, we are apt to
overlook the work itself which is truly monumental; being a summary of the papal epistolary
decrees, the synodal canons of 150 councils,
selections from various regal codes, extracts from
the Fathers, and comments of Schoolmen; all
methodically arranged and digested so as to
facilitate its use as a manual for the schools. It
is said to have occupied the compiler incessantly
for twenty-five years. Immediately on its completion in 1151 it was at once authorised by the
Pope Eugenius III. as the only text-book to be used
in the public schools, and to govern the decrees
of the Ecclesiastical Courts. Hence its celebrity.
Its transcripts are very numerous, and it has been
often printed. As to the Sext and Clementines
they are merely additional commentaries on supple-
mentary collections of decrees. Thus a new collection authorised by Boniface VIII. is called the
sext, *i.e.* the sixth book of the Decretals. The
Clementines were the constitutions of Clement V.
Other collections such as that of John XXII. are
called Extravagantes.

The most ancient MSS. of the Decretals bear
the title of *Concordantia discordantium Canonum* (a
"concordance of discordant decrees"); afterwards
The Book of Decrees; lastly, The Decretals. It
was considered, however, by some, jurists and

[1] See Add. 15274, British Museum.

others, to be not so much a concordance of dis
cordant canons as a subjugation of the ancient
canons to the decrees of the Papacy, and as
already stated, many of its decrees were found
to be false and fictitious. Nevertheless, it is by
no means an uncommon volume among the illuminators. Let us now return to the Laon example
—one of four or five of the species in that collection. The scene where the author is presenting
his work to the pope—we now know them both—
is quite a painting. Except for the defect that
kneeling figures are somewhat mis-shapen or ill-
proportioned in the lower limbs, the work is quite
comparable with contemporary mural painting,
both for composition and colour. It is almost
modern. It is quite realistic. In costume, expression, easy and appropriate attitude, it has
quite outrun French illumination altogether.

Another dated MS. (1332) in the same Library
(No. 357), " Rubrics of the Decretals," is a most
amusing example of the universal taste for irony
and satire in the initial figures and corner effigies.

A much-lauded MS. among these fourteenth-
century examples is one that has been carefully
and expensively reproduced by the late Cte.
Horace de Viel-Castel, namely, the " Statuts de
l'Ordre du Saint-Esprit au Droit Désir ou du
Nœud," an order instituted at Naples in 1352 by
Louis I. d'Anjou (called Louis of Taranto), King
of Jerusalem, Naples, and Sicily, cousin and husband of Queen Joanna of Naples. The style of
the illumination is precisely the same as those just
mentioned belonging to Laon, and as several

MSS. in the British Museum. Its stem and foliage ornament is very brightly coloured in fine green, scarlet, rose, ultramarine, and gold. The miniatures which occasionally contain evident attempts at portraiture, are painted in the manner of the school of Cimabue and the earlier Italian painters, more particularly that of Simone Memmi. It is substantially the Byzantine manner, but improved and enlivened by attention to natural attitude and expression. The greenish under-painting of the flesh-tints is often noticeable. The decorative portions are very skilful and elaborate, as well as extremely neat and symmetrical ; the gold profuse and brilliant. Indeed, the whole production may be studied as a typical example of its time. The text, though good, is not so beautiful as the Bolognese hand usually found in Italian MSS. of the following century. But perhaps this should add to its value as a proof of its being absolutely contemporaneous with the foundation of the Order, and therefore of its being the identical MS. ordered by the magnificent founder, Louis of Taranto, second husband of the too-celebrated Joanna of Naples. Their marriage took place in the August of 1346, and on the 27th of May, 1352, being Whitsun Day, they were crowned. In memory of this happy event, Joanna founded the Church of the Virgin, Louis instituted the Order of the Holy Spirit, or of the Knot, the symbols of which appear frequently in the illumination of the MS. It was named in honour of the Day of Pentecost— " L'Ordre de la Chevalerie du Saint-Esprit." The phrase "au droit désir" had reference to the circumstances preceding the marriage. The knot was worn in token of the "perfect amity" of the members of the Order.[1]

Other works of the fourteenth century are enthusiastically praised by Italian writěrs, as, *e.g.*, those of Don Silvestro, a Camaldolese monk, who flourished at the same time as the illuminator of this MS. of Louis of Taranto, and who worked on the great choir books of the Monastery "degli angeli," in Florence, so loudly commended by Vasari and others who had seen them. They have long been broken up and dispersed, and it is not improbable that cuttings from them were among those bought by Ottley, Rogers, and other amateurs. A fragment of an Antiphonary of Nocturnal Services, now in the Laurentian Library at Florence, finished in 1370, shows the style of work to be of the kind just described. Other great choir books of the earlier period are preserved in the Academy at Pisa. But the number of MSS. to which reference might be made is legion. Those of this date are chiefly civil law books; next to these come the canon law, and divinity. Among the intermediate class are the copies of the Rationale of Durandus, one of these being in the British Museum (Add. 31032). Now and then a fine Missal, like the "Stefaneschi," or the Munich Missal of 1374, which may be referred to as being one of the models of the school of Prag. On the whole, perhaps, the law books are

[1] See reproduction, published at Paris by Englemann and Graf in 1853, l. fol.

more numerous than liturgical ones, and are referable generally to Bologna or Padua. The name of Nicholaus of Bologna occurs more than once in these books. A book of offices of the Virgin, by Nicholaus, is now at Kremsmünster, and a New Testament, dated 1328, in the Vatican. Tommaso di Modena, another distinguished Italian illuminator, also had much to do with altering the style of the artists who worked for Charles IV. at Prag. Some of his work, or work presumed to be his, is still to be seen in the Bohemian capital. Next to these Bolognese MSS. we may place those of Florence—copies of the Divina Commedia and the Triumphs and Sonnets of Petrarch, which, with historians and copies or translations of the classics, chiefly occupied the illuminators of Florence and Siena, with one notable exception. Whoever has visited any of the North Italian cities cannot fail to have noticed and admired the magnificent choir-books still to be seen in the cathedrals and cathedral libraries. At Siena the Piccolomini service-books are truly splendid ; those in San Marco, the Riccardi, the Laurentian, and other collections in Florence, are no less admirable. Verona's best work is chiefly elsewhere, at Florence, Siena, etc. At Milan the Brera Graduals—each of them a man's load to carry—are simply gorgeous in the lavish richness of their letters, miniatures, and decorations. Venice, again, has another grand collection of MSS. of the highest class in her Attavantes and Gerard Davids ; Rome, in a crowd of princely libraries, has multitudes—literally multitudes—of exquisitely illuminated volumes. Naples also has some noble examples of the great craftsmen. We have not yet mentioned the Ambrosian Library in Milan, nor, except the Vatican, a single library by name in Rome. The mere names of the Corsini, Sciarra, Barberini Libraries are enough to those who have ever explored their contents to remind them of work that can nowhere else be seen so perfect, so profuse, as in beautiful Italy.

As specimens of local centres the British Museum offers many examples. Thus Add. 15813, though ordered for Sta. Justina of Padua, was probably illuminated at Venice ; 15814 at Bologna ; 15260 probably at Ferrara ; 18000 at Venice ; most of the fragments in 21412 in Rome ; 20927 in Rome ; 21591 at Naples ; 28962 at Naples ; 21413 at Milan ; the majority of the Ducali, of which the museum contains a large collection, in Venice. Some of the Spanish-looking MSS. executed for Alphonse V. of Aragon were actually produced in Naples.

It is not safe to assert that because a work is ordered for a monastery or a prince that the copyists or illuminators always went to the monastery or palace to do the work, though frequently they did so. Most of the MSS. executed for Matthias Corvinus, King of Hungary, were produced in Florence. There was more than one atelier of illuminators in Florence. There were others in Bologna, others in Rome, and quite a large establishment in Naples. Others resided in Milan, Ferrara, and Verona. Those at Ferrara lived chiefly at the Ducal Palace.

MISSALE

C. 1530

Brit. Mus.   Add. MS. 15813, fol. 27

KATHOLISCHES GEBETHBUCH
1584
Brit. Mus.   Add. MS. 17525, fol. 155

Those at Verona were the guests of the great Ghibelline leader, Can della Scala, and his immediate successors. Those at Naples, in the time of Alphonso the Magnanimous, and especially of his son, Ferdinand I., were maintained solely for the augmentation and embellishment of the Royal Library.[1] A list of seventeen copyists, including the famous names of Antonio Sinibaldo, Giovanni, Rinaldo, Mennio, and Hippolito Lunensis, and of fourteen or fifteen illuminators, all of distinguished ability, is given by Signor Riccio from the archives of the city. The splendid work they achieved may still occasionally be met with. In the British Museum (Add. 21120) there is a beautiful copy of the Ethics of Aristotle, with very peculiar initials and ornaments; and in the National Library, at Paris, many other very fine examples of Neapolitan work. Of the handwriting of Mennius we have a fine example in Add. 11912, which is a quarto copy of Lucretius, written on 160 leaves of vellum. Fol. 1 has a grand border on a gold ground, with a miniature containing a handsome initial E suspended over the author's head, who is seated at a desk writing. The first three lines of the text are in Roman capitals, alternately gold and blue. The illumination is of a transitional character, inclining rather towards the candelabra style of the Milanese and Neapolitan Renaissance—the Heures d'Aragon, executed for Frederick III., show a similar taste for candelabra, etc. On the other

[1] Riccio, C. W., *Cenno Storico dell' Accademia Alfonsina*. Naples, 1865.

hand, the initials are of the older white stem type, with coloured grounds. The writing is a small and very neat Roman minuscule, and dates probably about 1485, or between 1480 and 1490. The penmanship of Hippolito Lunensis appears in Ficino's Translation of Plato; also in the British Museum, Harl. 3481, and in Add. 15270, 15271.

The Heures d'Aragon referred to above are a rich example of the Neapolitan Renaissance preserved in the National Library at Paris. Writers on Italian miniatures are very numerous, and a good deal of interesting information about Italian MSS. may be found in M. Delisle's *Cabinet des MSS.*, etc.

There is one style of Italian illumination made very popular by the illuminators of the works of Petrarch, many of which are found in various libraries. That is the one called the vine-stem style. It consists of gracefully coiled stems, usually left uncoloured or softly tinted with yellow, and bearing here and there peculiar ornamental flowerets, while the grounds are picked out with various colours, on which are fine white triads of dots or traceries in delicate white or golden tendrils. A later variety of this style makes the stems of some pale but bright tint, and the grounds of deep colour. The vine-stem style seems to have prevailed throughout the whole of Italy just previous to the classic revival brought about by the Medici in throwing open their museums of sculptures, coins, and other antiquities, and by the liberal patronage of the new classic work by Matthias Corvinus, King of Hungary, and the Dukes of Urbino. After 1500 the vine-stem style seems to have gradually died out, and thenceforward only varieties of the revived antique became the fashion.

To the Italian Renaissance we shall revert in a later chapter.

CHAPTER VII

GERMAN ILLUMINATION FROM THE THIRTEENTH TO THE SIXTEENTH CENTURY

Frederick II., *Stupor Mundi,* and his MS. on hunting—The Sicilian school mainly Saracenic, but a mixture of Greek, Arabic, and Latin tastes—The Franconian Emperors at Bamberg—Charles of Anjou—The House of Luxembourg at Prag—MSS. in the University Library—The Collegium Carolinum of the Emperor Charles IV.—MSS. at Vienna—The Wenzel Bible—The Welt-chronik of Rudolf v. Ems at Stuttgard—Wilhelm v. Oranse at Vienna—The Golden Bull — Various schools — Hildesheimer Prayer-book at Berlin—The Nuremberg school—The Glockendons—The Brethren of the Pen.

IN a former chapter we brought up the story of German illumination to the time of the Hohenstaufen emperors. We may now make a new start with Frederick II., the eccentric, resolute, intractable, accomplished *Stupor Mundi* (1210-50). Not only was he a patron and encouraged art, but also an author. The work which he composed is still extant, and is preserved in the Vatican Library under the title *De arte venandi cum avibus.* Paintings of birds and hunting scenes embellish its pages. The art is not specially high class, and though in courtesy it may be called German, seeing that he was the German

Emperor, and in some respects is like the Imperial MSS. of the Saxon period, in point of fact it is Italian or Sicilian.[1] This Sicilian school is peculiar, and exhibits very slight traits of relationship with the rest of Italy. After the Arab conquest of the island in 827, whilst new ideas were imported, still the old Greek cities kept their ancient traditions and methods in art, especially in those branches we term industrial, and just as both Greek and Arabic tongues existed as vernaculars beside the Latin, so the arts and industries bore the features of three artistic tastes.

The silk-weaving of the Greek craftsmen was embellished with the designs of embroidery from Damascus, and these were mingled with patterns in which the foliages of Carolingian and German origin are distinctly traceable. Examples of the kind of manufacture here referred to may be seen in the robes of the Emperor Henry II., still preserved in the Cathedral Treasury at Bamberg. Also the coronation mantle of St. Stephen of Hungary, husband of Henry's sister Gisela — originally a closed *casula* covering the body, but now an open cloak richly embroidered with figures of prophets, animals, and foliages, and even portraits of the King and Queen. It has sometimes been thought, from the inscription on its border, that, like the Bayeux tapestries of Queen Matilda, the needlework was from the Queen's own hand;

[1] (Bibl. Vatican, Palatina, No. 1071). Notice in Kobell, *Kunstv. Miniaturen*, p. 44.

but no doubt both these attributions are mistaken.[1] Still more Saracenic in taste are the mantle and alb now in the Imperial Treasury at Vienna, of the twelfth century, and executed at Palermo. Sicilian in some respects is intermediate between Italian and German, hence we deem this a proper place to speak of it, and rather as a transient phase than a style, for it perished with the Hohenstauffen dynasty.

The cruel tyranny of the cold-blooded despot, remembered, but execrated, in Sicily as Charles of Anjou, extinguished the last *scintilla* of native art, and when the Italian revival of the thirteenth century took place, it was confined entirely to the North, except when such patrons as Robert or Ferdinand or Alfonso encouraged Tuscan artists by inviting them to Naples. Palermo was no longer of importance, though a capital, and Sicily existed merely as a portion of the kingdom of Naples.

Let us pass, then, to the great German capital. Changes here, too, have taken place. It is not Bamberg but Prag, for the Imperial crown has passed from the House of Suabia through the Hapsburgs to that of Luxembourg, and among its territories is the picturesque old city with its historic bridge and gate-towers, a Slavonic not a German city in its origin. The ten German circles of Suabia and Franconia, Westphalia, Bohemia, and the rest did not as yet exist—they were the later

---

[1] See description in Bock, *Die Kleinodien des heiligen Römisches Reichs*, pl. 17.

creation of Maximilian ; the Fatherland consisted
of some two or three hundred dukedoms, counts,
marquisates, and lordships, all absolute sovereign-
ties, but all pledged to support the Holy Roman
Empire.   Very thinly, perhaps, but still the
Imperial sceptre meant a real supremacy, and in
the hands of such emperors as Henry of Luxembourg, a supremacy maintained with real and becoming dignity.

Prag, as we have said, is in a Slavonic country,
and one sometimes hostile to the Empire.   It was
the capital of Bohemia.   In 1310 its King was
John, the restless son of the new Emperor Henry
VII. of Luxembourg.   Hence we find it at the
moment we begin the study of its art a nominally
German city.   Shortly before this time were produced several examples of German work ; as, for
instance, the "Minnelieder," with more than a
hundred miniatures of hunting scenes and similar
outdoor amusements, which are useful as studies
of costume, but otherwise of little interest.   But
it is not until 1312—the new King being then, for
the sake of acquiring the crown, though only, it
is said, thirteen years of age, already the husband
of the Princess Elizabeth, the late King's second
daughter, yet neither a favourite with his wife
nor with her father's people—that the Abbess of
St. George's in Prag, the Princess Cunigunda,
composed a Passionale, richly illustrated with
interesting miniatures.   The saints, histories, and
allegories are painted in tender water-colours, the
architectural details being in Gothic taste.   It is
still preserved in the University Library at Prag,

No. xiv., A. 17.[1] The Emperor Charles IV., son of the valorous but impracticable John (born 1316, died 1378), and who has already been spoken of in connection with English illumination, was the founder of the Bohemian school, or, rather, of the school of Prag. Owing probably his fine tastes and many accomplishments rather to his mother than his father, he devoted himself to art and literature, inviting painters and scholars from other countries to reside in the Bohemian capital. For the Collegium Carolinum, of which he was the founder, he caused many noble volumes to be executed, and among the vast treasures and curiosities of his celebrated Schloss Karlstein was a fine collection of illuminated MSS. In the Museum at Prag and other local libraries are still kept some relics of his library. The "Liber Viaticus" of Bishop John of Newmarkt—the "Orationale" of Bishop Arnestus (under French influence)—the "Pontificale of Bishop Albert von Sternberg" (in the library of the Præmonstrant Monastery of Strahow)—the Missal of Archbishop Ozko von Wlaschim (library of the Metropolitan Chapter in Prag)—the Evangeliary of Canon John von Troppau (Johannes de Oppavia), written and illuminated at Brunn, in Moravia, now in the Imperial Library at Vienna. All these illuminated MSS. are examples of the great variety of styles in which the Bohemian colony produced their work under

---

[1] Wocel, *Mittheil. der Central.-Commiss.*, v., 1860, p. 75, with illustrations.

the auspices of their liberal patron, yet not without peculiarities which mark the individuality of the artist. Thus while the Orationale of Arnestus is almost French, the Passionale of Cunegunda is entirely free from French influence. For costumes the Welt-chronik of Rudolf von Ems, 1350–85, and now in the Royal Private Library at Stuttgard, is almost an encyclopædia. Similar is the "Legenda Aurea" of 1362 in the Public Library at Munich (Cod. Germ. 6). A very interesting MS. with miniatures of costumes and curious usages is the "Bellifortis" of Conrad Kyeser (Göttingen, Public Library, Philos., No. 63). The Evangeliary of Troppau is most beautifully written; its text is a model of elegant and perfect penmanship; its ornaments distinctly Bohemian. Three or four Prag MSS. executed for Charles's son Wenzel (1378–1409) are, it may be said, typical. Of these the grandest, though incomplete, is the illuminated Bible, called the Wenzel Bible, executed by order of Martin Rotlöw for presentation to the Emperor. The choice of illustrations in this singular performance are rather more than on a par with the woodcuts of the great English Bible of Cranmer. The "Wilhelm von Oranse" of 1387, now in the Ambras Museum at Vienna (No. 7), affords splendid examples of the fine embroidered and richly coloured backgrounds we so often see towards 1400 in English MSS., and the Golden Bull of Charles IV., also in the Imperial Library at Vienna (j. c. 338), has the softly curling foliages variously coloured, which form the characteristic difference between the

French and English illumination of the fifteenth century.

Another rich example of German as distinct from French or Italian work of this period is the grand Salzburg Missal now at Munich (Lat. 15710). When we reach the fifteenth century German illumination begins to grow gaudy, especially in the revived taste for parti-coloured border-frames, in which green and scarlet are often to be seen. The Kuttenberg Gradual at Vienna (Imp. Lib., 15501) is of the Bohemian type. Now and then a MS. will show the influence of Westphalian treatment of foliage—and, again, of the school of Cologne or Nuremberg or Augsburg. These all differ, whilst still keeping an unmistakable German character. The Hildesheimer Prayer-book at Berlin points to Cologne. The Frankendorfer Evangeliary at Nuremberg is characteristic of that city. The Choir-book of St. Ulrich and Afra in their abbey at Augsburg is typical of its locality. The Missal of Sbinco, Archbishop of Prag, inclines to Nuremberg rather than Prag (Imp. Lib., Vienna, No. 1844). It is eighty years earlier than the Augsburg and Hildesheim MSS. Passing actively onwards, we find illumination still in vogue in the sixteenth century, notwithstanding that Germany was the cradle of the printing press.

In fact, it seems to wax more and more sumptuous—the books more profusely ornamented than ever. The Missal and Prayer-book of Albert of Brandenburg, Archbishop of Mainz, once at Aschaffenburg, executed about 1524 are among the finest productions of the illuminator's art. While perhaps we may complain that design has given way to profusion and the border flowers and insects—a contemporary characteristic of Netherlandish art also—are neither more nor less than portraiture applied to flowers, fruits, and the insect world. The larger miniatures are modern paintings, including portraits, differing in nothing but dimensions from the works of the greatest masters of the schools of painting. In ignorance of the strict rules of the gilds, some writers have gone so far as to say that miniatures also such as these were the work of the Van Eycks, the Memlings, and the Lucas van Leydens of our public galleries. This particular MS. was the work of a famous Nuremberg miniaturist, one of a distinguished family of artists — Nicolas Glockendon.

A very similar, but perhaps still richer, MS., is the Prayer-book of William of Bavaria, still kept in the Imperial Library at Vienna (No. 1880), painted by Albert Glockendon. It is one of the most exquisite volumes possibly to be met with. A Prayer-book in the British Museum (Add. 17525), though far inferior, may give some idea of the sumptuous character of the Glockendon work.

The first Archbishop of Prag, Arnestus or Ernest von Pardubitz, was an industrious collector of MSS. and employed many scribes. Another of the famous patrons in Prag was Gerhard Groot, who employed one of the best penmen to copy St. John Chrysostom's *Commentary on St. Matthew.*

In 1383 he founded at Deventer the famous House
of the Brothers of the Common Life, who made
a business of transcribing books; and, indeed,
so profitably, that, for instance, Ian van Enkhuisen
of Zwolle received five hundred golden gulden for
a Bible.   On account of the goose-quill which the
brothers wore in their hats, they were familiarly
known as the Brethren of the Pen.[1]

[1] Wattenbach, *Schriftwesen im Mittelalter*, p. 264.

CHAPTER VIII

NETHERLANDISH ILLUMINATION

IN speaking of the Netherlands we have to
bear in mind that some portions of what are
now called the Netherlands were once parts of
Germany, while others were parts of France. In
the thirteenth century Netherlandish art was
simply a variety either of Northern German or
Northern French. The earlier schools of Flanders
and Hainaut, and perhaps of Brabant, belong
rather to France, while Holland, Limburg, Luxembourg, and the Rhine districts were more inclined
towards Germany. But as soon as the schools of
Ghent and Bruges and other Burgundian centres
began to assert their claims, it was speedily
apparent that they had an individuality of their

own. In no country had the study of nature a more direct influence on the character of illumination. The allegorical method which so long had characterised both French and German art was promptly abandoned, and direct realism both in figure and landscape became the prevailing characteristic. Symbolism, it is true, remained in the representation of cities and other generalities of pictorial composition, but the details were in all cases direct imitations of contemporary facts. Half a dozen soldiers or houses might indicate an army or a city, and even some particular army or city named in the text, but the individual soldiers, though representing the army of Alexander or Roland, would wear the equipment or armour of the artist's military acquaintances, or his overlord's own company. The city, whether Ghent or Bagdad, would consist of the same sort of houses peaked and parapeted, the same towers and pinnacles that the illuminator saw before him in his daily walks. His conception of a scene from Scripture history would probably be framed more or less upon the traditions of the schools transmitted from the Sphigmenou Manual or the master's portfolio of "schemes," but while a prophet, an angel, or a divinity would wear ideal raiment, Abraham and Pharaoh would be arrayed in the costume of a contemporary burgomaster, and an almost contemporary French king. In one memorable instance, we are told, so realistic was the scene that Isaac was about to be despatched with a horse-pistol; and in another, representing the birth of Cain, Adam was bringing to the French tester bedside a supply of hot water from the kitchen boiler in a copper saucepan. This kind of anachronism, it is true, is to some degree chargeable on all early work; we see it among the early Italian painters no less frequently perhaps, but mostly accompanied with so much of allegory or imagination that we scarcely notice it, or if we do, we wink at it as part of the times of ignorance. It is really a mark of over-haste to be truthful, or at least to be understood, and at the worst it is no more than the natural rebound from the evil constraint of the old Byzantine tyranny over scheme and costume and invention. It is often truly diverting in its very *insouciance*. But its priceless value to us—and here the same remark applies to all styles of pictorial art before the fifteenth century—is the ocular record of dress, architecture, implements of peace and war, incidents of daily life, etc., for which no *Encyclopædia Britannica* of verbal explanation could ever be more than the poorest makeshift. As we say, this same happy anachronism is common to other schools of illumination, and we cannot fail to notice it from Byzantium to Britain, but it is the intense realism of the Netherlands that forces it upon us so strongly that we are bound to speak of it.

The oldest notice of illuminated work in the Netherlands is in a Benedictine chronicle of the ninth century, where mention is made of two ladies, daughters of the Lord of Denain, named Harlinda and Renilda,[1] who were educated in the

[1] Or Relinda.

convent of Valenciennes. " In 714 they left their native province to found a monastery on the banks of the Maas—among the meadows of Alden and Maas-Eyck. They there consecrated their lives to the praise of God and the transcription of books, adorning them with precious pictures."[1] About the year 1730 an Evangeliary of great age was discovered in the sacristy of the church by the Benedictine antiquary, Edmond Martène, which on good ground has been attributed to the two sisters. The MS. is still in existence, and was exhibited in Brussels in 1880. It is a small folio, and contains a great number of miniatures in the Carolingian or, perhaps more strictly, Franco-Saxon manner. On the first leaf is a Romanesque colonnade of arches surmounted by a larger one. Under the smaller arches are the figures of saints, demons, and monsters, and in the tympanum scrolls of foliage and birds. Between the columns are the reference numbers to the chapters.

The evangelist portraits are dignified and saintly, recalling the earliest work of the Byzantine school and that of the catacombs. Draperies and other details are heavy, dull, and ill drawn. In short, the work is of the same class as the early Carolingian. The blue, red, green, and gold of the borders, etc., have all kept their brilliancy.[2] It is somewhat curious that the Van Eycks, the founders of Flemish painting, were

---

[1] Bradley, *Dict. of Miniaturists,* ii. 87.
[2] See *Messager des Sciences,* etc., 110, 1858, and Deshaines, *L'Art Chrétien en Flandre,* 34 (Douai, 1860, 8°).

natives of this little town—then, doubtless, pretty and rural, now a busy place of breweries, oil-factories, tanneries, and other fragrant nuisances. Some miles further northward lie Deventer and Zwolle and Kempen, the land of the Brothers of the Pen, and of the immortal Thomas à Kempis. There is a style of calligraphic ornament deriving its origin from these Northern Hollandish founda-tions such as Zwolle, which is confined almost en-tirely to the painting of the initial letters and the decorating of the borders with flourished scrolls of pen-work very neatly drawn and terminating in equally neat but extremely fanciful flowers finely painted. It seems to have been brought at some time from the neighbourhood of Milan, where a similar kind of initial and exceedingly neat pen-manship also is found in the choir books. Many South German choir books are similarly orna-mented, so that it is not easy to say at once where the work was done. The Dutch illumina-tors, however, may usually be recognised by the Netherlandish character of the miniatures com-bined with neat and sometimes rigidly careful penmanship in the scrolls and tendrils and a hardness in the outline of the flowers. Sometimes the large initials are entirely produced by the pen, the labyrinthine patterns in blue or vermilion being filled in with circlets, loops, and other designs with infinite patience and excellent effect. Some of the border scrolls are exceedingly pretty, and the borders differ from Flemish in mixing natural flowers painted in thin water-colours with the more conventional flowers painted with a different medium, not in the later Flemish manner where the flowers are frankly direct imitations of nature, and painted in the same medium as the rest of the illumination.

After the Maas-Eyck Evangeliary the work of these northern foundations may well reckon either with the French or German schools until the fifteenth century. Where otherwise they are not distinguishable, the Netherlandish miniatures are usually such as prefer plain burnished gold backgrounds to diapered ones, or have a plain deep blue paled towards the horizon, and lastly replace the background by a natural, or what was intended to be a natural, landscape. As a test between French or German influence generally, the use of green shows the latter, that of blue the former. Not that this was any æsthetic point of difference in taste, but somehow the Germans had the green paint when the French had not, and so they used it. It is an open question whether Flanders or Italy first introduced the landscape background, but Flemish artists were so numerous, so ubiquitous, that we can hardly say where they were not at work—in France, Italy, or Spain. Plenty of so-called Spanish illumination is really the work of Flemish craftsmen. This was largely owing to the political conditions of the times. The Dukes of Burgundy and the Austrian Archdukes both ruled over Flemish municipalities, and employed the gildmen as their household "enlumineurs." And, of course, the success of the Van Eycks, Rogier van der Weide (de la Pasture), Derrick Bonts, and Hans Memling, stirred up the spirit of rivalry among the illuminators. They all worked in the same minutely, careful manner, and one could almost take a corporal oath on the identity of illuminations and panels which are really the work of different artists. Even yet the illuminations of the Grimani Breviary are attributed in part to Hans Memling—and no wonder! Only the best qualified judges can distinguish them. It is known that Gerard David of Oudewater, in Holland, a master painter, belonged also to the gild of miniaturists. But no miniatures are known to be from the hands of either Ian, or Hubert, or Marguerite van Eyck, or Hans Memling. The supposed identifications are merely guesses. But while this is so there is still no lack of illuminators, not to mention the illustrious few who were employed by the brothers of Charles V., King of France; and when we come to the days of his grandson, Philip of Burgundy (1419-67), we might name quite a crowd of distinguished illuminators. From 1422 to 1425 Ian van Eyck was "varlet de chamber" to Duke John of Bavaria, first bishop of Liége, and Regent of Luxembourg, Holland, and Brabant. In 1425 he passed into the service of Philip. He died in 1440. In court service there were besides, Jean de Bruges, David Aubert, Jean Mielot, Jean Wanguelin, Loyset Lyeder, and others connected more or less closely with the Maas valley and the province of Limburg. This valley seems to have been the cradle of Netherlandish miniature art. It is from this neighbourhood that Paris was supplied with craftsmen in the days of the brilliant if reckless administration of the uncles of Philip the Good. There were schools of illuminating artists in Maestricht and Liége, and within a very brief period the style of the Netherlander surpassed that of all competitors for facility, clearness, and realism. A marked feature in this mastery is the free use of architectural and sculptural design. All Gothic draperies are in some degree sculpturesque, and in miniatures we find sculpture to be the ruling principle. Perhaps it was the practice of uniting the crafts of painter and "imagier" in one person that fostered this peculiarity. But certain it is that Netherlandish illumination, in its border foliages, after the taste for the larger vine and acanthus leaf had superseded the ivy, the drawing is studiously sculpturesque. Many of the Gantois borders are like undercut wood carvings. Even as to colour we find either the gilded wood brown or the stone grey, quite as frequently as gayer colours, and much more so than any natural green. The after-fashion for grisailles or *camaieu gris* has reference probably rather to stained glass than to carving. Before the fifteenth century we do not often meet with individual illuminators by name, but in the Limburg Chronicle under 1380 is this entry : "There was at this time in Cologne a celebrated painter (he was probably a native of Herle in Limburg), the like of whom was not in the whole of Christendom," and more to his praise. His name was Wilhelm. In the municipal expense book, under 1370–90, page 12, is written,

" To Master Wilhelm for painting the Oath Book, 9 marks." The Oath Book still exists, but unfortunately the miniature has been cut out.[1]

Of course, it may be expected that some of the best examples of Netherlandish illumination are to be found in the Royal Library at Brussels. The *Bibliothèque de Bourgogne*, as it is called, contains, indeed, a great number of them. Some, of course, may be classed as Burgundian. There are, for instance, the grand "Chroniques de Hainaut" in three immense folio volumes, written from 1446 to 1449 (Nos. 9242-4). Also Jean Mansel's "Fleur des Histoires" in three grand folios (Nos. 9231-3), written about 1475. The frontispiece to the "Chroniques" shows the Duke Philip with his son the Count of Charolais receiving the work from the author, perhaps the best illumination in all three volumes.

Another (9245), the Book of the Seven Sages of Rome, is an example of the last quarter of the fourteenth century. Still another (9246), the History of St. Graal, or of the Round Table, is dated 1480. A Missal and Pontifical (9216, 9217) shows miniatures dating about 1475.

But other public libraries also possess admirable examples. The Imperial Library at Vienna possesses a most masterly production in the fragments of a folio Chronicle of Jerusalem (No. 2533), in which both figures and architectural details are most delicately and minutely finished, so that the miniatures form a most valuable treasury of costumes, armour, and architecture,

---

[1] Woltmann, *Hist. of Painting,* Eng. transl., i. p. 412.

correctly drawn and exquisitely painted. The
figure of Baldwin, King of Jerusalem, shows the
pointed toes which Anne of Bohemia is said to
have introduced into England. At Vienna, also,
is the richly illuminated History of Gérard de
Roussillon in French (No. 2549). At Paris we find
the "Champion des Dames" (No. 12476). Round
the first miniature in this MS. are splendidly
emblazoned the armorials of the various countries
and cities of his dominions—Burgundy, Brabant,
Flanders, Franche-Comte, Holland, Namur, Lower
Lorraine, Luxembourg, Artois, Hainaut, Zealand,
Friesland, Malines, and Salins. On either side
are scenes from the story, and beneath a symbolical crown is the motto of Philip's grandfather,
Philip le Hardi, *aultre n'aray*. The same motto
appears in the Chronicle of Jerusalem at Vienna,
and on the velvet of the daïs of Isabella of
Portugal, Philip's third consort.

It may be interesting to note, as a means of
distinguishing these Burgundian princes or their
MSS., that the arms of Philip II. the Good differ
from those of his father, during the latter's lifetime, by having in chief a label of three points,
and from those of his grandfather, Philip the
Bold, by having an inescutcheon of pretence on the
centre of the arms of Margaret de Maele, first
assumed by his father, John the Fearless, that is,
"or, a lion rpt. sa; for Flanders." As we have just
said, many of the MSS. claimed as Netherlandish
may be classed as Burgundian. The difference lies
mainly in the miniatures. Where the latter are
manifestly French with the mixed Brugeois bor-

HORÆ
15TH CENT. (LATE)

Brit. Mus. Add. MS. 17280. fol. 21

VALERE MAXIME, TRAD. PAR SIMON DE HESDIN
15TH CENT. (LATE)

Brit. Mus. Harl. MS. 4375, fol. 68

ders, they may pass as Burgundian ; but with similar borders yet distinguishably Netherlandish, that is, broad-nosed, square-jawed, and excited faces as compared with the finer features and placid expression of the French artists, the work may still be Burgundian, but it will be also Nether-landish. The individuality of Netherlandish illumination above every other quality establishes its identity. Look at the expression of the on-lookers in a Crucifixion, or a Christ before Pilate, or a Stoning of St. Stephen—the diabolical ferocity, the fiendish earnestness, the downright intentional ugliness put on some of the characters are in direct contrast to the sweet indifference, the calm complaisance, and blank unconcern of a crowd as shown in similar scenes by French illuminators.

We have seen something of the earlier kind of Netherlandish MSS. in those already referred to. It now remains to take a rapid glance at a few of the later ones, and here the difficulty is that of selection.

In 1484 Gerard David appears on the list of illuminators of Bruges,[1] and it appears that he, and not Hans Memling, was the painter of those marvellous miniatures in the Grimani Breviary at Venice usually attributed to the latter, and there-fore may be considered as one of the founders of the school of Bruges, or at least of the later style that may be referred to the Grimani Breviary as its most perfect example. Executed in much

[1] Cf. his "Judgement of Cambyses" in the museum at Bruges.

the same manner is a Book of Offices in the British Museum, containing portraits of Philip the Fair and his wife, the unhappy Juana *la Loca*, son and daughter-in-law of the Emperor Maximilian. Similar, again, are the " Offices of the Elector, Albert of Brandenburg," possibly the work of the same artists who produced the Grimani Breviary. There are also some fragments in a guard-book in the British Museum (Add. 24098), which may compare with any of the preceding examples. But perhaps to many book-lovers no better specimen of the highest class of Netherlandish art could be more welcome or more interesting than the celebrated copy of the "Roman de la Rose," also in our great national collection (Harl. 4425). This justly famous MS. is a real masterpiece in every department, whether we consider the expression in its miniatures or the consummate technical skill displayed in the drawing and colour of the borders. These secondary embellishments consist of fruit, flowers, birds, beetles, and butterflies. But, of course, the great interest of this book lies in its miniatures, scenes from the poet's allegory, and in the little statuesque figures of the various characters in the poem.

Two marvellous little volumes there are in the National Museum at Munich (861-2) which are surely unapproachable. One of the borders in 861 consists of the eyes of peacock feathers so absolutely perfect that we can only wonder at its rainbow hues and pearly sheen of colour. Something similar to it exists in a fragment (No. 4461) in the Victoria and Albert Museum at South

Kensington. The "Isabella Breviary" of the British Museum (Add. 18851) ought not to pass unmentioned, but space forbids us to add more on this inexhaustible topic. There is, however, the class of work alluded to early in the chapter, and in that on French work, which must be at least mentioned. We refer to what the Italians call *chiaroscuro* and the French *grisaille; i.e.* painting executed in tones of grey, in which the lights are given in white or gold and the backgrounds in rich blue. Occasionally the draperies and ornaments also are touched with gold, and the flesh tints as in life. Grisaille is not limited to Netherlandish illuminations. We find it both in French and Italian, but perhaps it is among the Netherlandish books we meet with it most frequently. Several examples are to be seen in the Royal Library at Brussels, and there is at least one in the British Museum (Add. 24189).

CHAPTER IX

THE FRENCH RENAISSANCE

WHEN the new ideas derived from the Italian revival first reached France, it would be difficult to say. There must have been communication with Italy going on the whole time that Cimabue and Giotto, Memmi and the rest were astonishing their fellow-citizens with their divine performances. The roads from Lyons, Poictiers, Dijon, and Paris were well known, and frequently trodden by both artists and merchants as well as by soldiers. The Renaissance, therefore, was no sudden convulsion. Perhaps a very careful examination of some of our Burgundian MSS. might reveal the presence of notions derived from Italian travel, for it is in the details of ornament that we find the traces of a new movement, and when the great change of style is clearly noticeable it is when the habits of society themselves have been remodelled, and when the once strange and foreign element has become a familiar guest.

In the fixing of schools and centres much is owing, of course, to the residential choice of princes, on whose patronage depends the very existence of art. This explains the schools of Bruges and Dijon, of Paris and Tours, for while the earlier dukes of Burgundy and the earlier kings of France had lived at Bruges and Paris, the later dukes had preferred Dijon, and Louis XI., Charles VIII., and Louis XII. lived mostly at Tours. So that while Dijon became the new centre of Burgundian illumination, Tours became to the new movement from Italy what Paris had been at the commencement of the Gothic period. Tours, in fact, became the centre of the Renaissance. The influence of Dijon was on the wane, Burgundy itself was going down. Michel Coulombe, the great Breton sculptor, who had been trained at Dijon, left it for Tours, and probably illuminators and other artists followed his example. As we know from examples, the Burgundian art of Dijon had the Flemish stamp strongly marked—the Flemish artists had a way of making strong impressions.

Tours, on the other hand, had had an entirely different training. The artists of Touraine had no shadow of Flemish influence in their practice. Their sculptures, enamels, colour-scheme were of another bias. Their stamp came from Italy, and if not so deep as that of Flanders or Dijon, it was equally inevitable and more permanent.

The first name that we meet with among the

illuminators of Touraine who are expressly connected with the Renaissance is that of Jean Fouquet. Of his origin or training nothing seems to be known, but he was born probably about 1415. He must have acquired distinction even as a youth, for some twenty-five years afterwards (1440–3) he was invited to Rome to paint the portrait of Pope Eugenius IV., and he stayed in Italy until 1447. On his return to France he was made *valet de chambre* and painter to Charles VII. at Tours, and continued in the same office under Louis XI. It was part of the business of the *paintre du roy* to design and provide decorations and costumes, banners and devices for all state ceremonies, and this became Fouquet's duty at the funeral of Charles VII., and when Louis instituted the Order of St. Michel in 1470, and the last trace of him as an artist occurs about 1477. His sons, Louis and Francis, were both painters, and, like himself, worked much at the illumination of books. It is curious that this great master—one of the greatest miniaturists of any school, and one of the founders of the French school of painting—became entirely forgotten until the discovery of some fragments of a Book of Hours painted for Estienne Chevalier, the King's treasurer.

Forty miniatures of the most masterly description came into the hands of M. Louis Brentano-Laroche, of Frankfort-on-the-Maine. Their uncommon excellence led to a most diligent search for information respecting the artist, which resulted in the unearthing of many other examples

of his unequalled pencil. We now know of a
dozen most precious examples. Besides the
Brentano miniatures, two other fragments of the
same Book of Hours have been found, and
several large and important MSS. Among these
we may name the "Antiquities of the Jews," by
Josephus, in the National Library at Paris (MSS.
Des. 6891), and a Book of Hours, executed for
Marie de Clève, widow of Charles Duke of
Orleans, in 1472. Attributed to him are the
"Versailles" Livy (Nat. Lib., Paris, 6907); the
"Sorbonne" Livy (fds. de Sorb. 297). A Livy
in the public library at Tours also passes under
his name, and the famous "Boccaccio" of
Estienne Chevalier at Munich, containing ninety
miniatures, is also confidently assigned to him.
Other MSS. that are imputed to him are probably
the work of his sons or scholars.

The Paris Josephus is generally considered his
masterpiece. The volume (which contains only
the first fourteen books) is in folio, written most
beautifully in two columns, and is adorned with
miniatures, vignettes, and initials, but much
of its interest lies in the note at the end, placed
there by Robortet, secretary to the Duc de Bourbon: "En ce liure a douze ystoires les troys
premieres de l'enlumineur du duc Iehan de Berry,
et les neuf de la main du bon paintre et enlumineur du roy Loys XIᵉ Iehan Foucquet, natif de
Tours." And we gather from another note that
the book had been entrusted to Fouquet for completion by Jacques d'Armagnac duc de Nemours.
A further note informs us that the book belonged

to the Duc de Bourbon. It seems to have been one of the rich presents made by the Duc de Berry to Jacques de Nemours. The first three miniatures are by the illuminator of the Duc de Berry, and this artist was probably Andrieu Beauneveu, though other illuminators did work for him, as Jacques de Hesdin and Pol de Limburg. The fourth miniature is by Fouquet, and represents a battle; the rest to the seventh are either not his best work or else the work of his pupils, but the seventh on folio 135 gives us a good idea of Fouquet at his best. It represents David receiving with his crown the news of the death of Saul. The eighth, ninth, and tenth are very fine, but the eleventh M. Paulin Paris (MSS. du Roy) thinks the most beautiful of all. Its subject is the clemency of Cyrus towards the captive Jews in Babylon.[1] Of the other MSS. space forbids us reluctantly to forego description.

The characteristics of the school of Tours as seen in the work of the greatest of its expositors is (1) The clearly marked influence of Italy and the antique. (2) A masterly understanding of French landscape (see fine instances of this understanding also in "Trésor des Histoires," now in the British Museum, Cott., Aug. 5). (3) A complete freedom from Gothic influence and from the domination of the school of Bruges. The colours for which Fouquet seems to have a preference are, first, a clear orange-vermilion,

---

[1] See Mrs. Mark Pattison s (Lady Dilke) *The Renaissance in France*, i. 273, etc. ; Bradley, *Dict. of Miniaturists*, art. "Fouquet," i. 346.

supported by golden brown and gold, clear blue
and green, lemon-yellow ; and then, as a contrast,
grey of various tones in walls and buildings, soft
landscape greens, and aërial tints of distance and
sky. Perhaps the technical skill of Fouquet has
never been surpassed. It is so perfect that some
have tried to explain it by supposing that he was
trained in a Flemish studio. His sons and pupils
continued his methods, and thus while Paris
remains under the influence of Flemish masters,
Tours was carrying forward a quite different type
of traditions.

The Valerius Maximus (Harl. 4374) of the
British Museum will give an idea of the later
Paris school. Its date is about the end of the
fifteenth century.

We ought not in this place to forget the
influence brought into French art through the
marriage of the murdered Duke of Orleans
with Valentina of Milan, not only directly through
books and artists, but by the hereditary trans-
mission of that love of art and beautiful things
for which Valentina and her family were well
known. It was in art, letters, and books that the
widowed princess sought such consolation as was
possible.[1] In her best days she had united in
herself a seductive grace of carriage, beauty of
person, and dignity of rank, which made her the
ornament of the French Court. She was almost
the only one about the unfortunate Charles VI.
who could influence him in his moments of mental

[1] She assumed as her impresa the *chantepleure*, with the
sorrowful motto : " Plus ne m'est rien : rien ne m'est plus."

aberration. Coming from the luxury of the most splendid court in Italy, she brought into France the most refined taste in matters connected with the arts. The inventory of her jewels at the time of her marriage includes three Books of Hours, three German MSS., and a volume called *Mandavilla*. Like her husband she was an employer both of copyists and illuminators, and before her death had collected at her Castle of Blois a very fine collection of beautiful books.

Her son Charles, the poet, inherited her tastes, and added to her collections. We are not surprised, therefore, to find her grandson Louis, afterwards Louis XII., supporting the great artistic movement which he and his Queen Anne of Brittany helped so effectually to identify with the Court of France.

About the time that we hear the last of Fouquet we have the earliest notices of another illuminator who plays an important part in the illuminations executed for Anne of Brittany, the noble and gifted Queen of France, and wife, first of Charles VIII. and then of his successor, Louis XII.

In 1472 Jean Perréal is entrusted with the glass paintings of the Carmelite church at Tours. Lemaire, in his *Légende des Vénitiens*, calls him a second Zeuxis or Apelles. During the reigns of Charles VIII. and Louis XII. he is the chief artist of the time. In 1491, and perhaps earlier, he is engaged in the usual duties of a *valet de chambre*, *i.e.* designing and preparing the requisite devises, arms, and banners for public functions. In 1502 he went to Italy. In 1509 his name occurs in connection with that of Jean Bourdichon, of whom we shall hear more when we come to the work done for the Queen. In 1523 in the household of Francis I. he is still *valet de chambre.* Twenty-four years previously it was as *valet de chambre* that he prepared the decorations for Louis XII.'s entry into Lyons. On the death of Anne of Brittany also he performed similar duties, and again on that of Louis XII. He even came to England in 1514, sent by Louis XII., to superin-tend the trousseau of Mary Tudor, "pour aider à dresser le dict appareil à la mode de France," previous to her wedding journey to Paris.[1] Four months afterwards he was summoned to direct the funeral obsequies of Louis himself. No illumi-nated work can be really identified as the work of Perréal, but Mrs. Patteson (Lady Dilke) strongly urges the probability that he painted the *Bible Historiée* of Corpus Christi College, Cambridge, bequeathed by General Oglethorpe.[2] She con-siders it quite the sort of work that would grow out of that of Fouquet, and dwells upon the fact of his official duties as *valet de chambre* giving him just that minute facility in the decora-tion of armour and furniture in the miniatures which the MS. displays. Whether this be so or not, it is certain that the *Bible Historiée* is a fine example of the school of Tours.

Another court painter and *valet de chambre* to Louis XI. and his successors was Jean Bour-dichon, an artist born at Tours in 1457, and there-

---

[1] See Vespas, b. 2 (Brit. Mus.).
[2] See her *Renaissance of Art in France,* i. 303.

fore as a youth probably one of the scholars in
the atelier of Jean Fouquet. He is first noticed
in the accounts in or about 1478 : "A Jehan
Bourdichon, paintre, la somme de vingt liures dix
sept solz ung denier tournois pour avoir paint le
tabernacle fait pour la chapelle du Plessis du
Parc, de fin or et d'azur."[1]   Later on, after
naming the painting of a statute of St. Martin,
for which he received twenty golden crowns, is a
note of his painting a MS., which we translate :
"To the said Bourdichon for having had written
a book in parchment named the Papalist—the
same illuminated in gold and azure and made in
the same 19 rich histories (miniatures) and for
getting it bound and covered, thirty crowns of
gold.   For this by virtue of the said order of the
King and by quittance of the abovenamed written
the 5th April One thousand four hundred and
eighty (milcccciiii[xx]) after Easter, here rendered
the sum of £19 1. 8."

Another quittance shows him to have been
employed on the decorations of the château of
Plessis les Tours. We may easily see how it is
that these artists, when they came to illuminate
the books entrusted to them, had such special
knowledge of embroideries and decoration of
armour when we read in the accounts how they
were constantly employed in designing dresses
for weddings, tournaments, and funeral obsequies,
and making "patterns for the dress and equipment of war."

A notice in 1508 tells us that Anne of Brittany

[1] Comptes de l'Hôtel de Louis XI., 1478–81.

made an order of payment to Bourdichon of *1,050 livres tournois* for having "richly and sumptuously historiated and illuminated a great Book of Hours for our use and service to which he has given and employed much time, and also on behalf of other services which he has rendered hitherto." This refers to the celebrated "Hours of Anne of Brittany," now in the National Library at Paris.

This volume, peerless of its kind, has been re-produced in colour lithography by Curmer of Paris—the result, however, is disappointing from the flat and faded look of the prints as compared with the brilliancy of the original pages. The MS. is an invaluable monument of French Renaissance illumination. It is French of Touraine rather than of Paris, yet bearing traces in its flowers and fruit borders of Flemish modes of ornament. It has also reminiscences of Italian painting. But the French neatness and restraint from over-decoration have kept it in a manner unique. It has not quite the softness of Italian, and is far from the intensity of Flemish. Indeed, its fault, if it be faulty, is in its want of force. With the exception of Anne's own portrait given with her patrons, St. Anne, St. Helena, and St. Ursula. The Queen's gown is of brown gold brocade trimmed with dark brown fur. Her hair is brown, like the fur. She wears a necklace of gems set in gold. On her head is a black hood edged with gold and jewels, beneath which and next her face is a border of crimped white muslin, She has brown eyes and finely pencilled eyebrows. As to nose and mouth, she and the two younger

saints are pretty much alike. With the allowance
of blue for black, St. Anne wears the dress of a
Benedictine abbess.   A dark crimson cloth covers
a table before which the Queen is kneeling,
and on which lies open a finely illuminated
Service-book.   The Calendar which follows this
portrait is for each month enclosed in a margin
of ornament. To the outer margin of every other
page of the book is placed a broad tablet or
pilaster containing flowers, fruits, insects, etc.,
from five to six inches high, each having the
Latin name of the plant, etc., at top in red, and
the French one in red or blue at the bottom.
These names may have been put in later. It must
be admitted that the fruits, flowers, and insects
are painted with the greatest care and neatness,
though sometimes a little assisted by the imagination of the painter. The text and initials are rather
heavy and commonplace. Now and then a border
surrounds the text completely, where flowers or
fruits are scattered—somewhat recklessly at times,
but usually with good design—over a ground of
plain gold, on which the branches, etc., cast
heavy shadows. This part of the design is certainly Flemish. Where "histories" occur the
border is a plain brown gilt frame within a black
border.   Undoubtedly the "Hours of Anne of
Brittany" is a very precious volume. The figure
subjects are of various degrees of excellence.
The four evangelists are vivid, and recall the portraits of Ghirlandaio, and it is to Italy also that
the illuminator is indebted for his architectural
and sculptural details.   Yet Bourdichon is in-

ferior to Fouquet in colouring, as the latter is to the Italians in design and composition. Perhaps he is most successful in his flowers and insects. "Nothing," said Muntz, "is less like the elegant foliages of Ghirlandaio and Attavante, and nothing is more worthy of being put in comparison with them."[1]

An illuminator of the name of Jehan Poyet is said to have assisted in the "Hours," thus while Bourdichon painted the miniatures, Poyet put in the flowers and fruit, etc.; but this share of work is by some believed to belong to a smaller Book of Hours executed for the Queen. Flowers and fruit are said to have been Poyet's speciality, and it is quite possible that he may have had the painting of the borders of the "Grandes Heures," while Bourdichon did the rest. The writer of the MS. was another native of Tours, named Jehan Riveron. During the reign of Francis I. the school of Tours was removed to Paris because the Court had settled there. Louis XII. had died in the Hôtel des Tournelles, and Francis, though full of plans for *plaisances* elsewhere, lived mostly in Paris. Fontainebleau is the dream of the near future. Il Rosso, the Italian architect, painter, poet, and musician, was busy there amid a crowd of other artists from Florence and Rome—the refuse of a once brilliant sodality. It was the frivolous, pretty, graceful side of Italian art that came northward in that great migration—the graver and more dignified elements were left behind. To see what Italian art became in

[1] *La Renaissance en Italie, etc.*, 547–8.

France, we have only to enter the Grand Gallery
at Fontainebleau, and we see it at its best in architecture, sculpture, and painting. And we cannot
help admiring it, for it is amazingly beautiful.
Yet it is not Italian—the Italian of the Medici and
Farnese palaces. Il Rosso was neither a Michel-
angelo nor a Carracci ; but he set a fashion. He
changed the face of art for France. Nor was it in
painting and sculpture only. The Italian passion
for devises, anagrams, emblems, and mottoes
became the rage in Paris. It first came in with
the return of Charles VIII. from his Neapolitan
campaign. Louis XII. adopted the hedgehog or
porcupine, with the motto "Cominus et eminus."
His Queen Claude's motto was "Candida candidis."
The Princess Marguerite's emblem was a mari-
gold or heliotrope ; others assigned her the daisy.
Her motto: "Non inferiora secutus." The well-
known emblem of Francis was a salamander—
why, is a mystery—with the motto, "Nutrisco et
extinguo." All this entered into the taste of the
illuminator, and elegant cartouche frames—probably of Dutch origin, as we see in the old map-
books of Ortelius Cluverius and Bleau, imported
by Ortelius and his friends into Italy, and made
use of by Clovio, and thence transferred to France
—were made into border-frames for miniatures,
varied with altar-forms, doorways, and other
fanciful frameworks from the new architecture
decorated with flowers, ribbons, panels, mottoes.
Another new thing, too, no doubt afforded plenty
of suggestion to the illuminator. This was stained
glass. Jean Cousin was in his glory in glass-

painting ; Robert Pinagrier also. But it was Cousin who adopted the new Italian ideas, and whose works were models for the illuminator. In the backgrounds and details of his glass-paintings at Sens, Fleurigny, Paris, and elsewhere, we may trace his progress ; and an excellent model, too, was Jean Cousin. He has other claims to remembrance in sculpture, engraving, authorship, but it is as the glass-painter that his influence is seen in illumination. Indeed, Mr. A. F. Didot strongly urged the probability that Cousin was himself the illuminator of the splendid Breviary or Hours of Claude Gouffier.[1] The drawing is in his best manner, the frame-border of *caryatides* in camaieu is of a richness of ornamentation in keeping with the rest of the volume. The arms and motto of Gouffier are painted in it. It is objected that Cousin's name does not appear in the Gouffier account-books, while those of other artists are given. But only a portion of the accounts is extant. Cousin may, perhaps, only have designed the book, and the other miniaturists carried out his designs. At any rate, the accounts give us the names of three miniaturists which we may here record — Jean Lemaire, of Paris (1555), Charles Jourdain, and Geoffroy Ballin (1359). These "enlumineurs" are stated to have decorated two Books of Hours for Gouffier's wedding. As a good example of the style employed in the decoration of title-pages, we may quote the chimney-piece of the Château d'Anet, executed for Diane de Poitiers, where a sculptured marble frame

---

[1] Now belonging to M. le Vicomte de Tanzé.

surrounds a painted landscape. Many of the books of the time of Francis I. and Henry II. are ornamented in this style.

In the British Museum are several fine MSS. illustrative of this period of French illumination, viz. Add. 18853, 18854, and 18855. These three MSS. formed part of the purchase which included the Bedford Offices. 18853 is a Book of Offices executed apparently for Francis I. In some of the borders is a large F with the *Cordelière* of the third Order of St. Francis and a rayed crown, and on folio 97 v. a large monogram consisting of the letter F, with two crossed sceptres and palm branches, surmounted by the crown-royal of France.

Nothing is known of the history of the MS. from 1547 to 1723, when it was in possession of the Regent Philippe d'Orleans. Possibly it had remained as an heirloom in the family. Philippe gave it to his natural son the Abbé Rothelin, a great lover of rare books and a noted collector, at whose death it was bought by Gaignat, another collector, who sold it to the Duc de la Vallière, and so, step by step, it came at length to Sir John Tobin, of Liverpool, and thence to the British Museum.

The partly sculpturesque character of the border-frames are of the kind just referred to, with festoons and garlands of flowers, and drapery, monograms, and emblems in full rich colours ; the architecture and other ornaments sometimes finished with pencillings of gold. The miniatures are of excellent design and colour, finely modelled,

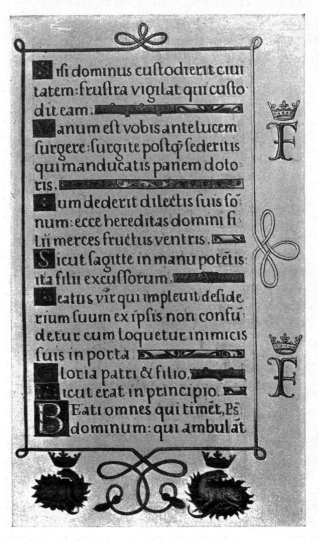

isi dominus custodierit ciui
tatem: frustra vigilat qui custo
dit eam.
anum est vobis ante lucem
surgere: surgite postq̃ sederitis
qui manducatis panem dolo
ris.
um dederit dilectis suis ſõ
num: ecce hereditas domini fi
lii merces fructus ventris.
Sicut sagitte in manu potẽtis
ita filii excussorum.
eatus vir qui impleuit deside
rium suum ex ipsis non confu
detur cum loquetur inimicis
suis in porta.
loria patri & filio.
icut erat in principio.
Beati omnes qui timet, Pſ
dominum: qui ambulát

OFFICM. B. MARIÆ VIRGINIS
C. 1530
Brit. Mus. Add. MS. 18853, fol. 52

OFFICM. MORTUORUM.
16TH CENT. (EARLY)
Brit. Mus. Egert. MS. 2125, fol. 183

and quite in the manner of the paintings of
Fontainebleau. The text is a combination of
Jarry-like Roman with italic. It may be compared
with 18854, similar in some respects, but the
smaller miniatures and the frames look more like
the older school of Tours. This MS. is also a
Book of Offices, and was written for François de
Dinteville, Bishop of Auxerre, in 1525, as appears
from an inscription in gold letters on fol. 26 v.

Some of the border-frames are drawn in sepia,
others in red-brown or burnt siena, and highly
finished with gold. The writing is a small Roman
hand. On the whole it is richer in illustration
than 18853, but not so perfect in drawing, yet it
is a very fine MS. Sometimes it has a border like
those in the "Hours of Anne of Brittany." On
fol. 26 v. is a curious border of twisted ribbons
covered with mottoes, such as "Virtutis fortuna
comes," "Ingrates servire nephas," etc.

Some of the tiny miniatures of the saints in the
Memoriæ are very charmingly painted : St. Mary
Magdalene, for instance, on fol. 147 v. The pillar
architecture of some of the borders, with pendant
festoons of flowers, is also very handsome.

18855, folio, is a Book of Offices written in a
Gothic text. The miniatures are large full-page
paintings within architectural frames or porches,
with coloured pillars or pilasters with panels of
rich blue, covered with golden traceries, bronze
gold pendants at side,—occasional borders as in
the "Hours of Anne of Brittany." The work is of
the older school of Tours, but loaded with ornamental details from North Italian pilaster-work.

Among the best miniatures are the Nativity
(34 v.), the Adoration of the Magi (42 v.), and the
Bathsheba. The last perhaps a little too open a
scene for a lady's bathroom, but placed within a
most gorgeous architectural window or doorway
(fol. 62 v). Compare also Harl. 5925, No. 574, for
a title-page of French Renaissance style from a
printed book, which suggests Venice as the source
of the style of 18853.

In the National Library at Paris are, of course,
a number of this class of MSS., such as the
Offices (MS. Lat. 10563), "Officium Beatæ Mariæ
Virginis ad usum Romanor" (1531), or the exquisitely painted "Heures de Henry 2^d" (fds. Lat.
1429), or the magnificent "Epistres d'Ovide" of
Louisa of Savoy (fds. fr. 875), and others.

By no means of less importance we may cite
the beautiful volume belonging to the late Comte
d'Haussonville, now in the Musée Condé at
Chantilly, called the "Heures du Connétable Anne
de Montmorency," and the "Heures de Dinteville"
(MS. Lat. 10558), the decoration of which is quite
on a par with the "Heures de Montmorency," or
those of Henry II., also the Psalter of Claude
Gouffier (Arsenal Lib., 5095), containing the Psalms
of Marot.

It is scarcely worth while to carry the subject
further. What is done later than Francis II. does
not grow finer or better : it only becomes more
overloaded with ornament, too much gold, too
much richness. Even foliages are often variegated
like pearls, or change gradually from colour to
colour on the same sweep of acanthus as in a

MS. in the British Museum attributed to Pierre Mignard (" Sol Gallicus," Add. 23745). Compare also the " Heures de Louis XIV." Now and then an exceptional work, like that of D'Eaubonne at Rouen, belongs to no particular school.

CHAPTER X

SPANISH AND PORTUGUESE ILLUMINATION

Late period of Spanish illumination — Isidore of Seville —
Archives at Madrid — Barcelona—Toledo—Madrid—Choir-
books of the Escorial—Philip II.—Illuminators of the choir-
books—The size and beauty of the volumes—Fray Andrés
de Leon and other artists—Italian influence—Giovanni
Battista Scorza of Genoa—Antonio de Holanda, well-known
Portuguese miniaturist in sixteenth century — His son
Francesco—The choir-books at Belem—French invasion—
Missal of Gonçalvez—Sandoval Genealogies—Portuguese
Genealogies in British Museum — The Stowe Missal of
John III.

SINCE all the best and best-known work of
Spanish or Portuguese illuminators was
executed in the sixteenth century, and is manifestly a reflection with peculiar mannerisms of
either Flemish or Italian illumination of the same
period, it may seem almost superfluous to devote
a separate chapter to the subject. Yet there is a
goodly list of both Spanish and Portuguese artists
who practised the art of illumination.

So early as the time of Isidore of Seville we
find notices of libraries, copyists, and the like
(see book iv. of his Encyclopædia), and an able
writer of the last century, Don José Maria de
Eguren, published a work on the MS. rarities of
Spain.[1] The most important of the miniatures in

[1] *Memoria de los Codices notables conservados en los
archivos ecleseasticos de Espana.* Madrid, 1859, L. 8°.

the famous Codex Vigilano are also reproduced in " El Museo Español de antiguedades," most interesting respecting the calligraphy and miniature art of the eleventh century.

One of the earliest instances of royal patronage bestowed on painting in Spain is a document in the Royal Library at Madrid, containing the expenses of King Sanchez IV. in 1291–2. Thus " to Rodrigo Esteban, painter of the king for many paintings done by the king's orders in the bishop's palace 100 golden maravedis." Again, in the archives at Barcelona we find that Juan Cesilles, painter of history, was engaged 16th March, 1382, to paint the " History of the twelve apostles for the grand altar of the Church at Reps for 330 florins." In 1339 one Gonzalez Ferran had some reputation both as a wood engraver and a painter. He was probably a miniaturist. In 1340–81, Garcia Martinez, a Spanish illuminator, worked at Avignon. A copy of the Decretals, dated 1381, in the Cathedral Library of Seville is by his hand.

In the fifteenth century we have many notices of painters, especially in Toledo, whither the taste was in all likelihood brought from Naples after the conquest of that kingdom by Alphonso V. of Aragon in 1441.

It has been observed by those familiar with native Spanish art that its chief characteristic is that it is gloomy. This may be so, but it is not fairly chargeable to the artists but to the tyranny of the Spanish Inquisidor, who laid the embargo on the illuminator that he should not follow the wicked gaiety of the Italians, nor the sometimes too realistic veracity of the Flemings. This accounts usually for backgrounds of black where the Fleming would have had rich colour or gold, for the prevalence of black in the draperies and for the sombre tone in general of Spanish painting. It is not always in evidence, as may be seen in many of the miniatures of the famous choir-books in the Escorial. The sombre period began under Ferdinand the Catholic, and it has left its mark on the schools of the fifteenth century. The six-teenth began a new era, and under Philip II. several, both Netherlandish and Italian, miniatur-ists were invited to assist in the production of the enormous choir-books ordered by the King for San Lorenzo of the Escorial, between 1572 and 1589. The volumes are bound in wooden boards covered with leather, stamped and bossed with ornaments of gilded bronze. It is said that 5,500 lbs. of bronze and 40 lbs. of pure gold were used in the bindings. The actual dimensions of the volumes are 115 by 84 centimetres. Every volume has at least seventy folios, and every folio is splendidly illuminated, thus affording more than 30,000 pages covered with richly ornamented initials, miniatures, and borders. The illuminators and copyists of these choir-books were Cristobal Ramirez, who planned the work, fixed the size and other details of the volumes and the character of the handwriting, Fray Andrés de Leon, Fray Julian de Fuente del Saz, Ambrosio Salazar, Fray Martin de Palencia, Francisco Hernandez, Pedro Salavarte, and Pedro Gomez. Ramirez was engaged at the Escorial from 1566 to 1572. In the latter year he presented a Breviary with musical notation to the King, and was then engaged for the great undertaking mentioned above.

Andrés Cristobal was also an illuminator of note at Seville, where he worked from 1555 to 1559. Andrés de Leon worked at the Escorial from 1568, and is especially mentioned by Los Santos in his well-known description of the monastery of San Lorenzo : "Son de gran numero y excelencia las iluminaciones que tienen de mano nuestro Fray Andrés de Leon, que fue otro Don Julio en el Arte."[1] The allusion is to the celebrated Don Giulio Clovio, then in the height of his fame in Italy. Fray Julian received similar praise for a *capitolario* for the principal festivals of the year, especially for the grand dimensions of the miniatures, the like of which the writer says had never been seen before, either in Spain or Italy. Andrés de Leon died at the Escorial in 1580. Salazar continued working on them till they were completed, and in 1590 went to Toledo, where he finished two Missals for the Cathedral, which had been begun by the famous Juan Martinez de los Corrales. He was still engaged on similar work until his death in 1604. Two other illuminators, Esteban and Julian de Salazar, were working at the Escorial in 1585. Bermudez[2] mentions Fray Martin de Palencia as having executed a volume in a fine handwriting

[1] Fr. Francisco de los Santos, *Descripcion breve del Monasterio de S. Lorenzo el Real del Escorial,* 24.
[2] *Diccionario,* iv. 24.

and with beautiful miniatures for the monastery of Saso. Thus we see there were numerous miniaturists in Spain in the latest years of the existence of the art that had been imported chiefly from Italy.

After most of these great choir-books had been finished there were still others in progress. In 1583 Giovanni Battista Scorza of Genoa, who is celebrated in the "Galleria" of the Cavaliero Marini, was invited by the King to take part in his great choir-book scheme. Scorza was then thirty-six years of age, and in the height of his reputation as a painter of small animals and insects. After a little time he returned to Genoa, where he lived to be ninety years old. He had a brother, Sinibaldo, who was equally skilful in miniature, and especially in scenes from history. The Scorzas were pupils of Luca Cambiaso. It may be noticed that all this work in miniature, although so late in its own history, is accomplished before the greatest names in Spanish painting are known. Josefo Ribera was born in 1588; Zurbaran in 1598; Velasquez in 1599; Alonzo Cano in 1601; Murillo in 1617. This, in a sense, is the natural course of things, as, generally, illumination has preceded the other kinds of painting.

With regard to Portugal, very little is recorded that does not in some way connect itself with Spain. So we find that Antonio and Francesco de Holanda, seemingly of Netherlandish origin, are mentioned in relation to the books illuminated for the Royal Monastery of Thomar; Francesco also

worked for the monastery of Belem. Francesco
de Holanda was a great admirer and imitator of
Clovio, but he always insisted that his father
Antonio was the inventor of the method of
"stippling," as the finishing with minute points of
colour is technically called, which was brought to
such perfection by Clovio and his scholars and
imitators.

Taken altogether, the work of the Spanish
illuminators at the Escorial and those of Toledo
and Seville is really the same, with just the variations we might expect from pupils and imitators,
as that of their masters in Genoa, Rome, Venice,
or Bruges. Examples of it may be seen occasionally in diplomas, such as are found in the British
Museum and other public libraries, as, *e.g.* Claud.
B. x. Lansd. 189, Add. 12214, 18191, 27231, etc.

In 1572, the same year in which Luiz de
Camoens published his Lusiades, an accomplished calligrapher, Miguel Barata, published
an elaborate treatise on his own art, then in high
repute.

In the fourteenth century the Cancioniero of
Don Pedro Affonso Ct. de Barcellos affords an
example of the calligraphy (for which Spain and
Portugal have always been famous) and illumination which is precious for the student. It is still
in existence in the Palace of Ajuda. Its date is
1320-40. And there are MSS. in the Torre do
Tombo of Lisbon that are richly illuminated.
Again, in Seville there is the "Juego de las
Tablas," executed under Alphonso the Wise in
1283, with its Gothic arcades and ornaments.

M. Joaquin de Vasconcellas has made a study of this MS. The miniatures of the Torre do Tombo of the thirteenth and fourteenth centuries are mostly of the French school.

About 1428–33 was executed a splendid MS. entitled "Leal Conselheiro," which is attributed to a famous miniaturist in his time named Vasco. It is, however, simply a monument of penmanship, as it contains no miniatures. The MS. has been edited by L'Abbé Roquete in 1842. The Portuguese MSS. of the fifteenth century betray a decided Flemish influence, as well they may, for probably the producers of them were Flemings. Constant intercourse with the Court of Burgundy had something to do with this.

The "Chronica do descobrimento e conquista de Guiné," now at Torre do Tombo, is clearly a Flemish work. It was begun about 1440, and finished in 1453. The portrait of the Enfante Don Henrique, called the Navigator, is set in a border evidently by a pupil or imitator of J. Van Eyck. The calligraphy of the MS. is most beautiful. This influence of the Netherlands on Portuguese art is, indeed, confirmed by the political diplomatic relations of the fifteenth century, and is of some importance in the history of art. We shall refer again to this matter when dealing with another MS.

Among all the calligraphic monuments of Portugal it is claimed that the most splendid is the "Bible of the Hieronymites." (See *Revista universal Lisbonense*, 1848, pp. 24–8.) This work, it is said, was a present from the Court of

Rome to Emanuel, successor of John II., in remembrance of the homage made to the Holy See,
of the first gold brought from the Indies, but the
story is very doubtful.   The King, in bequeathing
the seven volumes to the convent of Belem, says
nothing about such an origin.   They are manifestly in great part the work of foreign artists.
One well-known miniaturist, Antonio de Holanda,
the father of the better-known Francesco, took
part in the work, and having a good conceit of
his own abilities (we shall probably hear of him
again), reserved an entire volume to himself in
order to give proof of them.   The seven volumes
which then were covered with crimson velvet and
silver bosses and enamels, are now simply bound
in red morocco.   In the middle of each cover are the
arms of Emanuel King of Portugal. Vols. v. and
vii. have those of Doña Isabel, his Spanish wife.

The initials and ornaments show that the art of
Italy is freely mixed with that of Portugal.   Indeed, from the signatures in the volumes it is
seen that the work of the penman was Italian;
vol. i. being written at Ferrara by Sigismundo de
Sigismundis, the well-known Italian calligrapher,
in 1495.   The second volume, also finished in
1495, bears the name of Alessandro Verazzano,
another famous copyist, who wrote several of the
volumes illuminated by Attavante.   Vol. iii. is
dated 1496, and is unsigned.   The next three
volumes are also without signature.   Vol. vii.
is the work of Antonio de Holanda, who from his
name appears to have been of Dutch descent.
His work is certainly excellent, and renders this

volume a very precious monument of the art of
Portugal. He was the official herald of the King,
and he and his son Francesco gave their whole
time to the practice of illumination. His son's
Memoirs give a most interesting account of his
travels and intercourse with Giulio Clovio and the
other Italian artists whom he met with in Rome.[1]
For some years the Hieronymite Bible was in
Paris, having been brought thither by Marshal
Junot, where it remained unnoticed for several
years. Being called for by the Portuguese
Government, Louis XVIII. paid 50,000 francs to
the family of Junot, and restored it to the
monastery of Belem. A splendidly illuminated
atlas by an illuminator and cartographer named
Fernando Vas Dourado was published in the year
of his death, 1571.

As an important example of what we may
fairly call native art, we will now briefly refer to
the celebrated Missal of Estevam Gonçalvez Neto,
one of the productions of the busy second half of
the sixteenth century. The clever amateur who
achieved this beautiful series of paintings, for
paintings they are, in addition to the writing and
other ornamentation of the MS., was descended
from a noble family of Sêrem, in the parish of
Macinhata, forty-three leagues from Lisbon. He
became Canon of Viseu, and during his leisure,
after this appointment, executed the Pontifical
Missal which bears his name. It is dedicated to
Don Josè Manuel, of the House of Tancos, Bishop
of Viseu, afterwards of Coimbra, and lastly Arch-

[1] See my Life of Clovio.

bishop of Lisbon.   This prelate gave the book to
the Church of Viseu.   The original MS. was
afterwards in the library of the Convent of Jesus,
and is now in the Academy of Sciences at Lisbon.
Stephen Gonsalvez died July 29th, 1627.   The
Missal is signed : "Steph. Glz. Abbas Sereicencis
fac. 1610."   It has been very well reproduced in
colours by Macia, of Paris.

The "Genealogies of the House of Sandoval,"
written and painted in Lisbon in 1612, is now in
Paris.   It is called "Genealogia universal de la
Nobilissima casa de Sandoval Ramo del Generoso
tronco de los soberanos Reyes de Castilla y Leon.
Por Don Melchior de Teves del Conseio Real de
Castilla del Rey Dō Philippe III."

At the foot of the page is written "Eduardus
Caldiera Vlisspone scripsit, Anno Dn̄ī MDCXII."
This magnificent MS., which measures forty-six by
thirty centimetres, is numbered in the Catalogue
of the National Library as 10015. A grand frontispiece, formed of two columns of the Composite
Order, occupies the first page, representing a king
in royal robes and crown arresting the wheel of
Fortune.   Two lions accompany the scene, and
the motto of the picture is "Virtute duce non
comite Fortuna."   Page 2 contains the various
escutcheons of the family of the Count of Lerma,
for whom the book was written.   It contains a
great number of portraits.   A final instance of
the influence, or rather the inroad, of Flemish art
in Portugal in the fifteenth century may be shown
in the MS. called the Portuguese Genealogies in
the British Museum.

The work consists of eleven large folio sheets separately mounted and measuring eighteen by ten inches. · It commences with a prologue, with the arms of Portugal supported by two savages, having clubs and shields. Outside the inner frame are three scenes : (1) wild animals in combat ; (2) a sea-nymph being rescued ; (3) a fight among sylvan savages. Next comes a series of portraits painted in the most finished and life-like style, beginning with Dom Garcia F° del rey Abarca and Doña Constancia on a fruitful tree with foliage, fruits, and birds, a cat, and other things. The tree is an oak, beside it are apple and cherry trees. On the oak are green acorns. The birds are very beautiful, the cat simply perfect. These details recall the highly finished and lovely work of Georg Hoefnagle on the great Missal at Vienna. Gothic brown-gold architecture and three battle scenes complete the page.

Then follow the genealogical tables, and more portraits, the whole showing the most patient and careful work. Letters on the borders of the robes recall the same kind of ornament in the Grimani Breviary at Venice. No one has been able to explain these curious inscriptions. In the Grimani Breviary they were thought to be either Croatian or merely ornament. Here they cannot well mean anything but decoration. The portraits are fanciful but interesting mementoes of the period, and include several personages noted in history.

The last MS. to be mentioned in this hasty sketch is one in the British Museum (Stowe 597). It is a " Missale Romanum," and is said to have been illuminated for John III. in 1557. It was once the property of the Abbé Garnier, chaplain for near thirty years, of the French factory at Lisbon. The binding is red morocco, and once had silver clasps.

It commences with a large mirror-like oval tablet, containing the title, set between two pillars of pink-veined marble with bronze-gold capitals and bases. The tablet is crimson with a violet-slate frame moulding of egg and dart pattern. At foot are two Roman legionaries, one seated as supporting the tablet, on each side. On folio 3 is the index in a rose-wood panel and pale green frame. The peculiar forms of the frames and the scroll-work on them are of the fantastic kind, differing from Italian, which is characteristic both of Spanish and Portuguese ornament. The chief colours are a bright emerald green and blue, with ochre, gold, and crimson. The initials are still more fantastic—partly human, partly plant or fish-form, sometimes sculptured ornament and plant-forms combined—but all so sweetly painted and so delicately finished as to be most attractive. The text is a fine and elegant Roman minuscule interspersed with italic.

Here and there are exquisite little drawings of ecclesiastical utensils, etc., but the everlasting variety among the quaint and fanciful initials provides an unwearying fund of interest. Tiny birds of the loveliest plumage sit among and beneath the limbs of the letters, or elegant scrolls of pencilled gold cover the little coloured panels on which the plain gold Roman initials are placed.

Some of the larger initials are very finely executed, and contain full-length figures of saints, bishops, or queens.   One lovely initial B has a graceful girl simply clad in blue tunic and pale yellow skirt with a silken coil of pale rose forming the upper loop of the letter, the lower being formed of the curved body of a green dragon.   Her left hand lifts the silk-work, her right, hanging by her side, holds a little golden pitcher.   The whole is painted on a panel of bright gold.   Another (L) shows a peasant rushing laughingly, with a hare slung over his shoulder, past the figure of a guardian terminus of bronze.   But the Missal should be seen to be properly understood, for though in a general way it has a look of Italian influence, its originality is beyond question.

CHAPTER XI

ILLUMINATION SINCE THE INVENTION OF PRINTING

The invention of printing—Its very slight effect on illuminating —Preference by rich patrons for written books—Work produced in various cities in the sixteenth century—Examples in German, Italian, and other cities, and in various public libraries up to the present time.

THE art of printing, as the reading world has been frequently informed, was invented in the fifteenth century, and undoubtedly had, to a considerable extent, a destructive effect upon the craft of professional copyists. But in the fifteenth century the art of the writer and that of the illuminator had long been separate professions. There was no particular reason, therefore, why the invention of printing should interfere with the illuminator. As a matter of fact, it made little difference. Nor, indeed, did printing entirely put a stop to the professional career of the scribe. It was prophesied, before practical experience of facts proved the contrary, that the invention of the railway engine would abolish the horse. The printing-press did not abolish the penman, but it certainly spoiled his trade. We have seen in the course of the preceding chapters that it did not spoil the trade of the illuminator. Nor was it quite owing to the fact that many printed books were so adorned as to appear like illuminated MSS. More than one wealthy patron absolutely declined to have anything to do with printed books. The matter was too vulgar and too cheap. The last Duke of Urbino was a prince of this lofty way of thinking, and scarcely a court in Europe but continued to have MSS. produced as if no such thing as the printing-press were known. How they were multiplied in Spain and France we have seen in detail. We will now proceed to take a farewell look at the German and Italian libraries, in order to see how the illustrious presses of Mainz, Strassburg, Augsburg, Köln, Munich, Vienna, Venice, Milan, Florence, and Rome affected the ateliers of the great schools of illumination established in most of these cities. What do we find? In point of fact, some of the richest, most magnificent books ever produced by the illuminator, not only whilst the press was still a novelty, but long after it had become perfectly familiar to everybody. For several of the cities aforesaid we have the means of proof: thus for Mainz, at the end of the superb copy of the Mazarine Bible, now at Paris, is the following inscription: "Iste liber illuminatus, legatus and completus est ⚜ henricum Cremer vicariū ecclesie collegiate Sancti Stephani Moguntini sub anno dn̄ī Melesimo quatring entesimo quinquagesimo Sexto, festo assumptiois gloriose Virginis Marie. Deo gratias alleluya." This was in 1456, the year before the first press was set up. In 1524 we have two most splendidly illuminated MSS.—a Missal and a Prayer-book— executed by order of Albert of Brandenburg,

Archbishop of Mainz. Two richer examples of
the German Renaissance cannot easily be imagined.
We cannot dilate upon them. We may, however,
truly say that together with very many other examples of illuminated work, both in manuscripts
and printed books, they show the art of the illuminator to be no less splendid or elaborate after
the invention of printing than it was before.

On the last page of the Missal is written: "Ich
Niklas Glockendon zu Nurenberg hab dieses Bhuch
illuminiert ond vollent im jar 1524."

The Prayer-book is similarly adorned with miniatures and brightly coloured borders. On the cover
is a copy of the Archbishop's portrait, painted
by Dürer, and on folio 1 is written by the
Archbishop himself: "Anno domini MDXXXI
completum est presens opus, Sabbato post 'Invo-
cavit.' Albertus Cardinalis moguntinus manu
propria scripsit."

Other Glockendon books exist in other libraries.
Then there is the Beham Prayer-book at Aschaffenburg and a Bible in the library at Wolfenbüttel in two thick 4° volumes—a work well
worth examination. At Nuremberg is the Service-
book executed by Conrad Frankendorffer, of
Nuremberg, in 1498.

In the British Museum is the fine German MS.
—the Splendor Solis, a sixteenth century MS.
(Harl. 3469).

In the National Library at Paris is the Prayer-
book of William of Baden (10567–8) executed
at Strassburg by Frederic Brentel in 1647.

Augsburg was producing illuminated Service-books ten years after Günther Zainer had set up the press in that city.

Munich, also, with the Penitential Psalms, etc., by Hans Mielich. Vienna, too, can show a magnificent Missal by Georg Hoefnagel, bearing the dates 1582 to 1590. Venice is represented in the work of Benedetto Bordone and the Ducali. Florence in the splendid Missals, etc., of Attavante and his contemporaries.

Milan shows the gorgeous Graduals of the Brera belonging to the sixteenth century and the Sforziadas of London and Paris. So we might pass from city to city almost all over Western Europe. The great Spanish choir-books were almost all produced under Philip II. Several Papal Service-books are represented in the fifteenth- and sixteenth-century examples of the scrap-book 21412 of the British Museum; and the works of Clovio, the most noted of Italian illuminators, all belong to the sixteenth century.

These instances are amply sufficient to prove that in every city in Europe where printing was in full practice the art of the illuminator continued to flourish until the progress of modern inventions and various processes, added to the general cheapening of books, led to its disuse. Its present application seems to be almost solely to diplomas and testimonials, and in point of quality, usually as poor and spiritless as the incapacity of most of its professors can make it.

There seems, however, no reason why the artistic skill and elaborate methods of reproduction of the present day should not produce magnificent books — indeed the " Imitation " of Thomas à Kempis, and other continental examples prove that this is amply possible.

The next few years will probably show that readers are still desirous of possessing beautiful books, and that artists are still found capable of producing them.

MANUSCRIPTS THAT MAY BE CONSULTED AS EXAMPLES

(Partly taken by permission from the Victoria and Albert Museum Handbook)

CLASSICAL AND EARLY CHRISTIAN

No.	Name.	Where Produced.	Where Kept.	Date.	Remarks.
1	Vergil (fragment)	.....	Vatican Lib., Rome, Cod. Vat. 3225	3rd or 4th cent.	Doubtful which is the older.
2	Vergil	.....	Vat. Lib. 3867	4th cent.	
3	Rom. Calend.(f.)	.....	Imp. Lib., Vienna	,,	
4	Genesis(f.).	.....	,, ,,	5th cent.	Gold and silver text on purple vellum; 88 miniatures.
5	Genesis(f.).	.....	Brit. Mus., Cott. Oth. B. 6	,,	Much burnt in 1731.
6	Iliad (f.)	.....	Ambros. Lib., Milan	,,	Fine handwriting and clever pictures.
7	Joshua (f. of Roll)	.....	Vat. Lib., Rome	.....	15 leaves, 32 ft. long, 11 in. wide. Contains from ch. 2^{22} to 10^{26}, brush outlines to miniatures. Rivers, etc., personified in Byzantine manner.

8	Dioscorides, etc.	.....	Imp. Lib., Vienna	c. 500-5	Personifications of abstract qualities.
9	Bible of Montamiata	.....	Laurent. Lib., Florence	c. 540	Valuable as a theological document, but poor work, and in bad condition.
10	Syriac Gospels	Monastery of Zagba, in Mesopotamia	" "	c. 586.	Brought to Florence in 1497. Remarkable Crucifixion, see Byzantine, I.
11	Terence	.....	Nat. Lib., Paris	9th cent.	Copy of a 5th-cent. MS. pen-drawings.
12	Pentateuch	Tours	Nat. Lib., Paris, Nouv. acq. 2334	7th cent.	Called the Ashburnham Pentateuch; 19 large miniatures.

BYZANTINE

1	Syriac Gospels	Zagba, in Mesopotamia	Laur. Lib., Florence	c. 586.	Shows Byzantine influence.
2	Gospel-book (f.)	Byzantium	Brit. Mus., Add. 5111	6th cent.	Lettering, etc., on gold ground.
3	Menologium	"	Vat. Lib., Gr. 1613	9th cent.	A typical Byzantine MS.

BYZANTINE—(continued)

No.	Name.	Where Produced.	Where Kept.	Date.	Remarks.
4	Gregory of Nazianzum	Byzantium	Nat.Lib.,Paris— Gr. 510	9th cent.	Fine antique design and composition.
5	,,	,,	Gr. 543	,,	Good small figures.
6	,,	,,	Gr. 550	,,	Good small figures and headings.
7	Evangeliary	......	Brit. Mus.— Arund. 547	,,	
8	,,	......	Burney 19, 20.	,,	
9	Lectionary.	......	Harl. 5598	10th cent., end	Fine initials.
10	Chrysostom	......	Nat.Lib.,Paris— Gr. 654	10th cent.	Remarkable initials.
11	Simeon Meta-phrastes	......	Brit. Mus.— Add. 11870	11th cent.	Fine ornaments.
12	Evangeliary	......	Add. 11838	12th cent.	Beautiful headings.
13	Psalter	......	Add. Egert. 1139	,,	Executed for Melisenda, daughter of King of Jerusalem.

IRISH OR CELTIC

No.	Name.	Where Produced.	Where Kept.	Date.	Remarks.
1	Gospels of St. Columba	......	Trin. Coll., Dublin	7th cent.	

2	Gospels of St. Arnoul, of Metz	St. Arnoul's Abbey, Metz	Nuremberg Museum	7th cent.	
3	Book of St. Columbanus	......	Roy. Lib., Naples	,,	Curious Crucifixion.
4	Bible of St. Kilian	......	Cath. Lib., Wurzburg	8th cent.	Signed "Thomas scribsit."
5	Gospels of "Thomas"	Monastery of Hanow	Pub. Lib., Trèves	,,	Anglo - Irish, with arched frame-border.
6	Psalter	......	Brit. Mus., Cott. Vesp. a. 1	,,	See Westwood, *Palaeographia Sacra Pict.*, pl. 16.
7	Gospels of MacRegol	......	Bodl. Lib., Oxford	9th cent.	P. 103. Remarkable.
8	Book of Armagh	......	Roy. Irish Acad., Dublin	,,	Fine Anglo-Irish.
9	St. Chad's Gospels	......	Lichfield Cath. Lib.	,,	Anglo-Celtic—a very fine example.
10	Lindisfarne Gospels	Lindisfarne Monastery	Brit. Mus., Cott., Nero D. 4	7th cent.	
CAROLINGIAN					
1	Sacramentary.	Abbey of Gellone	Nat. Lib., Paris, MS. Lat. 12048	c. 750.	Symbolism. Given by Ct. William of Toulouse.
2	Ada-Codex	Abbey of St. Mesmin, of Trèves	Municip. Lib., Trèves	c. 775.	Written for Ada, sister of Charlemagne, Abbess of St. Mesmin.

CAROLINGIAN—(continued)

No.	Name.	Where Produced.	Where Kept.	Date.	Remarks.
3	Psalter of Dagulfus	.....	Imp. Lib., Vienna Theol. Lat. 1861	c. 780.	Written for Queen Hildegardis, wife of Charlemagne.
4	Evangeliarium of Godescale	Abbey of St. Sernin, of Toulouse	Nat. Lib., Paris, nouv. acq. 1203	,,	Written for Charlemagne and Hildegardis. Has gold and silver letters on purple vellum. Franco-Saxon.
5	Sacramentary of Gelasius.	Abbey of St. Gall	Abb. St. Gall, No. 348	,,	
6	Evangeliarium of St. Angilbert	Abbey of St. Riquier	Town Lib., Abbeville	c. 793.	On purple vellum.
7	Alcuin Bible	Abbey of Tours	Brit. Mus., Add. 10546	c. 800.	Coronation gift to Charlemagne. Very fine example.
8	Bible	Tours	Cantonal Lib., Zurich	,,	Like 7.
9	,,	,,	Bamberg Roy. Lib.	,,	Said to be an exact copy of 7.

10	Gospels of Charles the Great (Charlemagne)	Tours	Imp. Lib., Vienna	c. 800.	Found by Emperor Otho III. in tomb of Charlemagne.
11	Sacramentary of Drogo, Abp. of Metz	Abbey of Metz, or Tours	Nat. Lib., Paris, Theol. Lat. 9428	c. 814.	The gift of Charlemagne to his natural son Drogo.
12	Golden Gospels of Athelstan	.....	Brit. Mus., Harl. 2788	c. 835.	A splendid example.
13	Golden Gospels of Charles the Bald.	.....	Roy. Lib., Munich	c. 850.	Ditto, written in gold letters.
14	Evangeliary of Lothaire	Abbey of St. Martin's, Tours	Nat. Lib., Paris, Theol. Lat. 266	,,	Remarkably beautiful.
15	Golden Gospels	Abbey of St. Médard, of Soissons	Nat. Lib., Paris, Theol. Lat. 8850	,,	One of most beautiful Carol. MSS. known.
16	Bible of Count Vivien	Abbey of St. Martin, of Tours	Nat. Lib., Paris, Theol. Lat. 1	,,	Presented to Charles the Bald in 850. Miniature of presentation.
17	Bible of St. Paul's	......	Monastery of St. Calixtus, Rome	c. 860.	Written for Charles the Bald by Ingobert.

CAROLINGIAN—(continued)

No.	Name.	Where Produced.	Where Kept.	Date.	Remarks.
18	Prayer-book (or Hours) of Charles the Bald	......	Nat. Lib., Paris	c. 866.	Written by Ingobert and presented to Charles the Bald in 866.
19	Golden Gospels of St. Gall	Abbey of St. Gall	Lib. at St. Gall—No. 22	c. 870.	Written for Abbot Grimwold, or Hartmut.
20	Psalter of Folchard	"	No. 23	" .	Written for Abbot Hartmut. Gold and silver initials.
21	Evangeliarium Longum	St. Gall	Lib., St. Gall.	c. 920.	Written by Sintramn of the "Wondrous Hand." Profile foliages in gold and silver.
22	Evangeliary	......	Roy. Lib., Brussels, No. 16383	c. 925.	
23	"	......	Nat. Lib., Paris	c. 940.	Large 4°, written entirely in gold letters; 5 miniatures and 12 porticoes.
24	Psalter	......	Brit. Mus., Harl. 2904	c. 995.	Transition to the style of the Benedictionals.

WINCHESTER WORK AND SIMILAR

1	King Edgar's Charter	Hyde Abbey, Winchester	Brit. Mus., Cott. Vesp. A. 8	966	Style of the Benedictionals of Æthelwold and Robert.
2	Breviarium Cassinense	Monte Cassino?	Mazarine Lib., Paris, 759	......	Tendency to same style colouring as in school of Metz.
3	Æthelwold's Benedictional	Hyde Abbey, Winchester	Lib. of Duke of Devonshire	c. 970.	Best example known.
4	Benedictional of Abp. Robert	,,	Pub. Lib., Rouen	c. 980.	Drawing bold, but colouring unequal to 3.
5	Gospels	......	Trin. Coll., Camb.	c. 900.	Borders like Winchester work.
6	Psalter	......	Brit. Mus.— Harl. 2904	......	Fol. frames similar.
7	,,	Winchester	Tib. C. 7	c. 1000	Init. D on f. 115.
8	,,		Arund. 60	,,	
9	,,	,,	Roy. 1 D. 9	,,	
10	Cnut's Gospels	,,	155	c. 1017	Fine example.
11	Leofric Missal	......	Bodl. Lib., Oxford No. 579	10th cent.	Byzantine influence.

MONASTIC STYLES

No.	Name.	Where Produced.	Where Kept.	Date.	Remarks.
1	Weissobrun Prayer-book	Weissobrun .	Roy. Lib., Munich	c. 814.	Netherlandish.
2	Gospels .	......	Nat. Lib., Paris, 8851	c. 975.	Medallions of Emperors Henry I. and Otho I. and II.
3	Egbert Codex	Reichenau .	Pub. Lib., Trèves, No. 24	977–93	Beautiful initials.
4	Gospels .	Echternach .	Gotha Museum .	c. 990.	Portrait of Otho III. and Theophanu. Jewelled covers.
5	Otho Codex	......	Roy. Lib., Munich Cimel. 58	c. 998.	See p. 91.
6	Gospels .	......	Brit. Mus., Egert. 608	10th cent.	Branch-work initials.
7	Bernward's Gospels	Hildesheim .	Cath. Lib., Hildesheim	993–1022.	
8	Ellinger's Gospels	Tegernsee .	Roy. Lib., Munich No. 31	c. 1056.	
9	Hortus Deliciarum	Landsberg .	Formerly at Strassburg	c. 1175–80 .	Burnt in 1870.
10	Life of Virgin	Tegernsee .	Roy. Lib., Berlin	1173–1200 .	Written, etc., for the Emperor Frederick I. by Werinher.

11	Plenarium	Quedlinburg	Town Lib., Quedlinburg	1184–1203	Written for Abbess Agnes.
12	Passionale	Arnstein, near Trèves	Brit. Mus.— Harl. 2800–2	c. 1194.	
13	Bible	,,	Harl. 2803	c. 1190.	
14	,,	Floreffe	Add. 17737–8	c. 1153	Chronological tables in coloured inks.
15	Missal	St. Bavon of Ghent	Add. 16949	1150–1175.	
16	Chronicle of Jerusalem	.....	Roy. Lib., Brussels, No. 11142	.....	Fine miniatures—costumes.
17	Psalter	.....	Brit. Mus.— Arund. 157	12th cent.	Transition from Winchester to Othonian.
18	,,	.....	Lansd. 420	,,	
19	,,	.....	Lansd. 431	,,	
20	,,	.....	Roy. 1 D.X.	,,	
21	Bible	St. Nicholas, of Arnstein	Harl. 2798	,,	Typical 12th cent. MS.
22	Vauclere Psalter	.....	Pub. Lib., Laon, No. 29	.....	A perfect type of 12th cent. illumination.
23	Mater Verborum	Scheyern	Roy. Lib., Munich	.....	By Conrad of Scheyern, with all manner of diagrams, etc.

FRENCH AND ANGLO-FRENCH GOTHIC

No.	Name.	Where Produced.	Where Kept.	Date.	Remarks.
1	Psalter of Queen Ingeburga	.....	Musée Condé, Chantilly	1193-1236	27 large miniatures. Transitional to Gothic.
2	Psalter of Queen Blanche, mother of Louis IX.	.....	Arsenal Lib., Paris, Theol. Lat. 165 B.	c. 1220	Hieratic, and transitional to Gothic.
3	Psalter of St. Louis (IX.)	.....	Nat. Lib., Paris, No. 10525	c. 1250	Transitional to Gothic. 78 delicate miniatures.
4	Joinville's Credo		Nat. Lib., Paris	1287	Gothic portrait of St. Louis.
5	Alfonso Psalter (Tenison)	Blackfriar's, London	Brit. Mus.— Add. 24686	c. 1284	See article in *Fine Arts Qu. Rev.*, i. 77, and *Bibliographica*, pt. 4.
6	Bible	.....	Burney 3	1225-52	Richly illuminated.
7	Somme le Roy	.....	Add. 28162	c. 1300	9 large illuminations.
8	Life of St. Denis	.....	Nat. Lib., Paris, fds. fr. 2090-2.	1316-22	Contains view of Paris, and portrait of Philip V. Drolleries, coloured shading of draperies.

9	Bible	......	Brit. Mus., Roy. 1 D. 1	c. 1310-15	Typical work, English.
10	Ormsby Psalter	Norwich	Bodl. Lib., Oxford, Douce 366	c. 1295	English work.
11	Bible	......	Brit. Mus.— Add. 17341	Late 13th cent.	A typical MS.
12	Psalter	......	Roy. 2 B. 7	Early 14th cent.	Drolleries and interesting scenes.
13	Miroir Historiale	......	Arsen. Lib., Paris	c. 1356	Large folio richly illuminated.
14	Louterell Psalter	......	Lulworth Castle	c. 1340	Fine diapered backgrounds.
15	Missal	......	Westreenen Mus., The Hague	1366	"Gouache" painting in miniatures.
16	Chronicle of St. Denis	......	Nat. Lib., Paris, 8395	1375-80	Miniature in gold and grey.
17	Hours of John, Duke of Berry	......	Roy. Lib., Brussels, 11060	Finished 1380	Illuminated by André Beauneveu and Jacquemart de Hesdin.
18	Epistle to Richard II.	Paris	Brit. Mus.— Roy. 20 B. 6	1370-80	Fine ivy-branch style.
19	Offices B. M. V.	......	Harl. 2897	......	Prayer-book of Margaret of Bavaria. A typical MS.
20	Little Hours of Berry	......	Nat. Lib., Paris, 18014	c. 1400	113 beautiful miniatures.

FRENCH AND ANGLO-FRENCH GOTHIC—*(continued)*

No.	Name.	Where Produced.	Where Kept.	Date.	Remarks.
21	Psalter of the Duke of Berry	Paris ·	Nat. Lib., Paris, No. 13091	1401 ·	Contains 24 fine miniatures by André Beauneveu.
22	Grandes Heures de Berry	,, ·	Nat. Lib., Paris, fds. Lat. 919	1409 ·	By Jacquemart de Hesdin, André Beauneveu, and Pol de Limbourg.
23	Heures de Berry	,, ·	Musée Condé, Chantilly	1410 ·	Considered the finest example known.
24	Poems of Christine de Pisan	......	Brit. Mus.— Harl. 4431	1400–6	Fine miniatures—costumes and portraits.
25	Talbot Romances	......	Roy. 15 E. 6	1400 ·	Curious miniatures, portraits of Henry VI., etc.
26	Bedford Offices	......	Add. 18850	c. 1435	Richly illuminated. Contains French, English, and Netherlandish work.
27	Bedford Breviary	......	Nat. Lib., Paris, fds. Lat. 17294	c. 1430	Contains English and French work.
28	Pontifical ·	......	Brit. Mus.— Add. 16610	c. 1450	Fine borders.
29	Valerius Maximus	......	Harl. 4375	,,	Northern French and Netherlandish.
30	Girart de Nevers	......	Nat. Lib., Paris, fds. fr. 4092	c. 1470	Netherlandish — costumes, etc.

GERMAN AND BOHEMIAN

1	Minnelieder	......	Nat. Lib., Paris, fds. fr. 7266	c. 1300	Hunting scenes, costumes.
2	Wilhelm von Oranse	......	Pub. Lib., Cassel	1334	Written for Henry Landgrave of Hesse. French influence.
3	Picture Bible	......	Lib. of Prince Lobkowitz, Prag	c. 1300.	
4	Passionale of Abbess Cunigunda	Prag	Univ. Lib., Prag, xiv. A. 17	1312	Transparent water-colour. No French influence.
5	Weltchronik of Rudolf v. Hohen-Ems	......	Roy. Lib., Stuttgart	c. 1350	Old Cologne school.
6	Liber Viaticus	Prag	Bohem. Mus., Prag	c. 1360	Written for John v. Neumarkt, Bishop of Leitomischl.
7	Mariale	”	”	c. 1345	Written for Arnestus v. Pardubitz, Archbishop of Prag (1344–64). Bohemian school.
8	Orationale	”	”	c. 1345	Written for same prelate, in French Gothic style.
9	Bible of Emperor Wenzel	”	Imp. Lib., Vienna, No. 2759	......	Executed by order of Martin Rötlow for presentation to the Emperor.

GERMAN AND BOHEMIAN—(*continued*)

No.	Name.	Where Produced.	Where Kept.	Date.	Remarks.
10	Gospels of John of Oppavia	Prag .	Imp. Lib., Vienna	1368 .	Beautiful penmanship and ornaments.
11	Wilhelm von Oranse	,, .	Ambras Museum, Vienna, No. 7.	1387 .	Fine diapered backgrounds, costumes, and armour.
12	Salzburg Missal	......	Roy. Lib., Munich, Lat. 15710	c. 1350 .	In 5 fol. vols. Splendid colouring.
13	Weltchronik of Rudolfv. Hohen-Ems	......	Pub. Lib., Stuttgart	c. 1383 .	Large folio. Westphalian school.
14	Durandus	......	Imp. Lib., Vienna, No. 2765	1384 .	Written for Albert III., Duke of Austria. Illuminated in later Bohemian.
15	Golden Bull of Charles IV.	Prag .	Imp. Lib., Vienna, jus. c. 338	c. 1399 .	Rich soft-leaved foliages. Ornament superior to miniatures.
16	Wurzburg Bible	......	Brit. Mus., Arund. 106	After 1400 .	Large foliages, fine initials, bright colours.
17	Missal of Emperor Frederick III.	......	Imp. Lib., Vienna	1448 .	German work.

18	Gospels	......	Pub. Lib., Nuremberg	1498	43 miniatures and splendid borders, etc., by Conrad Frankendorfer.
19	Choir-book of SS. Ulrich and Afra, Augsburg	Abbey of St. Ulrich, Augsburg	Lib., Augsburg	1489	Written by L. Wagner, and illuminated by G. Beck.
20	Miniature of presentation of 19	Augsburg	Vict. and Alb. Mus., South Kensington	c. 1489	Taken from 19.
21	Offices B.M.V.	Upper Carinthia	Brit. Mus., Add. 15711	1513.	
22	Prayer-book of Albert of Brandenburg	Nuremberg	Aschaffenburg Castle Library	1524	Illuminated by A. Glockendon.
23	Prayer-book of William IV. of Bavaria	"	Imp. Lib., Vienna, No. 1880	1535	Illuminated by Albert Glockendon.
24	Prayer-book	"	Brit. Mus., Add. 17525 Harl. 3469	1584	School of Glockendon.
25	Splendor Solis	......		Late 16th cent.	Astrological diagrams, etc., scenes.
26	Penitential Psalms	Munich	Roy. Lib., Munich, Cimel. Saal	1570	Painted by Hans Mielich.

GERMAN AND BOHEMIAN—(continued)

No.	Name.	Where Produced.	Where Kept.	Date.	Remarks.
27	Horæ	......	Brit. Mus., Egert. 1146	Late 16th cent.	Fine foliages and initials.
28	Prayer-book of William of Baden	Strassburg	Nat. Lib., Paris, Nos. 10567-8	1647	2 vols., 8°. Renaissance by Frederic Brentel.

SICILIAN AND ITALIAN

No.	Name.	Where Produced.	Where Kept.	Date.	Remarks.
1	De arte venandi cum avibus	Palermo	Vat. Lib., Rome, palat. 1071	c. 1225	Composed by Emperor Frederick II. (1212–50). Paintings of birds and hunting scenes.
2	Offices, "ordo offic. Senensis"	Gubbio	Acad. Lib., Siena	......	Attributed to Oderigi.
3	Legends	Florence?	Canon. Lib., Rome	c. 1327–43	Attributed to Giotto.
4	Vergil	Florence?	Ambros. Lib., Milan	c. 1310	Attributed to Simone Martini.
5	Durandus	Siena?	Brit. Mus.— Add. 31032	c. 1330	Fine work.
6	Aristotle	Bologna?	Harl. 6331	c. 1335	Like the "Avignon" Decretals.

7	Stefaneschi Missal	Rome?	Canon. Lib., Rome	1327–43	In same vol. with 3, and attributed to Giotto.
8	Poems of Convenevole da Prato[1]	Naples?	Brit. Mus., Roy. 6 E. 9	1309–43	Bold "gouache" painting. Executed for King Robert of Naples. Fine initials.
9	Breviarium Romanum	Florence?	Brit. Mus., Harl. 2903	c. 1400	
10	Concordantiæ Canonicæ	Bologna?	Nat. Mus., Naples	c. 1350	Allegorical figures and "gouache" painting.
11	Statuts de l'Ordre du St. Esprit	Naples	Nat. Lib., Paris, fds. fr. 4274	c. 1354	Executed for Louis I., of House of Anjou, King of Sicily and Jerusalem.
12	Romance of Meliadus	Avignon?	Brit. Mus.— Add. 12228	c. 1355	Executed for Louis II. of Naples.
13	Triumphs of Fr. Petrarch	......	Harl. 3109	c. 1370	Small miniatures and initials in older style. Miniatures of triumphs.
14	,,	......	Nat. Lib, Paris	......	
15	Joannes Andreae, Lib. VI. Decretalium	......	Abp. of St. Florian	c. 1370	Fine Bolognese miniatures.
16	Glossa Joannis Andreae in Clementinas	Bologna?	Laon, No. 382	c. 1330–43	Very finely illuminated.

[1] Petrarch's tutor.

SICILIAN AND ITALIAN—(*continued*)

No.	Name.	Where Produced.	Where Kept.	Date.	Remarks.
17	Rubrics on the Decretals	Bologna ?	Laon, No. 357	1332	Many grotesque figures.
18	Decretum Gratiani	,,	Brit. Mus., Add. 15274, 15275	c. 1375	Exquisitely illuminated.
19	Missale Romanum	,,	Roy. Lib., Munich, Lat. 10072	c. 1374	By Nicolaus de Bononia.
20	,,	,,	St. Mark's, Venice, cl. iii. xcvii.	c. 1370	,, ,,
21	,,	Florence ?	Brit. Mus.— Add. 21973	c. 1380–1400	Fine penwork diapers and initials.
22	Latin Bible	Bologna ?	Add. 18720	c. 1375–1400	Sweet colouring and fine foliages.
23	Hymnarium Heremitarum	Sienese ?	Add. 30014	c. 1400	Fine initials.
24	Questions on 4 Books of Sentences by Joh. Scot, Franciscan	Naples	Add. 15270–3	c. 1458–94	Written by Hippolytus Lunensis for Ferdinand I., King of Naples, and finely illuminated.

No.	Title	Place	Brit. Mus.—	Date	Notes
25	Platonis Opera	Naples	Harl. 3481	c. 1470	Written for Ferdinand I., King of Naples. Finely illuminated. White stem-work.
26	Cæsar	......	Add. 16082	1462	Executed for Pius II. Roman Renaissance (1458–64).
27	,,	Rome ?.	Harl. 2683	c. 1460	White stem-work. Written by J. And. Mussolini.
28	Petrarch Sonnets, etc.	......	Harl. 3411	c. 1465	A pretty little volume of Milanese work.
29	Offices	Milan ?.	Add. 19417	c. 1475	Like MSS. executed for the Dukes of Ferrara. Very fine.
30	Missale Romanum	......	Add. 15260	,,	Of Florentine type.
31	Officium B.M.V.	Florence	Harl. 2875	c. 1480	A small volume, but rich initials.
32	,,		Add. 15528	c. 1475	Like 32, but finer.
33	Missale Romanum	Bologna	Add. 15814	c. 1495	Written by Jo. de Lyvonia for one of the Visconti.
34	Josephus	Rome	Harl. 3699	c. 1490	Roman Renaissance.
35	Herodean	Florence	Add. 23773	1487	Written by Alexander Verazzanus.
36	Scrapbook of cuttings	Rome and Florence	Add. 21412	1480–1500	A very interesting collection. Roman and Florentine.

SICILIAN AND ITALIAN—(continued)

No.	Name.	Where Produced.	Where Kept.	Date.	Remarks.
37	Grant of Ludovico Sforza (il Moro)	Milan	Brit. Mus.— Add. 21413	1494	Illuminated by Antonio da Monza.
38	Offices	Naples	Add. 21591	1500	Written and illuminated for Frederick of Aragon, King of Naples. Finest Neapolitan work. Portraits (1416–58).
39	Prayer-book of Alfonso I.	,,	Add. 28962	c. 1455	
40	Orations of Cicero	,,	Imp. Lib., Vienna	c. 1490	Executed for Ferdinand I., King of Naples (1458–94). Very fine.

RENAISSANCE ILLUMINATION

ITALIAN

No.	Name.	Where Produced.	Where Kept.	Date.	Remarks.
1	Life of Manetti	Florence	Brit. Mus.— Add. 9770	1506	Neat in execution.
2	Life of St. Francis	,,	Harl. 3229	c. 1505	Very fine illumination.
3	Eusebius	,,	Harl. 3308	c. 1515.	
4	Life of Manetti	,,	Lansd. 842	c. 1525.	
5	Eusebius	Milan	Roy.	,,	
6	Missale	Venice	Add. 15813	c. 1530	Attributed to Benedetto Bordone.

		Naples or Calabria			
7	Ethics of Aristotle		Imp. Lib., Vienna	c. 1490-1510	Fine Renaissance work. Elaborately designed frames, and fine miniatures painted in a strong "gouache," by Rinaldo Piramo, for And. Matt. Acquavira, 8th Duke of Atri.
8	St. Jerome on Ezechiel	Florence	Imp. Lib., Vienna, No. 654	c. 1490-1520	Illuminated by Attavante for Matt. Corvinus, King of Hungary (1443-90).
9	Philostratus (Latin)	"	Imp. Lib., Vienna, No. 25	"	Illuminated probably by Attavante for Matt. Corvinus.
10	Missale Romanum of Corvinus	"	Roy. Lib., Brussels	"	Illuminated by Attavante for Corvinus. Used for admission oaths of Governors of Netherlands.
11	Augustine: Epistles	"	Imp. Lib., Vienna	c. 1495	Illuminated by Attavante for Matt. Corvinus. Signed "Attavantes pinsit."
12	Martianus Capella	"	Lib. St. Mark's, Venice	c. 1500	Illuminated by Attavante for Matt. Corvinus. Signed. Written by Al. Verazzanus

RENAISSANCE ILLUMINATION—(continued)

ITALIAN—(continued)

No.	Name.	Where Produced.	Where Kept.	Date.	Remarks.
13	Psalter	Florence	Ducal Lib., Wolfenbüttel	c. 1500	Illuminated by Attavante.
14	Diurnale	,,	Laurent. Lib., Florence	,,	Illuminated by Attavante or Gherardo.
15	Missal of Bp. of Dôle	,,	Pub. Lib., Lyons	,,	Illuminated by Attavante.
16	St. Gregory on Ezechiel	,,	Estense Lib., Modena.	,,	Illuminated by Attavante. Signed.
17	Dionysii Opp.	,,	Pub. Lib., Besançon	,,	,, ,,
18	"Gran" Breviary	,,	Nat. Lib., Paris, MS. Lat. 8879	,,	Probably illuminated by Boccardino il Vecchio, though attributed to Attavante.
19	Hieronymi Breviar. in psalmos	,,	Nat. Lib., Paris, MS. Lat. 16839	1488-1500	Written for Matt. Corvinus by Anton. Sinibaldi, and illuminated by Attavante.
20	Poems of Eurialo d'Ascoli	Rome	Imp. Lib., Vienna	c. 1536	Illuminated by Giulio Clovio (1498-1578).
21	"Rothesay" Offices	,,	Brit. Mus., Add. 20927	c. 1546	Illuminated by Clovio.

22	Commentary on St. Paul's Epistles	Rome	Soane Mus., London	c. 1536	Executed for Cardinal Grimani by Clovio.
23	Psalter of Paul III.	,,	Nat. Lib., Paris, MS. Lat. 702.	c. 1542	Illuminated by Vincenzio Raimondi.
24	Papal Lectionary (Towneley Clovio)	,,	Lenox Lib., New York	c. 1546	By Clovio and his assistants.
25	Dante	,,	Vat. Lib., No. 365	c. 1555	Illuminated in part by Clovio.
26	Investiture from Duke of Urbino	,,	Brit. Mus., Add. 22660	c. 1560	Very fine ornament.
27	Triumphs of Petrarch	,,	Lib. of Capt. Holford, London	c. 1550	Fine miniatures.
28	Missal of Card. Colonna	,,	Rylands Lib., Manchester	c. 1520	Fine miniatures. Attributed, but without authority, to Raffaelle.
29	Prayer-book	Rome, or Florence	Barberini Lib., Rome, No. 324	c. 1500	Many fine miniatures.
30	Missal of Pius II.	Rome	Chigi Lib., Rome	c. 1460-70	Executed for Pius II.
31	Missal of Card. Corsini	,,	Corsini Lib., Rome, No. 1015	c. 1530	Fine framed miniatures.

RENAISSANCE ILLUMINATION—(continued)

ITALIAN—(continued)

No.	Name.	Where Produced.	Where Kept.	Date.	Remarks.
32	Missal of Card. Cornaro	Rome	Minerva Lib., Rome	c. 1520	Fine miniatures.
33	"Pavia" Graduals.	Milan	Brera Lib., Milan	1530–80	By several artists, especially G. Berretta. Enormous folios.
34	Prayer-book of Albert IV. of Bavaria	......	Roy. Lib., Munich, Cim. Saal. 42	c. 1574	Finest Roman Renaissance, but written by Hans Lenker, of Munich (not a Clovio).
35	Apologia di Colenuccio	Rome	Brit. Mus., Roy. 12, c. viii.	c. 1510	Executed for Henry VIII. of England.
36	Prayer-book Bianca Maria of Milan	Milan	Roy. Lib., Munich, No. 99A	c. 1450	Illuminated by Giovanni da Como. Contains Visconti and Sforza arms.
37	Hours of Bona Sforza of Milan	,,	Brit. Mus., Add. 34294	c. 1490	Finest Milanese Renaissance, with some Flemish additions.
			FRENCH		
1	The "Versailles" Livy	Tours	Nat. Lib., Paris, 6907	......	Attributed to Jehan Fouquet of Tours.

2	The "Sorbonne" Livy	Tours	Nat. Lib., Paris, fds. Sorb. 297	......	Attributed to Jehan Fouquet of Tours.
3	Antiquities of the Jews	,,	Nat. Lib., Paris, Resew. 6891	......	Fouquet's masterpiece.
4	Boccaccio	,,	Roy. Lib., Munich	......	Executed for Etienne Chevalier.
5	Trésor des Histoires	,,	Brit. Mus.— Cott. Aug. v.	c. 1490	Fine aërial perspective and landscape.
6	Valerius Maximus	Paris	Harl. 4374-5	,,	A very fine MS.
7	Hours of Anne of Brittany	,,	Nat. Lib., Paris	c. 1508	A magnificent example, eclectic in style, with natural flowers and insects in borders, and fine figure-painting.
8	Hours of Claude Gouffier	,,	Vicomte de Janzé	c. 1550	Attributed to Jean Cousin. Influence of glass-painting.
9	Offices	,,	Brit. Mus., Add. 18853	c. 1530	Probably executed for Francis I. of France. Excellent work, eclectic in style.
9a	Hours of Montmorency.	,,	Libr. of Count of Haussonville	1549	Same style as 8 and 9, and probably by J. Cousin,

RENAISSANCE ILLUMINATION—(*continued*)

FRENCH—(*continued*)

No.	Name.	Where Produced	Where Kept.	Date.	Remarks.
10	Offices	Tours?	Brit. Mus.—Add. 18854	c. 1525	Architectural details of School of Tours. Written for Fr. de Dinteville, Bp. of Auxerre.
11	,,	,,	Add. 18855	,,	Architectural frames to miniatures as in 10, but larger and more fanciful details, somewhat like 7 in portions.
12	,,	Paris	Nat. Lib., Paris, Lat. 10563	1531.	
13	Epistres d'Ovide	......	Nat. Lib., Paris, fds. fr. 875	c. 1500	Executed for Louise de Savoie, mother of Francis I.
14	Boece	Paris	Nat. Lib., Paris, u. fds. Lat. 6643	,,	Fine miniatures with Renaissance architectural details.
15	Epistres d'Ovide	,,	Nat. Lib., Paris, 6877	,,	Translated by Octavien de St. Gelay. Beautiful miniatures.
	Petrarch's Triumphs	......	Nat. Lib., Paris, f. fr. 7079	c. 1520	Very fine miniatures of triumphs. Italian influence.

17	Chants royaux	...... ·	Nat. Lib., Paris, 6987	c. 1520 ·	Fine miniatures.
18	Chants Royaux	Paris ·	Nat. Lib., Paris, f. fr. 379	" ·	Magnificent miniatures under Italian influence of Andrea del Sarto.
19	Petrarch ·	" ·	Nat. Lib., Paris, f. fr. 225	c. 1503 ·	Miniature of presentation to Louis XII. Many full-page miniatures.
20	Fleur des Histoires	" ·	Nat. Lib., Paris, f. fr. 54	c. 1505 ·	Executed for Cardinal d'Amboise.
21	Chron. de Monstrelet	" ·	Nat. Lib., Paris, 20360–2	" ·	Three large folio vols. Vol. i. contains five equestrian portraits of Louis XII.
22	Les Echecs amoreux	" ·	Nat. Lib., Paris, f. fr. 143	c. 1500 ·	Executed for use of Francis, d. of Angoulême, and his sister Marguerite.
23	Boccace de claris et nobilibus mulieribus	" ·	Nat. Lib., Paris, f. fr. 599	" ·	By same illuminator as 22. Executed for Louise de Savoie.
24	Reception de Marie d' Angleterre à Paris	" ·	Brit. Mus., Vesp. B. 2	c. 1514 ·	"Avec belles peintures."

RENAISSANCE ILLUMINATION—*(continued)*

FRENCH—*(continued)*

No.	Name.	Where Produced.	Where Kept.	Date.	Remarks.
25	Chants Royaux	Paris .	Nat. Lib., Paris, f. fr. 145	1515 .	Presented in 1515 to Louise de Savoie by the City of Amiens. The miniatures painted in grisaille by J. Plastel, and coloured by J. Pinchon. Contains portrait of Louise.
26	Comment-aires de César— Vol. i. .	,, .	Brit. Mus.	c. 1519	Attributed to Geoffroy Tory. Part grisaille. Written in Roman text. See *Dict. Miniat.* iii. 312.
	Vol. ii. .	,, .	Nat. Lib., Paris, 13429	,,	
	Vol. iii. .	,, .	Lib. of Duc d'Aumale	,,	
27	Dutillet, French Kings, etc.	......	Nat. Lib., Paris, 2848	......	Presented to Charles IX.
28	Hours of Henry IV.	......	Nat. Lib., Paris, Lat. 1171	c. 1595	Peculiar style and colouring.

29	Gospel of St. John	Boisleduc	......	Brit. Mus.—Roy., E. 5	Finely written, but not illuminated by Pet. Meghen.
30	"Sol Gallicus"	,,	c. 1682	Add. 23745	Painted by Pierre Mignard.
31	Psalter	London	1565	Roy. 2 B. 9	Written by Petrucco Ubaldini, a Florentine.
32	Book of Sentences for Lady Sumley	English? London?	c. 1600	Roy. 17 A. 23	Very elegant borders.

ENGLISH ILLUMINATION

FROM THE THIRTEENTH TO THE SIXTEENTH CENTURY

1	Offices and Prayers	Westminster	1240	Brit. Mus.—Roy. 2 A. 22	Imitation of stained glass. Typical MS.
2	Bible in Latin	Canterbury	1245	Burney 3	
3	,,	Salisbury	1254	Roy. 1 B. 12	Written by Will de Hales.
4	Tenison Psalter	London	1294	Add. 24686	Written and illuminated by order of Edward I.
5	Bible in Latin	......	13th cent.	Roy. 1 D 1	Written by Will of Devon.

ENGLISH ILLUMINATION—(continued)

FROM THE THIRTEENTH TO THE SIXTEENTH CENTURY

No.	Name.	Where Produced.	Where Kept.	Date.	Remarks.
6	Apocalypse in French	......	Brit. Mus.—Roy. 19 B. 15	c. 1330	See *Bibliographica*, pt. v. pl. 1.
7	Arundel Psalter	......	Arund. 83	,,	See *Bibliographica*, pt. v. pl. 2
8	Psalter of Joan of Kent	......	Roy. 2 B. 8	1380	Transition from French Gothic to Lancastrian.
9	Pontifical	......	Lansd. 451	c. 1400	Early Lancastrian.
10	Bible in Latin	......	Roy. 1 E. ix.	,,	Large folio. See *Bibliographica*, pt. v. pl. 4.
11	Breviary	......	Harl. 2975	,,	Something like 7.
12	Offices	......	Add. 16968	c. 1390–1400.	
13	,,	......	Add. 16998	c. 1410	Executed for Anne Mauleverer.
14	Liber Albus	London	Guildhall Lib., London	,,	Bracket borders.
15	Liber de Hyda	Winchester	Shirburn Castle Lib.	,,	Richly illuminated borders, some unfinished. See Rolls Series, 1866.
16	Offices	......	Brit. Mus., Roy. 2 B. 1	c. 1400–1410	Early Lancastrian.

17	Grandison Offices	.....	Brit. Mus.— Roy. 2 A. 18	c. 1410	Fine initials with Lancastrian brackets. See *Bibliographica*, v. pl. 5.
18	Occleve de Regim. Principum	.....	Ar. 38	c. 1415	Traceried backgrounds in Bohemian manner. Cf. Will. v. Oranse MS.
19	Ormonde Offices	.....	Roy. 2 B. 15	c. 1420	Similar to 17. Called by Humphreys (*Books of Middle Ages*) *Queen Mary's Breviary*. Lancastrian style.
20	Gower's Confessio Amantis	.....	Harl. 3490	„	
21	Psalter of Queen Mary	St. Alban's	Roy. 2 B. 7	1460	Fine English work. Presented in 1553 to Queen Mary.
22	Horæ	.....	Harl. 2884	c. 1460	Many mediocre illuminations.
23	Gospels and Epistles, etc.	London	Roy. 2 B. 12, 13	c. 1508	Given by Stephen and Margaret Jenyns to the church at Aldermanbury, London.
24	Bourchier Psalter	„	Roy. 2 B. 14	c. 1458	Contains Bourchier obituaries.
25	Psalter and Canticles, etc.	.....	Harl. 1749	c. 1470	Good text and many illuminated letters and borders.

SPANISH AND PORTUGUESE

No.	Name.	Where Produced.	Where Kept.	Date.	Remarks.
1	Hours, etc., Lat. and Catalan.	......	Brit. Mus.— Add. 18193	......	Netherlandish influence.
2	Offices B.M.V.	......	Add. 28271	......	Italian influence.
3	Hidalguia	......	Add. 12214	1604	In Genoese manner.
4	Diploma of Philip III.	......	Roy. Claud. B. x.	17th cent.	,,
5	Patent to Princ. de la Paz	......	Add. 1706	1797	Allegorical designs.
6	Ordo Miss. Pontificales	......	Add. 30857	17th cent.	Roman text, good initials.
7	Portuguese Missal	......	Stowe 597	......	Written for John III., King of Portugal.
8	Hidalguia de Gonsalo de Castro Cepeda	Spain	Add. 22143	1578	Granted by Philip II., with his portrait.

BIBLIOGRAPHY

Abrahams, N. C. L. *Description des MSS. françaises du Moyen Age de la Bibliothèque Royale de Copenhague.* 4to. Copenhagen. 1844.

Alt, H. *Die Heiligenbilder oder die bildende Kunst u. die Theologie.* 8vo. Berlin, 1845.

Astle, Thomas. *The Origin and Progress of Writing.* 4to. London, 1784, 1803.

Barrois, J. *Bibliothèque Protypographique ou librairies du roi Jean.* 4to. Paris, 1830. 6 plates.

Bastard, Aug. *Librairie de Jean de France duc de Berry . . . illustrée des plus belles miniatures de ses MSS., etc.* Folio. Paris, 1834. 32 plates.

Beissel, Stephan. *Des heiligen Bernward Evangelienbuch im Dome zu Hildesheim. Mit Hdschr. des 10 and 11 Jahrh., etc.* Third edition. 26 photo-lithographs (12 × 9). Hildesheim, 1894.

Beissel, Stephan. *Vaticanische Miniaturen.* Folio. Freiburg im Breisgau, 1893. Many lithographed plates.

Birch, W. de G. *History, Art, and Palæography of the MS. commonly styled the Utrecht Psalter.* 8vo. 3 facsimile plates in autotype. B. Quaritch, London, 1876.

Birch, W. de G., and Jenner, H. *Early Drawings and Illuminations* (in MSS., chiefly in the British Museum). 12mo. London, 1879.

Biscionii, A. M. *Catal. bibl. Medico-Laurentiana.* Folio. Florentine, 1752-7. (Valuable plates of facsimiles, etc.)

Bradley, J. W. *Life and Works of G. G. Clovio, Minia-turist, etc.* 8vo. London, 1891. 18 plates.

Bradley, J. W. *Dictionary of Miniaturists, Calligraphers, etc.* 8vo. 3 vols. Quaritch, London, 1887-90.

Bradley, J. W. *Venetian Ducali, in Bibliographica*, II. 257. 4 phototypes.

Bucher, B. *Geschichte des Technischen Künste, etc.*, vol. i. Miniatur, etc. 8vo. Stuttgart, 1875.

Cahier and Martin. *Nouveaux Mélanges d'Archéologie, etc.* Large 4to. Paris, 1874-77, etc. Many fine plates of miniatures, etc., mostly without colour.

Campori, G. *Gli artisti Italiani, etc., nelle Stati Estensi.* 8vo. Modena, 1855.

Campori, G. *Racconti artistici italiani.* 8vo. Firenze, 1858.

Caravita, A. *I codici e le Arti a Monte Cassino.* 8vo. Montec., 1869-71.

Carta, F. *Codici, corali e libri a stampa miniati della Biblioteca nazionale di Milano.* Folio. Roma, 1895. With 25 phototype facsimiles.

Chassant, Alph. *Paléographie des chartes et des MSS. du 11e au 17e Siècle.* 8vo. Paris, 1867, and companion vols.

Curmer, L. *Les Evangiles des Dimanches et Fêtes.* Large 8vo. Paris, 1864. Many facsimiles in gold and colours from illuminated MSS.

Delisle, L. *Mém. sur l'Ecole calligraphique de Tours au IXe Siècle.* Paris, 1885. 5 heliograv.

Delisle, L. *L'Evangéliaire d'Arras et la Calligraphie Franco-Saxonne du neuvième Siècle.* 4to. Paris, 1888. Large heliogravure facsimiles.

Delaunay (l'Abbé H.). *Le livre d'Heures de la reine Anne de Bretagne.* With facsimile of the whole MS. Large 8vo. Paris, 1861.

Della Valle, G. *Lettere Senese, Sopra le Belle Arti.* 3 vols. 8vo. Venezia, 1782–86. (Relating to Sienese miniaturists.)

Delisle, L. *Le cabinet des manuscrits de la bibliothèque impériale (in Hist. gén. de Paris).* 4to. Paris, 1868.

Denis, Ferd. *Histoire de l'ornementation des manuscrits.* 8vo. Paris, 1858. (143 pp., with illustrations.)

Deshaines, C. *Histoire de l'Art dans la Flandre, d'Artois, et le Hainaut.* 8vo. Lille, 1886.

Dibdin, T. F. *The Bibliographical Decameron.* 3 vols. 8vo. London, 1817.

Didron (edit.). *Annales Archéologiques.* Periodical 4to. 1844, etc. (P.P. 1931, d. a. Brit. Mus.)

Dorange, A. *Cat. descr. et raisonné des manuscr. de la bibl. de Tours.* 4to. Tours, 1875.

Durieux, A. *Les Artistes Cambrésiens du IXe à XIXe Siècle, etc.* 8vo. Cambray, 1874. (With plates in folio.)

Durieux, A. *Miniatures des manuscr. de la bibl. de Cambrai.* 8vo. Cambrai, 1861. 18 plates.

Du Sommerard, Andr. *Les Arts du Moyen-âge.* 6 vols. Folio. Paris, 1838–46.

Fleury, E. *Les MSS. à miniatures de la bibliothèque de Soissons.* 4to. Paris, 1865. Lithograph facsimiles.

Fleury, E. *Les manuscrits à miniatures de la bibl. de Laon.* 4to. Laon, 1863. 50 plates (good).

Gabelentz, H. von der. *Zur Geschichte der oberdeutschen Miniaturmalerei im 16ten Jahrhundert.* Large 8vo. Strassburg, 1899. 12 phototypes.

Garnier, J. *Catalogue descriptif et raisonné des MSS. de la bibl. de la ville d'Amiens.* 8vo. Amiens, 1843.

Girardot, B. de. *Cat. des manuscrits de la bibl. de Bourges.* Folio. Paris, 1859.

Gualandi, M. A. *Memorie originale Italiane risguardante le Belle Arti.* 8vo. Bologna, 1840–45.

Hardy, Sir Thomas D. *The Athanasian Creed in Connection with the Utrecht Psalter: being a Report, etc.* With autotype facsimiles. Folio. Spottiswoode and Co., 1872.

Hendrie, R. *Encyclopædia of the Arts of the Middle Ages by the monk Theophilus.* Translated, with notes. 8vo. London, 1847. One of the best collections of mediæval methods and recipes relating to illumination.

Humphreys, H. Noel. *The Illuminated Books of the Middle Ages.* Folio. London, 1849. 39 plates.

Husenbeth, F. C. *Emblems of Saints by which they are Distinguished in Works of Art.* 8vo. London, 1850. Second edition, 1860. Third edition, 1882.

Jäck, J. J. *Viele Alphabete und ganze Scriftmuster vom 8, bis zum 16, Jahrh. aus den Handschr. der öffentl. Bibl. zu Bamberg.* Folio. Bamberg, 1833–35.

James, M. R. *Descriptive Catalogue of the Illuminated MSS. in the Fitzwilliam Museum, Cambridge.* (Fine phototype facsimiles, and an excellent text.) Large 8vo. Cambridge University Press, 1895.

Jorand, J. B. J. *Grammatographie du neuvième siècle.* 4to. Paris, 1837. 65 plates, folio.

Kirchoff, Albr. *Handschriftenhändler des Mittelalters.* Second edition. 8vo. Leipzig, 1853.

Kondakov. *Hist. de l'Art Byzantin considéré... dans les miniatures.* 2 vols. Small folio. Paris, 1891. Plates and woodcuts.

Kugler. *Kleine Schriften.* 3 vols. 8vo. Stuttgart. 1853–54. (German illumination.)

BIBLIOGRAPHY 281

Labarte, Jules. *Historie des Arts industriels au Moyen-âge.* (Vol. iii.) 8vo. Paris, 1865.

Laborde, L. *La renaissance des arts à la cour de France.* 2 vols. 8vo. Paris, 1855–56.

Lacroix, P. *Military and Religious Life in the Middle Ages.* 8vo. London, 1874.

Lacroix, P. *The Arts of the Middle Ages.* 4to. London, 1870.

Lacroix, P. *Manners, Customs, and Dress during the Middle Ages.* 4to. London, 1874.

Lacroix, Paul, and Séré, Ferd. *Le Moyen-âge et la Renaissance.* 5 vols. 4to. Paris, 1848–52, 1874.

Lacroix, P., Fournier, Ed., and Séré, F. *Livre d'or des métiers.* 8vo. Paris, 1852.

Lambecius, P. *Commentar. de Bibliotheca Cæsarea Vindobonensi.* Folio. Vindobona (Vienna). 1670. Plates.

Langlois, E. H. *Mémoire sur la calligraphie les MSS. du Moyen-âge.* 8vo. Paris, 1841. 17 plates.

Le Arti. *Various Articles on Illuminated MSS., by Frizzoni, Venturi, etc.* (Italian Periodical. Roma, v. 7. From 1898.)

Lecoy de la Marche, A. *Les MSS. et la Miniature.* 12mo. Paris, 1884. Woodcuts.

Leitschuh, F. F. *Geschichte der Karolingischen Malerei, etc.* Berlin, 1894. Many prototype facsimiles.

Libri, Gul. *Monumens inédits.* Folio. London, 1864. 65 plates.

Madden, Sir Fred. *Universal Palæography.* 2 vols. 8vo. London, 1850.

Marchal, J. *Cat. des MSS. de la bibl. royale des ducs de Bourgogne.* 3 vols. 4to. Brussels, 1842.

Middleton, J. H. *Illuminated MSS. in Classical and Mediæval Times: their Art and their Technique.* Large 8vo. Cambridge University Press, 1892.

Milanesi, G. *Documenti per la Storia dell' arte Senese, etc.* 8vo. Siena, 1854-56.

Molinier, A. *Les MSS. et les Miniatures.* 12mo. Paris, 1892. Woodcuts.

Monte Cassino. *Paleografia artistica.* Monte Cassino, 1877. Folio. Facsimiles in gold and colours, etc., from Gothic and Lombardic MSS.

Montfaucon. *Palæographia Græca.* Small folio. *Parisiis,* 1708.

Mugnier, Fr. *Les MSS. à miniatures de la Maison de Savoie, etc.* 8vo. Moutiers-Tarantaise, 1894. 17 phototypes.

Ottley, W. Y. *History of Engraving.* 4to. London, 1816.

Peignot, Gabr. *Essai sur l'histoire du parchemin et du vélin.* 8vo. Paris, 1812.

Pinchart, A. *Miniaturistes, Enlumineurs, et Calligraphes Employés par Philippe le Bon, etc.* 8vo. Bruxelles, 1865.

Publications of the Palæographical Society of London. Folio. Vol. vii., etc. Very useful.

Quaritch, B. *Examples of the Art of Book-illumination during the Middle Ages.* 4to. London, 1899. Fine facsimiles in gold and colours.

Raczynski, A. (Cte.). *Les arts en Portugal.* 8vo. Paris, 1846.

Rahn, J. R. *Das Psalterium Aureum v. Sanct Gallen.* Folio. St. Gallen, 1878. 11 chromolithogr. in colours and gold. 7 lithogr. and many woodcuts. (A capital account of Carolingian and Irish MSS.)

Sacken, Ed. Frh. von. *Die Ambraser Sammlung.* 8vo. Wien, 1855.

Sakcinski, J. K. *Leben des Giulio Clovio.* 8vo. Agram, 1852.

Sakcinski, J. K. *Slovnik umjetnah Jugoslavenskih.* (*Biographical Dict. of South Slavonic Artists.*) 8vo. Uzagreba, 1858.

Sanftl, K. *Dissertatio in aureum ac pervetustum SS. Evangelior. Codicem MS. Monast. S. Emmerani.* 4to. Ratisbonæ, 1786. Gives a large folding plate of the Gospelbook cover, and facsimiles of illumination and writing.

Schönemann. *100 Merkwürdigkeiten des Herzoglichen Biblioth. zu Wolfenbüttel.* 8vo. Hannover, 1849.

Schultz, A. *Deutsches Leben in 14ten und 15ten Jahrh.* 2 vols. Large 8vo. Wien, 1892. (Contains many facsimiles in gold and colours, from German and Bohemian MSS.)

Serapeum. *Zeitschrift für Bibliothekens Wissenschaft.* 8vo. Leipzig. Vol. vii.

Seroux D'Agincourt, J. *Historie de l'Art par les Monuments.* Folio. 3 vols. Paris, 1823. London, 1847. Engravings.

Shaw, H. *The Art of Illuminating as Practised in the Middle Ages.* Second edition. 4to. London, 1845. Plates.

Shaw, H. *Alphabets, Numerals, and Devices of the Middle Ages.* Folio. London, W. Pickering, 1845. Many plates, some in gold and colours.

Silvestre, J. B. *Paléographie universelle.* 4 vols. Folio. Paris, 1841. 600 plates. (Plates very good.)

Smet, J. J. de. *Quelques recherches sur nos anciens enlumineurs, etc.* In *Bulletin de l'Academie de Belgique,* t. xiv., pt. 2, p. 78, and *Bullet. du Bibliophile Belge,* t. iii., p. 376, t. iv., p. 176.

Stokes, M. *Early Christian Art in Ireland.* 12mo.

London, 1887. Woodcuts. (Victoria and Albert M. Handbook.)

Swarzenski, G. *Die Regensburger Buchmalerei des X. und XI. Jahrhunderts.* Large 8vo. Leipzig, 1901. 35 phototypes.

Tambroni, G. *Cennino Cennini: Trattato della Pittura.* 8vo. Roma, 1821. Later edition (Milanesi), Firenze, 1859. (Contains many practical directions and recipes.)

Thompson, Sir Edward M. *English Illuminated MSS.* In *Bibliographica*, vol. i. pp. 129, 385, etc. Large 8vo. London, 1895.

Venturi, Ad. *La miniatura ferrarese nel secolo XV., etc.* Folio. Roma, 1899. 4 chromolithographs and 7 phototypes. In *Le Gallerie Nazionale Italiane.* Vol. iv., 187.

Viel-Castel, Cte. Horace de. *Statuts de l'Ordre du Saint-Esprit, etc. MS. du 14e Siècle avec une notice sur la peinture des MSS.* Large folio. Paris, 1853. 17 very fine facsimiles in gold and colours.

Vogelsang, W. *Holländische Miniaturen des späteren Mittelalters.* Large 8vo. Strassburg, 1899. Many phototype facsimiles.

Wailly, J. N. de. *Élémens de Paléographie.* 2 thick vols. 4to. Paris, 1838. Many plates of writing, seals, etc.

Wallther, J. L. *Lexicon diplomaticum.* Folio. 1751. Many examples of writings.

Waagen, G. F. *On the Importance of MSS. with Miniatures in the History of Art.* 8vo. Philobiblon Society. Vol. 1. London, 1854.

Waagen, G. F. *Die Vornehmsten Künstler in Wien.* 8vo. Wien, 1866. (MSS. in Imperial Library, etc., in Vienna.)

Warner, G. F. *Miniatures and Borders from the Hours*

of Bona Sforza, Duchess of Milan. Small 4to. London, 1894. 65 sepia facsimiles.

Warner, G. F. *Illuminated MSS. in the British Museum* 4to. London, 1899, etc. Many coloured facsimiles.

Wattenbach, W. *Das Schriftwesen im Mittelalter.* 8vo. Leipzig, 1871.

Westwood, J. O. *Palæographia Sacra Pictoria.* 4to. London, 1845. 50 facsimile plates, mostly in colours and gold.

Westwood, J. O. *Miniatures and Ornaments of Anglo-Saxon and Irish MSS.* Folio. Oxford, 1868. Many fine facsimiles in colours.

Wyatt, M. D., and Tymms. *The Art of Illuminating.* Large 8vo. London, 1860. Many facsimiles in gold and colours.

INDEX